Life and Meaning

A Reader

Edited by Oswald Hanfling
at the Open University

Basil Blackwell
in association with
The Open University

This reader is part of the Open University course A310 *Life and Death*. Opinions expressed in it are not necessarily those of the course team or of the University.

Selection and editorial material
copyright © The Open University 1987

First published 1987
First published in USA 1988

Basil Blackwell Ltd
108 Cowley Road, Oxford, OX4 1JF, UK

Basil Blackwell Inc.
432 Park Avenue South, Suite 1503
New York, NY 10016, USA

British Library Cataloguing in Publication Data

Life and meaning: a reader.
  1. Life
  I. Hanfling, Oswald   II. Open University
  128'.5   BD431

ISBN 0-631-15783-2
ISBN 0-631-15784-0 Pbk

Library of Congress Cataloging in Publication Data

Life and meaning.
  Includes index.
  1. Life. 2. Meaning (Philosophy)   I. Hanfling,
  Oswald. II. Open University.
  BD431.L417 1988   128'.5   87-20879

ISBN 0-631-15783-2
ISBN 0-631-15784-0 (pbk.)

Typeset in 10 on 12 pt Ehrhardt
by Photo·graphics, Honiton, Devon
Printed in Great Britain by Page Bros (Norwich) Ltd

Contents

Sources

The readings in this book are taken from the following:

'Vanity of Vanities' (chapter 1) from *Ecclesiastes*, Revised Standard Version of the Bible/New Oxford Annotated Bible. Copyright © 1846, 1952, 1971; reprinted by permission of the Division of Christian Education of the National Council of the Churches of Christ in the USA.

'My Confession' (chapter 2) by Leo Tolstoy. J. M. Dent and Sons Ltd, 1905.

'The Purpose of Man's Existence' (chapter 3) by Kurt Baier from *The Meaning of Life*, edited by E. D. Klemke, 1981. Reprinted by permission of the author.

'Has the Question about the Meaning of Life any Meaning?' (chapter 4) by Rudolf Wohlgennant from *Philosophie als Wissenschaft*, edited by E. Morscher, 1981. Used by permission of Edgar Morscher and Comes Verlag. Translated by O. Hanfling.

'The Meaning of Life' (chapter 5) from *Good and Evil* by Richard Taylor, 1970. Reprinted by permission of the author and Macmillan Publishing Company.

'The Absurd' (chapter 6) by Thomas Nagel from the *Journal of Philosophy*, 68 (20), 1971. Reprinted by permission of the author and the *Journal of Philosophy*.

'On the Meaning of Life' (chapter 7) by Moritz Schlick from *Philosophical Papers II*, 1979, pp. 112–18, 120–6, 128. Copyright © 1979, Albert M. Schlick and Barbara F. B. van de Velde Schlick. Reprinted by permission of Albert M. Schlick and Barbara F. B. van de Velde Schlick and D. Reidel Publishing Company.

'What is There in Horse Racing?' (chapter 8) by John Wisdom from the *Listener*, 10 June 1954. Reprinted by permission of the author and the *Listener*.

'We Have Nothing to Fear in Death' (chapter 9) from *On the Nature of the Universe* by Lucretius, trans. R. E. Latham, 1951, pp. 122–9. Copyright © R. E. Latham 1951. Reprinted by permission of Penguin Books Ltd.

'Death' (chapter 10) by Mary Mothersill from *Moral Problems*, edited by J. Rachels, 1971. Reprinted by permission of the author.

'Why We Should not be Biased towards the Future' (chapter 11) from *Reasons and Persons* by Derek Parfit, 1984. Reprinted by permission of Oxford University Press.

'The Vanity and Suffering of Life' (chapter 12) from *Essays and Aphorisms* by Arthur Schopenhauer, trans. R. J. Hollingdale, 1970, pp. 41–5, 53–4, copyright © R. J. Hollingdale; and from *The World as Will and Representation* by Arthur Schopenhauer. Reprinted by permission of Penguin Books Ltd and Dover Publications Inc.

'Murder' and 'A World without Human Beings' (chapter 13) from *Principia Ethica* by G. E. Moore, 1962. Reprinted by permission of Cambridge University Press.

'The Sanctity of Life' (chapter 14) from *Causing Death and Saving Lives* by Jonathan Glover, pp. 39, 45–57, 69–71, copyright © J. Glover 1977. Reprinted by permission of Penguin Books Ltd.

'What is Wrong with Killing People?' (chapter 15) by R. E. Ewin from the *Philosophical Quarterly*, 1972. Reprinted by permission of the author and Basil Blackwell.

'A Covenant for the Ark?' (chapter 16) by Peter Singer from the *Listener*, 14 April 1983. Reprinted by permission of the author and the *Listener*.

'The Tree of Knowledge' (chapter 17) from *Genesis*, Revised Standard Version of the Bible/New Oxford Annotated Bible. Copyright © 1846, 1952, 1971; reprinted by permission of the Division of Christian Education of the National Council of the Churches of Christ in the USA.

'The Origin of Inequality' (chapter 18) from *The Social Contract* by Jean-Jacques Rousseau, trans. G. D. H. Cole and revised 1955. Reprinted by permission of J. M. Dent and Sons Ltd.

'Of the Natural Condition of Mankind as Concerning their Felicity, and Misery' (chapter 19) from *Leviathan* by Thomas Hobbes, Fontana 1962.

'Man and the State' (chapter 20) from *The Politics* by Aristotle, trans. T. A. Sinclair, 1962, pp. 59–61, revised by Trevor J. Saunders, 1981, translation copyright © T. A. Sinclair 1962, 1981, revised translation copyright © Trevor J. Saunders 1981. Reprinted by permission of Penguin Books Ltd.

'Nature' (chapter 21) from *Three Essays on Religion* by John Stuart Mill. London 1875.

'Pleasure and Desire' (chapter 22) from *Georgias* by Plato, trans. Walter Hamilton, 1960, pp. 90–6, copyright © Walter Hamilton 1960. Reprinted by permission of Penguin Books Ltd.

'The Difference of Quality in Pleasures' and 'Of What Sort of Proof the Principle of Utility is Susceptible' (chapter 23) from *Utilitarianism* by John Stuart Mill.

'The Experience Machine' (chapter 24) from *Anarchy, State and Utopia* by Robert Nozick, copyright © Basic Books Inc. Publishers 1975. Reprinted by permission of Basil Blackwell Ltd and Basic Books Inc.

'How should a Man Live?' (chapter 25) from *Eudemian Ethics* by Aristotle, trans. Michael Woods, 1982; and from *Articles on Aristotle*, edited by J. Barnes, 1976. Reprinted by permission of Oxford University Press and Gerald Duckworth and Co. Ltd.

'My Station and its Duties' (chapter 26) from *Ethical Studies* by F. H. Bradley, Oxford University Press, 1962.

'Freedom and Bad Faith' (chapter 27) from *Existentialism and Humanism* by Jean-Paul Sartre, 1973; and from *Being and Nothingness* by Jean-Paul Sartre, 1958. Reprinted by permission of Eyre and Spottiswoode Ltd and Methuen and Co. and the Philosophical Library.

'Homo Ludens' (chapter 28) from *Homo Ludens* by J. Huizinga, 1949. Reprinted by permission of Routledge and Kegan Paul plc.

'Moral Tradition' (chapter 29) by John Kekes from *Philosophical Investigations*, 8, 4, 1985, pp. 252–68. Reprinted by permission of the author and Basil Blackwell Ltd.

Introduction

Questions about the meaning of life have not always troubled people as they do today. Their prominence now may be attributed to a number of related developments. There is the widespread loss of religious belief, of a kind that gave – or was thought to give – a meaning to life. Even those who continue to believe are likely to have a more critical attitude to religious answers than was previously the case. Then there is the more general questioning of accepted practices and traditions, whether religious or otherwise. The question 'Why?' obtrudes itself everywhere, and answers are not always available. Next, there is the profound change in man's conception of himself, due to modern scientific ideas. Our planet, we learn, is an insignificant entity compared to the vastness of the universe, and there is no reason to think that life and intelligence are peculiar to it. The origin of life, it appears, was due to some accidental combination of chemicals in a 'primeval soup', and the human species developed, like all others, by a mechanical process of natural selection. The very concept of *explanation* has changed, into a less 'meaningful' one. It was thought, prior to the age of modern science, that explanation must be in terms of *purpose*; an object or phenomenon was to be explained by saying what it was for, what purpose it served for man or beast or God. But modern laws of nature are not, by and large, couched in these terms; they are not about ends or purposes, but about observed regularities. Such an explanation says, in effect, no more than that a given phenomenon occurred because things always happen like that; referring one brute fact (a particular one) to another (a general regularity). Hence it is sometimes said that modern science is 'merely descriptive'; it tells us *how* things happen, but not *why*.

These are some of the ways in which there is, or appears to be, less meaning in ourselves and the world in which we live than was once the case. It would be a mistake, however, to think that questions about the meaning or purpose of life did not occur to anyone before modern times. Aristotle, for example, raised the question why one 'would choose to be born rather than not', and in reply quoted the view of a still earlier thinker, Anaxagoras. The purpose of life was, indeed, one of the main themes of

Aristotle's *Ethics*. He held that this purpose was to be found in the essential nature of *homo sapiens*. Human beings, he argued, have a special 'function', to do with rationality; and fulfilment was to be found by living in accordance with that function.

Another question that is by no means peculiar to modern times is about the meaning of death. This is, admittedly, affected by changing views about survival; but, whether we believe in survival or not, death is an important and permanent aspect of the human condition, affecting the meaning and value of life. The question whether death is an evil was discussed by the ancient Roman philosopher Lucretius (who did not believe in survival), and his views have been the subject of discussion recently.

Many modern philosophers have treated questions about the meaning or purpose of life with suspicion, and there are good reasons for this. A question like 'What is the meaning of life?' may itself be without meaning. Such questions sound highly important, and it may be thought that a philosopher who does not address himself to them is hardly worthy of his discipline. But this question, like others, ought not to be pursued before establishing what – if anything – it means. In this matter, as elsewhere in philosophy, it is advisable to follow Wittgenstein's recommendation 'to bring words back from their metaphysical to their everyday use' – in this case the word 'meaning' itself. (The concern about the meaning of 'meaning of life' is reflected in several of the readings in section one.)

If questions like 'What is the meaning (or purpose) of life?' have no clear meaning, they may still serve to express some kind of unease about the human condition – a feeling that there is (to put it vaguely) something wrong with life. Section one is mainly about claims that life is 'meaningless' or 'absurd', because of certain more or less permanent aspects of the human condition. Section two begins with a reading from Lucretius and some recent reactions to his views about death. There follows a reading from Schopenhauer, who gave probably the most sustained argument of any for a negative view of human life, taking into account our consciousness of death and the prevalence of suffering in our lives. This is followed by discussions of the *value* of human life and (in the last reading) of non-human life.

Sections three and four are largely about the purpose of life, in the sense of 'the good life'. The main question of section three is whether man is better or worse off after emerging from the 'state of nature' into the state of society (or political association). Rousseau argues that what is wrong with life as we know it is due to the emotional changes, the emergence of 'artificial passions', which must have taken place with the change away from nature. Hobbes, Aristotle and Mill are all, in their different ways, critical of the view that nature, or the state of nature, should be accorded moral approval.

In section four Mill, Aristotle and Bradley all provide answers to 'How should a man live?', drawn from essential facts, as they see them, about the human condition. But the assumption that such 'essentialist' arguments are applicable to human beings is challenged in the readings from Sartre. The concept of 'self-realization', with its implications for educational policies, is important in this section.

To a large extent I have followed chronological order within the sections, but sometimes the ordering is governed rather by thematic considerations. The literature in and around this subject, past and present, is very large, and I do not pretend that the present selection is an 'accurate' representation of it. For one thing, there is much that I have not read; and, for another, I have been guided by certain lines of enquiry of my own, with certain ways of approaching and organizing the topic (or topics). I hope, however, that the reader will find here at least a meaningful arrangement, and one that represents at least a fair number of the main lines of thought in this area.

Has Life a Meaning?

1

Vanity of Vanities

Ecclesiastes

Questions like 'What is the meaning of it all?' and 'What is it all for?' may arise in the context of observations about the 'vanity' of life, such as those made by the writer of Ecclesiastes. *If we accept that the ultimate prospect before us is that of non-being (death), we may feel that nothing we do really matters. (The same kind of view appears also in the extracts from Schopenhauer, in section two.)*

It is not easy to account for the inclusion of Ecclesiastes *in the Old Testament. In spite of some positive advice at the end of the book ('Fear God, and keep his commandments; for this is the whole duty of man'), its questioning and pessimistic tone seems at variance with the Jewish religious attitude. The book is thought to have been influenced by Greek ideas of about the third century BC.*

The words of the Preacher, the son of David, king in Jerusalem.

> Vanity of vanities, says the Preacher,
>   vanity of vanities! All is vanity.
> What does man gain by all the toil
>   at which he toils under the sun?
> A generation goes, and a generation comes,
>   but the earth remains for ever.
> The sun rises and the sun goes down,
>   and hastens to the place where it rises,
> The wind blows to the south,
>   and goes round to the north;
> round and round goes the wind,
>   and on its circuits the wind returns.
> All streams run to the sea,
>   but the sea is not full;
> to the place where the streams flow,
>   there they flow again.
> All things are full of weariness;
>   a man cannot utter it;
> the eye is not satisfied with seeing,
>   nor the ear filled with hearing.
> What has been is what will be,
> and what has been done is what will be done;
> and there is nothing new under the sun.

Is there a thing of which it is said,
    'See, this is new'?
It has been already,
    in the ages before us.
There is no remembrance of former things,
    nor will there be any remembrance
of later things yet to happen
    among those who come after. ...

I said to myself, 'Come now, I will make a test of pleasure; enjoy yourself.' But behold, this also was vanity. I said of laughter, 'It is mad,' and of pleasure, 'What use is it?' I searched with my mind how to cheer my body with wine – my mind still guiding me with wisdom – and how to lay hold on folly, till I might see what was good for the sons of men to do under heaven during the few days of their life. I made great works; I built houses and planted vineyards for myself; I made myself gardens and parks, and planted in them all kinds of fruit trees. I made myself pools from which to water the forest of growing trees. I bought male and female slaves, and had slaves who were born in my house; I had also great possessions of herds and flocks, more than any who had been before me in Jerusalem. I also gathered for myself silver and gold and the treasure of kings and provinces; I got singers, both men and women, and many concubines, man's delight.

So I became great and surpassed all who were before me in Jerusalem; also my wisdom remained with me. And whatever my eyes desired I did not keep from them; I kept my heart from no pleasure, for my heart found pleasure in all my toil, and this was my reward for all my toil. Then I considered all that my hands had done and the toil I had spent in doing it, and behold, all was vanity and a striving after wind, and there was nothing to be gained under the sun.

So I turned to consider wisdom and madness and folly; for what can the man do who comes after the king? Only what he has already done. Then I saw that wisdom excels folly as light excels darkness. The wise man has his eyes in his head, but the fool walks in darkness; and yet I perceived that one fate comes to all of them. Then I said to myself, 'What befalls the fool will befall me also; why then have I been so very wise?' And I said to myself that this also is vanity. For of the wise man as of the fool there is no enduring remembrance, seeing that in the days to come all will have been long forgotten. How the wise man dies just like the fool!

2

My Confession

Leo Tolstoy

Another source of ideas about the vanity of life is the role of purpose *in our lives.
We act, and are taught and expected to act, in reasonable ways; and a paradigm
of reasonable action is that in which we act for a purpose. This kind of activity
is the means to a desired end, and is given meaning by the end for which it is
done. But it may occur to us that ends cannot themselves be justified in this
satisfying way. We may do A for the sake of B, B for the sake of C, and so on,
but finally there must come a term which cannot be justified in this way,
'Something', as Hume observed, 'must be desirable on its account.' But 'on its
own account' is no justification; and many people have been assailed, from time
to time, by the thought that if the end cannot be justified then nothing else really
matters. Tolstoy, in the extracts presented below, gives eloquent expression to this
kind of scepticism. At a time when, by ordinary criteria, everything was going well
for him, he was suddenly assailed by the question 'Well, and what then?', to
which he could find no answer. He describes how he turned in vain to science to
provide a solution, finally concluding that 'in faith alone could we find the meaning
and possibility of life.' Tolstoy notes that although his problem was, in essence,
very simple, and could be grasped 'even by the simplest kind of men', it did not
usually trouble people of that kind; they 'continue living and never think of
doubting the reasonableness of life'. But it may also be said that, for most of us
most of the time (and whether we are simple or not), such problems do not present
themselves, because we are conditioned by nature to pursue various ends regardless
of the problem about reasonableness. Tolstoy recounts that when he suffered his
arrest of purpose, he still 'could not help breathing, eating, drinking and sleeping'.
There is also a sense in which we (most of us most of the time) cannot help
pursuing our various ends, and treating them as important. This is what 'keeps
us going' – but it does not provide an* answer *to those who are assailed by radical
questioning as described in this reading (or, to take another famous example, the
experience recounted by J. S. Mill in his* Autobiography*).*

Although I regarded authorship as a waste of time, I continued to write
during those fifteen years. I had tasted of the seduction of authorship, of
the seduction of enormous monetary remunerations and applauses for my

insignificant labour, and so I submitted to it, as being a means for improving my material condition and for stifling in my soul all questions about the meaning of my life and life in general.

In my writings I advocated, what to me was the only truth, that it was necessary to live in such a way as to derive the greatest comfort for oneself and one's family.

Thus I proceeded to live, but five years ago something very strange began to happen with me: I was overcome by minutes at first of perplexity and then of an arrest of life, as though I did not know how to live or what to do, and I lost myself and was dejected. But that passed, and I continued to live as before. Then those minutes of perplexity were repeated oftener and oftener, and always in one and the same form. These arrests of life found their expression in ever the same questions: 'Why? Well, and then?'

At first I thought that those were simply aimless, inappropriate questions. It seemed to me that that was all well known and that if I ever wanted to busy myself with their solution, it would not cost me much labour – that now I had no time to attend to them, but that if I wanted to I should find the proper answers. But the questions began to repeat themselves oftener and oftener, answers were demanded more and more persistently, and, like dots that fall on the same spot, these questions, without any answers, thickened into one black blotch.

There happened what happens with any person who falls ill with a mortal internal disease. At first there appear insignificant symptoms of indisposition, to which the patient pays no attention; then these symptoms are repeated more and more frequently and blend into one temporally indivisible suffering. The suffering keeps growing, and before the patient has had time to look around, he becomes conscious that what he took for an indisposition is the most significant thing in the world to him – is death.

The same happened with me. I understood that it was not a passing indisposition, but something very important, and that, if the questions were going to repeat themselves, it would be necessary to find an answer for them. And I tried to answer them. The questions seemed to be so foolish, simple and childish. But the moment I touched them and tried to solve them, I became convinced, in the first place, that they were not childish and foolish, but very important and profound questions in life, and, in the second, that, no matter how much I might try, I should not be able to answer them. Before attending to my Samára estate, to my son's education, or to the writing of a book, I ought to know why I should do that. So long as I did not know why, I could not do anything, I could not live. Amidst my thoughts of farming, which interested me very much during that time, there would suddenly pass through my head a question like this: 'All right, you are going to have six hundred desyatínas of land in the Government of Samára, and three hundred horses – and then?' And I completely lost my senses and did not know what to think farther. Or, when I thought of the education of my children, I said to myself: 'Why?' Or, reflecting on the manner in which the masses might obtain their welfare, I suddenly said to myself: 'What is that to me?' Or, thinking of the fame which my works would get me, I said to myself: 'All right, you will be more famous than Gógol, Púshkin, Shakespeare, Molière, and all the writers in the world – what of it?' And I was absolutely unable to make any reply. The questions were not waiting, and I had to answer them at once; if I did not answer them, I could not live.

I felt that what I was standing on had given way, that I had no foundation to stand on, that that which I lived by no longer existed, and that I had nothing to live by.

My life came to a standstill. I could breathe, eat, drink, and sleep, and could not help breathing, eating, drinking, and sleeping; but there was no life, because there were no desires the gratification of which I might find reasonable. If I wished for anything, I knew in advance that, whether I gratified my desire or not, nothing would come of it. If a fairy had come and had offered to carry out my wish, I should not have known what to say. If in moments of intoxication I had, not wishes, but habits of former desires, I knew in sober moments that that was a deception, that there was nothing to wish for. I could not even wish to find out the truth, because I guessed what it consisted in. The truth was that life was meaningless. ...

All that happened with me when I was on every side surrounded by what is considered to be complete happiness. I had a good, loving, and beloved wife, good children, and a large estate, which grew and increased without any labour on my part. I was respected by my neighbours and friends, more than ever before, was praised by strangers, and, without any self-deception, could consider my name famous. With all that, I was not deranged or mentally unsound – on the contrary, I was in full command of my mental and physical powers, such as I had rarely met with in people of my age: physically I could work in a field, mowing without falling behind a peasant; mentally I could work from eight to ten hours in succession, without experiencing any consequences from the strain. And while in such condition I arrived at the conclusion that I could not live, and, fearing death, I had to use cunning against myself, in order that I might not take my life.

This mental condition expressed itself to me in this form: my life is a stupid, mean trick played on me by somebody. Although I did not recognize that 'somebody' as having created me, the form of the conception that some one had played a mean, stupid trick on me by bringing me into the world was the most natural one that presented itself to me.

Involuntarily I imagined that there, somewhere, there was somebody who was now having fun as he looked down upon me and saw me, who had lived for thirty or forty years, learning, developing, growing in body and mind, now that I had become strengthened in mind and had reached that summit of life from which it lay all before me, standing as a complete fool on that summit and seeing clearly that there was nothing in life and never would be. And that was fun to him –

But whether there was or was not that somebody who made fun of me, did not make it easier for me. I could not ascribe any sensible meaning to a single act, or to my whole life. I was only surprised that I had not understood that from the start. All that had long ago been known to everybody. Sooner or later there would come diseases and death (they had come already) to my dear ones and to me, and there would be nothing left but stench and worms. All my affairs, no matter what they might be, would sooner or later be forgotten, and I myself should not exist. So why should I worry about all these things? How could a man fail to see that and live – that was surprising! A person could live only so long as he was drunk; but the moment he sobered up, he could not help seeing that all that was only a deception, and a stupid deception at that! Really, there was nothing funny and ingenious about it, but only something cruel and stupid.

Long ago has been told the Eastern story about the traveller who in the steppe is overtaken by an infuriated beast. Trying to save himself from the animal, the traveller jumps into a waterless well, but at its bottom he sees a dragon who opens his jaws in order to swallow him. And the unfortuante man does not dare climb out, lest he perish from the infuriated beast, and does not dare jump down to the bottom of the well, lest he be devoured by the dragon, and so clutches the twig of a wild bush growing in a cleft of the well and holds on to it. His hands grow weak and he feels that soon he shall have to surrender to the peril which awaits him at either side; but he still holds on and sees two mice, one white, the other black, in even measure making a circle around the main trunk of the bush to which he is clinging, and nibbling at it on all sides. Now, at any moment, the bush will break and tear off, and he will fall into the dragon's jaws. The traveller sees that and knows that he will inevitably perish; but while he is still clinging, he sees some drops of honey hanging on the leaves of the bush, and so reaches out for them with his tongue and licks the leaves. Just so I hold on to the branch of life, knowing that the dragon of death is waiting inevitably for me, ready to tear me to pieces, and I cannot understand why I have fallen on such suffering. And I try to lick that honey which used to give me pleasure; but now it no longer gives me joy, and the white and the black mouse day and night nibble at the branch to which I am holding on. I clearly see the dragon, and the honey is no longer sweet to me. I see only the inevitable dragon and the mice, and am unable to turn my glance away from them. That is not a fable, but a veritable, indisputable, comprehensible truth.

The former deception of the pleasures of life, which stifled the terror of the dragon, no longer deceives me. No matter how much one should say to me, 'You cannot understand the meaning of life, do not think, live!' I am unable to do so, because I have been doing it too long before. Now I cannot help seeing day and night, which run and lead me up to death. I see that alone, because that alone is the truth. Everything else is a lie.

The two drops of honey that have longest turned my eyes away from the cruel truth, the love of family and of authorship, which I have called an art, are no longer sweet to me.

'My family – ' I said to myself, 'but my family, my wife and children, they are also human beings. They are in precisely the same condition that I am in: they must either live in the lie or see the terrible truth. Why should they live? Why should I love them, why guard, raise, and watch them? Is it for the same despair which is in me, or for dulness of perception? Since I love them, I cannot conceal the truth from them – every step in cognition leads them up to this truth. And the truth is death.' …

But, perhaps, I overlooked something, or did not understand something right?' I said to myself several times. 'It is impossible that this condition of despair should be characteristic of men!' And I tried to find an explanation for these questions in all those branches of knowledge which men had acquired. I searched painfully and for a long time, and I searched not from idle curiosity, not in a limp manner, but painfully and stubbornly, day and night – I searched as a perishing man searches for his salvation – and I found nothing.

I searched in all the branches of knowledge, and not only failed to find anything, but even convinced myself that all those who, like myself, had been searching in the sciences, had failed just as much. They had not only not found anything, but had also clearly recognized the fact that that which had brought me to despair – the meaninglessness of life – was the only incontestable knowledge which was accessible to man.

I searched everywhere, and, thanks to a life passed in study, and also because through my connections with the learned world I had access to the most learned of men in every imaginable branch of knowledge, who did not refuse to disclose to me their knowledge, not only in books, but also in conversations, I learned everything which science replies to the question of life.

For a long time I could not believe that science had no answer to give to the questions of life, except what it gave. For a long time it seemed to me, as I looked at the importance and seriousness of tone which science assumed, when it enunciated its principles which had nothing in common with the questions of human life, that there was something in it which I did not understand. For a long time I was intimidated by science, and it seemed to me that the inapplicability of the answers to my questions was not the fault of science, but of my own ignorance; but the matter was for me not a joke, a trifle, but an affair of my whole life, and I was against my will led to the conviction that my questions were the only legitimate questions, which served as a foundation of all knowledge, and that not I with my questions was to blame, but science, if it had the presumption to answer these questions.

My question, the one which led me, at fifty years, up to suicide, was the simplest kind of a question, and one which is lying in the soul of every man, from the silliest child to the wisest old man – that question without which life is impossible, as I have experienced it, in fact. The question is: 'What will come of what I am doing to-day and shall do to-morrow? What will come of my whole life?'

Differently expressed, the question would stand like this: 'Why live, wish for anything, why do anything?' The question may be expressed still differently: 'Is there in my life a meaning which would not be destroyed by my inevitable, imminent death?'

To this one, differently expressed, question I searched for an answer in human knowledge. I found that in relation to this question all human knowledge seemed to be divided into two opposite hemispheres, at the opposite ends of which there were two poles: one, a negative, the other, a positive pole; but that at neither pole was there an answer to the questions of life.

One series of the sciences does not seem to recognize the question, but clearly and definitely answers its own, independently put questions: that is the series of the experimental sciences, and at their extreme point stands mathematics; the other series of knowledge recognizes the question, but gives no answer to it: that is the series of the speculative sciences, and at their extreme point stands metaphysics.

Ever since my early youth I had been interested in the speculative sciences, but later mathematics and the natural sciences attracted me, and so long as I did not clearly put my question, so long as the question did not of itself rise in me, insisting on an answer, I was satisfied with those fictitious answers which sciences give to the question.

In the sphere of the experimental sciences, I said to myself: 'Everything develops, is differentiated, moves in the direction of complexity and perfection, and there are laws which govern this progress. You are a part of the whole. Having, in so far as it is possible, learned the whole, and having learned the law of evolution, you will learn your place in this whole, and all about yourself.' I am ashamed to confess it, there was a time when I seemed to be satisfied with that. That was the time when I myself was growing more complex and was developing. My muscles grew and became stronger, my memory was being enriched, my ability to think and comprehend was increasing, I grew and developed, and, feeling within me that growth, it was natural for me to think that that was the law of the whole world, in which I should find a solution also to the questions of my life. But the time came when my growth stopped – I felt that I was not developing, but drying up, that my muscles were growing weaker and my teeth falling out – and I saw that that law not only explained nothing to me, but that there never was and never could have been such a law, and that I took for a law what I found within me at a certain period of life. I was more severe toward the definition of that law; and it became clear to me that there could be no law of endless development; it became clear to me that saying that in endless space and time everything was developing, perfecting itself, becoming more complex, differentiating, was tantamount to saying nothing. All those are words without any meaning, for in the infinite there is nothing complex, nor simple, nor in front, nor behind, nor better, nor worse.

The main thing was that my personal question, 'What am I with my desires?' remained entirely unanswered. And I understood that those sciences were very interesting, very attractive, but that the definiteness and clearness of those sciences were in inverse proportion to their applicability to the questions of life: the less applicable they are to the questions of life, the more definite and clear they are; the more they attempt to give answers to the questions of life, the more they become dim and unattractive. ...

In my search after the question of life I experienced the same feeling which a man who has lost his way in the forest may experience.

He comes to a clearing, climbs a tree, and clearly sees an unlimited space before him; at the same time he sees that there are no houses there, and that there can be none; he goes back to the forest, into the darkness, and he sees darkness, and again there are no houses.

Thus I blundered in this forest of human knowledge, between the clearings of the mathematical and experimental sciences, which disclosed to me clear horizons, but such in the direction of which there could be no house, and between the darkness of the speculative sciences, where I sank into a deeper darkness, the farther I proceeded, and I convinced myself at last that there was no way out and could not be.

By abandoning myself to the bright side of knowledge I saw that I only turned my eyes away from the question. No matter how enticing and clear the horizons were that were disclosed to me, no matter how enticing it was to bury myself in the infinitude of this knowledge, I comprehended that these sciences were the more clear, the less I needed them, the less they answered my question.

'Well, I know', I said to myself, 'all which science wants so persistently to know, but there is no answer to the question about the meaning of my life.' But in the speculative sphere I saw that, in spite of the fact that the aim of the knowledge was directed straight to the answer of my question, or because of that fact, there could be no other answer than what I was giving to myself: 'What is the meaning of my life?' – 'None.' Or, 'What will come of my life?' – 'Nothing'. Or, 'Why does everything which exists exist, and why do I exist?' – 'Because it exists.'

Putting the question to one side of human knowledge, I received an endless quantity of exact answers about what I did not ask: about the chemical composition of the stars, about the movement of the sun toward the constellation of Hercules, about the origin of species and of man, about the forms of infinitely small, imponderable particles of ether; but the answer in this sphere of knowledge to my question what the meaning of my life was, was always: 'You are what you call your life; you are a temporal, accidental conglomeration of particles. The inter-relation, the change of these particles, produces in you that which you call life. This congeries will last for some time; then the interaction of these particles will cease, and that which you call life and all your questions will come to an end. You are an accidentally cohering globule of something. The globule is fermenting. This fermentation the globule calls its life. The globule falls to pieces, and all fermentation and all questions will come to an end.' Thus the clear side of knowledge answers, and it cannot say anything else, if only it strictly follows its principles.

With such an answer it appears that the answer is not a reply to the question. I want to know the meaning of my life, but the fact that it is a particle of the infinite not only gives it no meaning, but even destroys every possible meaning. ...

Life is a meaningless evil – that was incontestable, I said to myself. But I have lived, still live, and all humanity has lived. How is that? Why does it live, since it can refuse to live? Is it possible Schopenhauer and I alone are so wise as to have comprehended the meaninglessness and evil of life?

The discussion of the vanity of life is not so cunning, and it has been brought forward long ago, even by the simplest kind of men, and yet they have lived and still live. Why do they continue living and never think of doubting the reasonableness of life?

My knowledge, confirmed by the wisdom of the sages, has disclosed to me that everything in the world – everything organic and inorganic – everything is constructed with surprising cleverness, only my own condition is stupid. And those fools, the enormous masses of people, know nothing about how everything organic and inorganic is constructed in the world, and yet live, and they think that their life is sensibly arranged!

And it occurred to me that there might be something I did not know, for ignorance acts in precisely that manner. Ignorance always says the same. When it does not know a thing, it says that what it does not know is stupid. In reality it turns out that there is a human entity which has lived as though understanding the meaning of its life, for, if it did not understand it, it could not live, and I say that the whole life is meaningless, and that I cannot live. ...

There resulted a contradiction, from which there were two ways out: either what I called rational was not so rational as I had thought; or that which to me appeared irrational was not so irrational as I had thought. And I began to verify the train of thoughts of my rational knowledge.

In verifying the train of thoughts of my rational knowledge, I found that it was quite correct. The deduction that life was nothing was inevitable; but I saw a mistake. The mistake was that I had not reasoned in conformity with the question put by me. The question was, 'Why should I live?' that is, 'What real, indestructible essence will come from my phantasmal, destructible life? What meaning has my finite existence in this infinite world?' And in order to answer this question, I studied life.

The solutions of all possible questions of life apparently could not satisfy me, because my question, no matter how simple it appeared in the beginning, included the necessity of explaining the finite through the infinite, and vice versa.

I asked, 'What is the extra-temporal, extra-causal, extra-spatial meaning of life?' But I gave an answer to the question, 'What is the temporal, causal, spatial meaning of my life?' The result was that after a long labour of mind I answered, 'None.'

In my reflections I constantly equated, nor could I do otherwise, the finite with the finite, the infinite with the infinite, and so from that resulted precisely what had to result: force was force, matter was matter, will was will, infinity was infinity, nothing was nothing – and nothing else could come from it.

There happened something like what at times takes place in mathematics: you think you are solving an equation, when you have only an identity. The reasoning is correct, but you receive as a result the answer: $a = a$, or $x = x$, or $0 = 0$. The same happened with my reflection in respect to the question about the meaning of my life. The answers given by all science to that question are only identities.

Indeed, the strictly scientific knowledge, that knowledge which, as Descartes did, begins with a full doubt in everything, rejects all knowledge which has been taken on trust, and builds everything anew on the laws of reason and experience, cannot give any other answer to the question of life than what I received – an indefinite answer. It only seemed to me at first that science gave me a positive answer – Schopenhauer's answer: 'Life has no meaning, it is an evil.' But when I analysed the matter, I saw that the answer was not a positive one, but that it was only my feeling which expressed it as such. The answer, strictly expressed, as it is expressed by the Brahmins, by Solomon, and by Schopenhauer, is only an indefinite answer, or an identity, $0 = 0$, life is nothing. Thus the philosophical knowledge does not negate anything, but only answers that the question cannot be solved by it, that for philosophy the solution remains insoluble.

When I saw that, I understood that it was not right for me to look for an answer to my question in rational knowledge, and that the answer given by rational knowledge was only an indication that the answer might be got if the question were differently put, but only when into the discussion of the question should be introduced the question of the relation of the finite to the infinite. I also understood that, no matter how irrational and monstrous the answers might be that faith gave, they had this advantage that they introduced into each answer the relation of the finite to the infinite, without which there could be no answer.

No matter how I may put the question, 'How must I live?' the answer is, 'According to God's law.' 'What real result will there be from my life?' – 'Eternal torment or eternal bliss.' 'What is the meaning which is not destroyed by death?' – 'The union with infinite God, paradise.'

Thus, outside the rational knowledge, which had to me appeared as the only one, I was inevitably led to recognize that all living humanity had a certain other irrational knowledge, faith, which made it possible to live.

All the irrationality of faith remained the same for me, but I could not help recognizing that it alone gave to humanity answers to the questions of life, and, in consequence of them, the possibility of living.

The rational knowledge brought me to the recognition that life was meaningless – my life stopped, and I wanted to destroy myself. When I looked around at people, at all humanity, I saw that people lived and asserted that they knew the meaning of life. I looked back at myself: I lived so long as I knew the meaning of life. As to other people, so even to me, did faith give the meaning of life and the possibility of living.

Looking again at the people of other countries, contemporaries of mine and those passed away, I saw again the same. Where life had been, there faith, ever since humanity had existed, had given the possibility of living, and the chief features of faith were everywhere one and the same.

No matter what answers faith may give, its every answer gives to the finite existence of man the sense of the infinite – a sense which is not destroyed by suffering, privation, and death. Consequently in faith alone could we find the meaning and possibility of life. What, then, was faith? I understood that faith was not merely an evidence of things not seen, and so forth, not revelation (that is only the description of one of the symptoms of faith), not the relation of man to man (faith has to be defined, and then God, and not first God, and faith through him), not merely an agreement with what a man was told, as faith was generally understood – that faith was the knowledge of the meaning of human life, in consequence of which man did not destroy himself, but lived. Faith is the power of life. If a man lives he believes in something. If he did not believe that he ought to live for some purpose, he would not live. If he does not see and understand the phantasm of the finite, he believes in that finite; if he understands the phantasm of the finite, he must believe in the infinite. Without faith one cannot live.

3

The Purpose of Man's Existence

Kurt Baier

The confrontation between science and religion is continued in the extract from Baier, who takes a very different view from that of Tolstoy. Baier concludes that, in so far as it makes sense to speak of a meaning or purpose of human life, it is Christianity rather than modern science that 'robs man of purpose'. The Christian answer to the problem is, he argues, really no answer at all. But there is a sense in which meaning and purpose can be found in our lives; and in that sense they are enhanced rather than undermined by the scientific world-view.

Our conclusion in the previous section has been that science is in principle able to give complete and real explanations of every occurrence and thing in the universe. This has two important corollaries: (i) Acceptance of the scientific world picture cannot be *one's reason for* the belief that the universe is unintelligible and therefore meaningless, though coming to accept it, after having been taught the Christian world picture, may well have been, in the case of many individuals, *the only or the main cause* of their belief that the universe and human existence are meaningless. (ii) It is not in accordance with reason to reject this pessimistic belief on the grounds that scientific explanations are only provisional and incomplete and must be supplemented by religious ones.

In fact, it might be argued that the more clearly we understand the explanations given by science, the more we are driven to the conclusion that human life has no purpose and therefore no meaning. The science of astronomy teaches us that our earth was not specially created about 6,000 years ago, but evolved out of hot nebulae which previously had whirled aimlessly through space for countless ages. As they cooled, the sun and the planets formed. On one of these planets at a certain time the circumstances were propitious and life developed. But conditions will not remain favourable to life. When our solar system grows old, the sun will cool, our planet will be covered with ice, and all living creatures will eventually perish. Another theory has it that the sun will explode and that the heat generated will be so great that all organic life on earth will be destroyed. That is the comparatively short history and prospect of life on earth. Altogether it amounts to very little when compared with the endless history of the inanimate universe.

Biology teaches us that the species man was not specially created but is merely, in a long chain of evolutionary changes of forms of life, the last link, made in the likeness not of God but of nothing so much as an ape. The rest of the universe, whether animate or inanimate, instead of serving the ends of man, is at best indifferent, at worst savagely hostile. Evolution, to whose operation the emergence of man is due, is a ceaseless battle among members of different species, one species being gobbled up by another, only the fittest surviving. Far from being the gentlest and most highly moral, man is simply the creature best fitted to survive, the most efficient if not the most rapacious and insatiable killer. And in this unplanned, fortuitous, monstrous, savage world man is madly trying to snatch a few brief moments of joy, in the short intervals during which he is free from pain, sickness, persecution, war or famine until, finally, his life is snuffed out in death. Science has helped us to know and understand this world, but what purpose or meaning can it find in it?

Complaints such as these do not mean quite the same to everybody, but one thing, I think, they mean to most people: science shows life to be meaningless, because life is without purpose. The medieval world picture provided life with a purpose, hence medieval Christians could believe that life had a meaning. The scientific account of the world takes away life's purpose and with it its meaning.

There are, however, two quite different senses of 'purpose'. Which one is meant? Has science deprived human life of purpose in both senses? And if not, is it a harmless sense, in which human existence has been robbed of purpose? Could human existence still have meaning if it did not have a purpose in that sense?

What are the two senses? In the first and basic sense, purpose is normally attributed only to persons or their behaviour as in 'Did you have a purpose in leaving the ignition on?' In the second sense, purpose is normally attributed only to things, as in 'What is the purpose of that gadget you installed in the workshop?' The two uses are intimately connected. We cannot attribute a purpose to a thing without implying that someone did something, in the doing of which he had some purpose, namely, to bring about the thing with the purpose. Of course, *his* purpose is not identical with *its* purpose. In hiring labourers and engineers and buying materials and a site for a factory and the like, the entrepreneur's purpose, let us say, is to manufacture cars, but the purpose of cars is to serve as a means of transportation.

There are many things that a man may do, such as buying and selling, hiring labourers, ploughing, felling trees, and the like, which it is foolish, pointless, silly, perhaps crazy, to do if one has no purpose in doing them.

A man who does these things without a purpose is engaging in inane, futile pursuits. Lives crammed full with such activities devoid of purpose are pointless, futile, worthless. Such lives may indeed be dismissed as meaningless. But it should also be perfectly clear that acceptance of the scientific world picture does not force us to regard our lives as being without a purpose in this sense. Science has not only not robbed us of any purpose which we had before, but it has furnished us with enormously greater power to achieve these purposes. Instead of praying for rain or a good harvest or offspring, we now use ice pellets, artificial manure, or artificial insemination.

By contrast, having or not having a purpose, in the other sense, is value neutral. We do not think more or less highly of a thing for having or not having a purpose. 'Having a purpose,' in this sense, confers no kudos, 'being purposeless' carries no stigma. A row of trees growing near a farm may or may not have a purpose: it may or may not be a windbreak, may or may not have been planted or deliberately left standing there in order to prevent the wind from sweeping across the fields. We do not in any way disparage the trees if we say they have no purpose, but have just grown that way. They are as beautiful, made of as good wood, as valuable, as if they had a purpose. And, of course, they break the wind just as well. The same is true of living creatures. We do not disparage a dog when we say that it has no purpose, is not a sheep dog or a watch dog or a rabbiting dog, but just a dog that hangs around the house and is fed by us.

Man is in a different category, however. To attribute to a human being a purpose in that sense is not neutral, let alone complimentary: it is offensive. It is degrading for a man to be regarded as merely serving a purpose. If, at a garden party, I ask a man in livery, 'What is your purpose?' I am insulting him. I might as well have asked, 'What are you *for*?' Such questions reduce him to the level of a gadget, a domestic animal, or perhaps a slave. I imply that *we* allot to *him* the tasks, the goals, the aims which he is to pursue; that *his* wishes and desires and aspirations and purposes are to count for little or nothing. We are treating him, in Kant's phrase, merely as a means to our ends, not as an end in himself.

The Christian and the scientific world pictures do indeed differ fundamentally on this point. The latter robs man of a purpose in this sense. It sees him as a being with no purpose allotted to him by anyone but himself. It robs him of any goal, purpose, or destiny appointed for him by any outside agency. The Christian world picture, on the other hand, sees man as a creature, a divine artefact, something halfway between a robot (manufactured) and an animal (alive), a homunculus, or perhaps Frankenstein, made in God's laboratory, with a purpose or task assigned him by his Maker.

However, lack of purpose in this sense does not in any way detract from the meaningfulness of life. I suspect that many who reject the scientific outlook because it involves the loss of purpose of life, and therefore meaning, are guilty of a confusion between the two senses of 'purpose' just distinguished. They confusedly think that if the scientific world picture is true, then their lives must be futile because that picture implies that man has no purpose given him from without. But this is muddled thinking, for, as has already been shown, pointlessness is implied only by purposelessness in the other sense, which is not at all implied by the scientific picture of the world. These people mistakenly conclude that there can be no purpose *in* life because there is no purpose *of* life; that *men* cannot themselves adopt and achieve purposes because *man*, unlike a robot or a watch dog, is not a creature with a purpose.[1]

However, not all people taking this view are guilty of the above confusion. Some really hanker after a purpose of life in this sense. To some people the greatest attraction of the medieval world picture is the belief in an omnipotent, omniscient, and all-good Father, the view of themselves as His children who worship Him, of their proper attitude to what befalls them as submission, humility, resignation in His will, and what is often described as the 'creaturely feeling'.[2] All these are attitudes and feelings appropriate to a being that stands to another in the same sort of relation, though of course on a higher plane, in which a helpless child stands to his progenitor. Many regard the scientific picture of the world as cold, unsympathetic, unhomely, frightening, because it does not provide for any appropriate object of this creaturely attitude. There is nothing and no one in the world, as science depicts it, in which we can have faith or trust, on whose guidance we can rely, to whom we can turn for consolation, whom we can worship or submit to – except other human beings. This may be felt as a keen disappointment, because it shows that the meaning of life cannot lie in submission to His will, in acceptance of whatever may come, and in worship. But it does not imply that life can have *no* meaning. It merely implies that it must have a different meaning from that which it was thought to have. Just as it is a great shock for a child to find that he must stand on his own feet, that his father and mother no longer provide for him, so a person who has lost his faith in God must reconcile himself to the idea that he has to stand on his own feet, alone in the world except for whatever friends he may succeed in making.

But is not this to miss the point of the Christian teaching? Surely, Christianity can tell us the meaning of life because it tells us the grand and noble end for which God has created the universe and man. No human life, however pointless it may seem, is meaningless because in being part of God's plan, every life is assured of significance.

This point is well taken. It brings to light a distinction of some importance: we call a person's life meaningful not only if it is worthwhile, but also if he has helped in the realization of some plan or purpose transcending his own concerns. A person who knows he must soon die a painful death, can give significance to the remainder of his doomed life by, say, allowing certain experiments to be performed on him which will be useful in the fight against cancer. In a similar way, only on a much more elevated plane, every man, however humble or plagued by suffering, is guaranteed significance by the knowledge that he is participating in God's purpose.

What, then, on the Christian view, is the grand and noble end for which God has created the world and man in it? We can immediately dismiss that still popular opinion that the smallness of our intellect prevents us from stating meaningfully God's design in all its imposing grandeur.[3] This view cannot possibly be a satisfactory answer to our question about the purpose of life. It is, rather, a confession of the impossibility of giving one. If anyone thinks that this 'answer' can remove the sting from the impression of meaninglessness and insignificance in our lives, he cannot have been stung very hard.

If, then, we turn to those who are willing to state God's purpose in so many words, we encounter two insuperable difficulties. The first is to find a purpose grand and noble enough to explain and justify the great amount of undeserved suffering in this world. We are inevitably filled by a sense of bathos when we read statements such as this: '... history is the scene of a divine purpose, in which the whole history is included, and Jesus of Nazareth is the centre of that purpose, both as revelation and as achievement, as the fulfilment of all that was past, and the promise of all that was to come. ... If God is God, and if He made all these things, why did He do it? ... God created a universe, bounded by the categories of time, space, matter, and causality, because He desired to enjoy for ever the society of a fellowship of finite and redeemed spirits which have made to His love the response of free and voluntary love and service.'[4] Surely this cannot be right? Could a God be called omniscient, omnipotent, *and* all-good who, for the sake of satisfying his desire to be loved and served, imposes (or has to impose) on his creatures the amount of undeserved suffering we find in the world?

There is, however, a much more serious difficulty still: God's purpose in making the universe must be stated in terms of a dramatic story many of whose key incidents symbolize religious conceptions and practices which we no longer find morally acceptable: the imposition of a taboo on the fruits of a certain tree, the sin and guilt incurred by Adam and Eve by violating the taboo, the wrath of God,[5] the curse of Adam and Eve and all their progeny, the expulsion from Paradise, the Atonement by Christ's bloody sacrifice on the cross which makes available by way of the sacraments God's Grace by which alone men can be saved (thereby, incidentally, establishing the valuable power of priests to forgive sins and thus alone make possible a man's entry to heaven,[6] Judgment Day on which the sheep are separated from the goats and the latter condemned to eternal torment in hell-fire.

Obviously it is much more difficult to formulate a purpose for creating the universe and man that will justify the enormous amount of undeserved suffering which we find around us, if that story has to be fitted in as well. For now we have to explain not only why an omnipotent, omniscient, and all-good God should create such a universe and such a man, but also why, foreseeing every move of the feeble, weak-willed, ignorant, and covetous creature to be created, He should nevertheless have created him and, having done so, should be incensed and outraged by man's sin, and why He should deem it necessary to sacrifice His own son on the cross to atone for this sin which was, after all, only a disobedience of one of His commands, and why this atonement and consequent redemption could not have been followed by man's return to Paradise – particularly of those innocent children who had not yet sinned – and why, on Judgment Day, this merciful God should condemn some to eternal torment.[7] It is not surprising that in the face of these and other difficulties, we find, again and again, a return to the first view: that God's purpose cannot meaningfully be stated.

It will perhaps be objected that no Christian to-day believes in the dramatic history of the world as I have presented it. But this is not so. It is the official doctrine of the Roman Catholic, the Greek Orthodox, and a large section of the Anglican Church.[8] Nor does Protestantism substantially alter this picture. In fact, by insisting on 'Justification by Faith Alone' and by rejecting the ritualistic, magical character of the medieval Catholic interpretation of certain elements in the Christian religion, such as indulgences, the sacraments, and prayer, while at the same time insisting on the necessity of grace, Protestantism undermined the moral element in medieval Christianity expressed in the Catholics' emphasis on personal merit.[9] Protestantism, by harking back to St Augustine, who clearly realized the incompatibility of grace and personal merit,[10] opened the way for Calvin's doctrine of Predestination (the intellectual parent of that form of rigid determinism which is usually blamed on science) and Salvation or Condemnation from all eternity.[11] Since Roman Catholics, Lutherans, Calvinists, Presbyterians and Baptists officially subscribe to the views just outlined, one can justifiably claim that the overwhelming majority of professing Christians hold or ought to hold them.

It might still be objected that the best and most modern views are wholly different. I have not the necessary knowledge to pronounce on the accuracy of this claim. It may well be true that the best and most modern views are such as Professor Braithwaite's who maintains that Christianity is, roughly speaking, 'morality plus stories', where the stories are intended merely to make the strict moral teaching both more easily understandable and more

K. Baier

palatable.[12] Or it may be that one or the other of the modern views on the nature and importance of the dramatic story told in the sacred Scriptures is the best. My reply is that even if it is true, it does not prove what I wish to disprove, that one can extract a sensible answer to our question, 'What is the meaning of life?' from the kind of story subscribed to by the overwhelming majority of Christians, who would, moreover, reject any such modernist interpretation at least as indignantly as the scientific account. Moreover, though such views can perhaps avoid some of the worst absurdities of the traditional story, they are hardly in a much better position to state the purpose for which God has created the universe and man in it, because they cannot overcome the difficulty of finding a purpose grand and noble enough to justify the enormous amount of undeserved suffering in the world.

Let us, however, for argument's sake, waive all these objections. There remains one fundamental hurdle which no form of Christianity can overcome: the fact that it demands of man a morally repugnant attitude towards the universe. It is now very widely held[13] that the basic element of the Christian religion is an attitude of worship towards a being supremely worthy of being worshipped and that it is religious feelings and experiences which apprise their owner of such a being and which inspire in him the knowledge or the feeling of complete dependence, awe, worship, mystery, and self-abasement. There is, in other words, a bi-polarity (the famous 'I–Thou relationship') in which the object, 'the wholly-other' is exalted whereas the subject is abased to the limit. Rudolf Otto has called this the 'creature-feeling'[14] and he quotes as an expression of it, Abraham's words when venturing to plead for the men of Sodom: 'Behold now, I have taken upon me to speak unto the Lord, which am but dust and ashes.' (Gen. XVIII.27.) Christianity thus demands of men an attitude inconsistent with one of the presuppositions of morality: that man is not wholly dependent on something else, that man has free will, that man is in principle capable of responsibility. We have seen that the concept of grace is the Christian attempt to reconcile the claim of total dependence and the claim of individual responsibility (partial independence), and it is obvious that such attempts must fail. We may dismiss certain doctrines, such as the doctrine of original sin or the doctrine of eternal hellfire or the doctrine that there can be no salvation outside the Church as extravagant and peripheral, but we cannot reject the doctrine of total dependence without rejecting the characteristically Christian attitude as such.

THE MEANING OF LIFE

Perhaps some of you will have felt that I have been shirking the real problem. To many people the crux of the matter seems as follows. How can there be any meaning in our life if it ends in death? What meaning can there be in it that our inevitable death does not destroy? How can our existence be meaningful if there is no after-life in which perfect justice is meted out? How can life have any meaning if all it holds out to us are a few miserable earthly pleasures and even these to be enjoyed only rarely and for such a piteously short time?

I believe this is the point which exercises most people most deeply. Kirilov, in Dostoyevsky's novel, *The Possessed*, claims, just before committing suicide, that as soon as we realize that there is no God, we cannot live any longer, we must put an end to our lives. One of the reasons which he gives is that when we discover that there is no paradise, we have nothing to live for.

'... there was a day on earth, and in the middle of the earth were three crosses. One on the cross had such faith that He said to another, "To-day thou shalt be with me in paradise." The day came to an end, both died, and they went, but they found neither paradise nor resurrection. The saying did not come true. Listen: that man was the highest of all on earth. ... There has never been any one like Him before or since, and never will be. ... And if that is so, if the laws of Nature did not spare even *Him*, and made even Him live in the midst of lies and die for a lie, then the whole planet is a lie and is based on a lie and a stupid mockery. So the very laws of the planet are a lie and a farce of the devil. What, then, is there to live for?'[15] And Tolstoy, too, was nearly driven to suicide when he came to doubt the existence of God and an after-life.[16] And this is true of many.

What, then, is it that inclines us to think that if life is to have a meaning, there would be an after-life? It is this. The Christian world view contains the following three propositions. The first is that since the Fall, God's curse of Adam and Eve, and the expulsion from Paradise, life on earth for mankind has not been worthwhile, but a vale of tears, one long chain of misery, suffering, unhappiness, and injustice. The second is that a perfect after-life is awaiting us after the death of the body. The third is that we can enter this perfect life only on certain conditions, among which is also the condition of enduring our earthly existence to its bitter end. In this way, our earthly existence which, in itself, would not (at least for many people if not all) be worth living, acquires meaning and significance: only if we endure it, can we gain admission to the realm of the blessed.

It might be doubted whether this view is still held to-day. However, there can be no doubt that even to-day we all imbibe a good deal of this view with our earliest education. In sermons, the contrast between the perfect life of the blessed and our life of sorrow and drudgery is frequently driven home and we hear it again and again that Christianity has a message of hope and consolation for all those 'who are weary and heavy laden.'[17]

It is not surprising, then, that when the implications of the scientific world picture begin to sink in, when we come to have doubts about the existence of God and another life, we are bitterly disappointed. For if there is no after-life, then all we are left is our earthly life which we have come to regard as a necessary evil, the painful fee of admission to the land of eternal bliss. But if there is no eternal bliss to come and if this hell on earth is all, why hang on till the horrible end?

Our disappointment therefore arises out of these two propositions, that the earthly life is not worth living, and that there is another perfect life of eternal happiness and joy which we may enter upon if we satisfy certain conditions. We can regard our lives as meaningful, if we believe both. We cannot regard them as meaningful if we believe merely the first and not the second. It seems to me inevitable that people who are taught something of the history of science, will have serious doubts about the second. If they cannot overcome these, as many will be unable to do, then they must either accept the sad view that their life is meaningless or they must abandon the first proposition: that this earthly life is not worth living. They must find the meaning of their life in this earthly existence. But is this possible?

A moment's examination will show us that the Christian evaluation of our earthly life as worthless, which we accept in our moments of pessimism and dissatisfaction, is not one that we normally accept. Consider only the question of murder and suicide. On the Christian view, other things being equal, the most kindly thing to do would be for every one of us to kill as many of our friends and dear ones as still have the misfortune to be alive, and then to commit suicide without delay, for every moment spent in this life is wasted. On the Christian view, God has not made it that easy for us. He has forbidden us to hasten others or ourselves into the next life. Our bodies are His private property and must be allowed to wear themselves out in the way decided by Him, however painful and horrible that may be. We are, as it were, driving a burning car. There is only one way out, to jump clear and let it hurtle to destruction. But the owner of the car has forbidden it on pain of eternal tortures worse than burning. And so we do better to burn to death inside.

On this view, murder is a less serious wrong than suicide. For murder can always be confessed and repented and therefore forgiven, suicide cannot – unless we allow the ingenious way out chosen by the heroine of Graham Greene's play, *The Living Room*, who swallows a slow but deadly poison and, while awaiting its taking effect, repents having taken it. Murder, on the other hand, is not so serious because, in the first place, it need not rob the victim of anything but the last lap of his march in the vale of tears, and, in the second place, it can always be forgiven. Hamlet, it will be remembered, refrains from killing his uncle during the latter's prayers because, as a true Christian, he believes that killing his uncle at that point, when the latter has purified his soul by repentance, would merely be doing him a good turn, for murder at such a time would simply despatch him to undeserved and everlasting happiness.

These views strike us as odd, to say the least. They are the logical consequence of the official medieval evaluation of this our earthly existence. If this life is not worth living, then taking it is not robbing the person concerned of much. The only thing wrong with it is the damage to God's property, which is the same both in the case of murder and suicide. We do not take this view at all. Our view, on the contrary, is that murder is the most serious wrong because it consists in taking away from someone else against his will his most precious possession, his life. For this reason, when a person suffering from an incurable disease asks to be killed, the mercy killing of such a person is regarded as a much less serious crime than murder because, in such a case, the killer is not robbing the other of a good against his will. Suicide is not regarded as a real crime at all, for we take the view that a person can do with his own possessions what he likes.

However, from the fact that these are our normal opinions, we can infer nothing about their truth. After all, we could easily be mistaken. Whether life is or is not worthwhile, is a value judgment. Perhaps all this is merely a matter of opinion or taste. Perhaps no objective answer can be given. Fortunately, we need not enter deeply into these difficult and controversial questions. It is quite easy to show that the medieval evaluation of earthly life is based on a misguided procedure.

Let us remind ourselves briefly of how we arrive at our value judgments. When we determine the merits of students, meals, tennis players, bulls, or bathing belles, we do so on the basis of some criteria and some standard or norm. Criteria and standards notoriously vary from field to field and even from case to case. But that does not mean that we have *no* idea about what are the appropriate criteria or standards to use. It would not be fitting to apply the criteria for judging bulls to the judgment of students or bathing belles. They score on quite different points. And even where the same criteria are appropriate as in the judgment of students enrolled in different schools and universities, the standards will vary from one institution to another. Pupils who would only just pass in one, would perhaps obtain honours in another. The higher the standard applied, the lower the marks, that is, the merit conceded to the candidate.

The same procedure is applicable also in the evaluation of a life. We examine it on the basis of certain criteria and standards. The medieval Christian view uses the criteria of the ordinary man: a life is judged by what the person concerned can get out of it: the balance of happiness over unhappiness, pleasure over pain, bliss over suffering. Our earthly life is judged not worthwhile because it contains much unhappiness, pain, and suffering, little happiness, pleasure, and bliss. The next life is judged worthwhile because it provides eternal bliss and no suffering.

Armed with these criteria, we can compare the life of this man and that, and judge which is more worthwhile, which has a greater balance of bliss over suffering. But criteria alone enable us merely to make comparative judgments of value, not absolute ones. We can say which is more and which is less worthwhile, but we cannot say which is worthwhile and which is not. In order to determine the latter, we must introduce a standard. But what standard ought we to choose?

Ordinarily, the standard we employ is the average of the kind. We call a man and a tree tall if they are well above the average of their kind. We do not say that Jones is a short man because he is shorter than a tree. We do not judge a boy a bad student because his answer to a question in the Leaving Examination is much worse than that given in reply to the same question by a young man sitting for his finals for the Bachelor's degree.

The same principles must apply to judging lives. When we ask whether a given life was or was not worthwhile, then we must take into consideration the range of worthwhileness which ordinary lives normally cover. Our end poles of the scale must be the best possible and the worst possible life that one finds. A good and worthwhile life is one that is well above average. A bad one is one well below.

The Christian evaluation of earthly lives is misguided because it adopts a quite unjustifiably high standard. Christianity singles out the major shortcomings of our earthly existence: there is not enough happiness; there is too much suffering; the good and bad points are quite unequally and unfairly distributed; the underprivileged and underendowed do not get adequate compensation; it lasts only a short time. It then quite accurately depicts the perfect or ideal life as that which does not have any of these shortcomings. Its next step is to promise the believer that he will be able to enjoy this perfect life later on. And then it adopts as its standard of judgment the perfect life, dismissing as inadequate anything that falls short of it. Having dismissed earthly life as miserable, it further damns it by characterizing most of the pleasures of which earthly existence allows as bestial, gross, vile, and sinful, or alternatively as not really pleasurable.

This procedure is as illegitimate as if I were to refuse to call anything tall unless it is infinitely tall, or anything beautiful unless it is perfectly flawless, or anyone strong unless he is omnipotent. Even if it were true that there is available to us an after-life which is flawless and perfect, it would still not be legitimate to judge earthly lives by this standard. We do not fail every candidate who is not an Einstein. And if we do not believe in an after-life, we must of course use ordinary earthly standards.

I have so far only spoken of the worthwhileness, only of what a person can get out of a life. There are other kinds of appraisal. Clearly, we evaluate people's lives not merely from the point of view of what they yield to the persons that lead them, but also from that of other men on whom these lives have impinged. We judge a life more significant if the person has contributed to the happiness of others, whether directly by what he did for others, or by the plans, discoveries, inventions, and work he performed. Many lives that hold little in the way of pleasure or happiness for their owners are highly significant and valuable, deserve admiration and respect on account of the contributions made.

It is now quite clear that death is simply irrelevant. If life can be worthwhile at all, then it can be so even though it be short. And if it is not worthwhile at all, then an eternity of it is simply a nightmare. It may be sad that we have to leave this beautiful world, but it is so only if and because it is beautiful. And it is no less beautiful for coming to an end. I rather suspect that an eternity of it might make us less appreciative, and in the end it would be tedious.

It will perhaps be objected now that I have not really demonstrated that life has a meaning, but merely that it can be worthwhile or have value. It must be admitted that there is a perfectly natural interpretation of the question, 'What is the meaning of life?' on which my view actually proves that life has no meaning. I mean ... that, if we accept the explanations of natural science, we cannot believe that living organisms have appeared on earth in accordance with the deliberate plan of some intelligent being. Hence, on this view, life cannot be said to have a purpose, in the sense in which man-made things have a purpose. Hence it cannot be said to have a meaning or significance in that sense.

However, this conclusion is innocuous. People are disconcerted by the thought that *life as such* has no meaning in that sense only because they very naturally think it entails that no individual life can have meaning either. They naturally assume that *this* life or *that* can have meaning only if *life as such* has meaning. But it should by now be clear that your life and mine may or may not have meaning (in one sense) even if life as such has none (in the other). Of course, it follows from this that your life may have meaning while mine has not. The Christian view guarantees a meaning (in one sense) to every life, the scientific view does not (in any sense). By relating the question of the meaningfulness of life to the particular circumstances of an individual's existence, the scientific view leaves it an open question whether an individual's life has meaning or not. It is, however, clear that the latter is the important sense of 'having a meaning'. Christians, too, must feel that their life is wasted and meaningless if they have not achieved salvation. To know that even such lost lives have a meaning in another sense is no consolation to them. What matters is not that life should have a guaranteed meaning, whatever happens here or here-after, but that, by luck (Grace) or the right temperament and attitude

(Faith) or a judicious life (Works) a person should make the most of his life.

'But here lies the rub,' it will be said. 'Surely, it makes all the difference whether there is an after-life. This is where morality comes in.' It would be a mistake to believe that. Morality is not the meting out of punishment and reward. To be moral is to refrain from doing to others what, if they followed reason, they would not do to themselves, and to do for others what, if they followed reason, they would want to have done. It is, roughly speaking, to recognize that others, too, have a right to a worthwhile life. Being moral does not make one's own life worthwhile, it helps others to make theirs so.

NOTES

1 See e.g. 'Is Life Worth Living?' BBC Talk by the Rev. John Sutherland Bonnell in *Asking Them Questions*, Third Series, ed. by R. S. Wright (London: Geoffrey Cumberlege, 1950).

2 See e.g. Rudolf Otto, *The Idea of the Holy* (London: G. Cumberlege, 1952), pp. 9–11. See also C. A. Campbell, *On Selfhood and Godhood* (London: George Allen & Unwin Ltd, 1957), p. 246, and H. J. Paton, *The Modern Predicament* (London: George Allen & Unwin Ltd, 1955), pp. 69–71.

3 For a discussion of this issue, see the eighteenth century controversy between Deists and Theists, for instance, in Sir Leslie Stephen's *History of English Thought in the Eighteenth Century* (London: Smith, Elder & Co., 1902), pp. 112–19 and pp. 134–63. See also the attacks by Toland and Tindal on 'the mysterious' in *Christianity not Mysterious* and *Christianity as Old as the Creation, or the Gospel a Republication of the Religion of Nature*, resp., parts of which are reprinted in Henry Bettenson's *Doctrines of the Christian Church*, pp. 426–31. For modern views maintaining that mysteriousness is an essential element in religion, see Rudolf Otto, *The Idea of the Holy*, esp. pp. 25–40, and most recently M. B. Foster, *Mystery and Philosophy* (London: SCM Press, 1957), esp. Chs IV and VI. For the view that statements about God must be nonsensical or absurd, see e.g. H. J. Paton, *The Modern Predicament*, pp. 119–20, 367–9. See also 'Theology and Falsification' in *New Essays in Philosophical Theology*, ed. by A. Flew and A. MacIntyre (London: SCM Press, 1955), pp. 96–131; also N. McPherson, 'Religion as the Inexpressible', ibid., esp. pp. 137–43.

4 Stephen Neill, *Christian Faith To-day* (London: Penguin Books, 1955), pp. 240–1.

5 It is difficult to feel the magnitude of this first sin unless one takes seriously the words 'Behold, the man has eaten of the fruit of the tree of knowledge of good and evil, and is become as one of us; and now, may he not put forth his hand, and take also of the tree of life, and eat, and live for ever?' (Genesis III.2).

6 See in this connection the pastoral letter of 2nd February, 1905, by Johannes Katschtaler, Prince Bishop of Salzburg on the honour due to priests, contained

in *Quellen zur Geschichte des Papsttums*, by Mirbt, pp. 497–9, translated and reprinted in *The Protestant Tradition*, by J. S. Whale (Cambridge: University Press, 1955), pp. 259–62.

7   How impossible it is to make sense of this story has been demonstrated beyond any doubt by Tolstoy in his famous 'Conclusion of A Criticism of Dogmatic Theology', reprinted in *A Confession, The Gospel in Brief, and What I Believe* (London: G. Cumberlege, 1940).

8   See 'The Nicene Creed', 'The Tridentine Profession of Faith', 'The Syllabus of Errors', reprinted in *Documents of the Christian Church*, pp. 34, 373 and 380 resp.

9   See e.g. J. S. Whale, *The Protestant Tradition*, Ch. IV, esp. pp. 48–56.

10 See ibid., pp. 61 ff.

11 See 'The Confession of Augsburg', esp. Articles II, IV, XVIII, XIX, XX; 'Christianae Religionis Institutio', 'The Westminster Confession of Faith', esp. Articles III, VI, IX, X, XI, XVI, XVII; 'The Baptist Confession of Faith', esp. Articles III, XXI, XXIII, reprinted in *Documents of the Christian Church*, pp. 294 ff., 298 ff., 344 ff., 349 ff.

12 See e.g. his *An Empiricist's View of the Nature of Religious Belief* (Eddington Memorial Lecture).

13 See e.g. the two series of Gifford lectures most recently published: *The Modern Predicament* by H. J. Paton, pp. 69 ff., and *On Selfhood and Godhood* by C. A. Campbell (London: George Allen & Unwin Ltd, 1957), pp. 231–50.

14 Rudolf Otto, *The Idea of the Holy*, p. 9.

15 Fyodor Dostoyevsky, *The Devils* (London: The Penguin Classics, 1953), pp. 613–14.

16 Leo Tolstoy, *A Confession, The Gospel in Brief, and What I Believe*, The World's Classics, p. 24.

17 See for instance J. S. Whale, *Christian Doctrine*, pp. 171, 176–8, etc. See also Stephen Neill, *Christian Faith To-day*, p. 241.

4

Has the Question about the Meaning of Life any Meaning?

Rudolf Wohlgennant

The article by Wohlgennant is also concerned, as its title implies, with the meaning *of the question about meaning. He points out that a person might describe his life as meaningful because he was successful and contented, and then the word 'meaning' would be understood in that sense. This was evidently not the way in which Tolstoy understood it, for he makes a point of telling us that his doubts assailed him when he was successful and lacked none of the ingredients of a happy life. However, Wohlgennant introduces another sense of 'meaning'. He describes how one might seek a kind of meaning that would not be contingent on the buffets of fortune, and claims that it would make sense, at least, for a religious person to believe such a meaning to be in the keeping of God – even if he did not know what it was.*

Most people, presumably, would regard the question about the meaning of life, or of existence, as meaningful – which is not to say that they would actually put this question to themselves. Others, especially the adherents of a certain philosophical tradition, would doubt or deny that it makes sense. Both groups demand that the question whether life has a meaning must form a meaningful sentence. If they did not agree about this, then they would have different concepts of meaning, and would not understand the same by the word 'meaning'.

Now, if someone thinks that the sentence in which we ask about the meaning of life is not meaningful because it cannot, even in principle, be answered, then his position is obviously different from those who merely believe it wrong to expect an answer with the *same* content, but who regard the question itself as answerable. On this view, to ask meaningfully about the meaning of life is to formulate a question which is answerable in principle, however difficult it may be in a concrete situation to find a satisfactory answer which will also be convincing for others.

But when is a question meaningful? Under what conditions does a question make sense? A question makes sense if it is possible to state conditions under which the answer will be true or false.

If, for example, I ask myself whether I am satisfied with the course of my life, then I may, as also in other cases or with other questions, be undecided, vacillate, doubt, etc.: even so, it is possible, in principle, to say clearly what I mean or feel. I *understand* the question, and other people understand it too. It is clear that the answer to this question must be regarded as true, if it corresponds with my judgement concerning my satisfaction. I may indeed be mistaken in thinking that I am really satisfied and, even more so, in thinking that human beings in general are satisfied with their lives; but what is meant by 'being satisfied', that I understand. I am therefore able to use this expression in accordance with these criteria of application or conditions of use. To be sure, what is to be understood by 'satisfied' must first be clarified and established. But this requirement applies to all concepts having such a role in a given context.

It is no different if I ask myself whether I regard the actions which represent my life, or the lives of human beings as such, as valuable with regard to certain objectives, i.e. as leading to those objectives; and whether I regard these objectives themselves as worthy of pursuit. This is a question that I understand and that I can answer in principle.

I can define 'meaning of life' as a *feeling* that human beings generally have when they achieve a sufficient number of objectives that they have set themselves, or when they can bring about the realization of values they recognize. Now it is obvious that here certain preconditions must be assumed. But, if these preconditions disappear or are irretrievably destroyed, then I shall ask myself what the new state of affairs (or the state of affairs of which I now become conscious) means to me. Perhaps I shall find that a life of this kind does not interest, please or satisfy me; and this may remain so if there is no prospect of replacing what has been lost by new aims or values, together with the preconditions for achieving or realizing them. If I now ask whether my life is meaningful under these conditions, then again I understand very well what is meant by the question (which might be put by myself or by others to me). I may be confused or uncertain, may vacillate and doubt, and perhaps not be able to find a way out of this oppressive, unsatisfactory situation; but I would at least know *when* the question is to be answered in the affirmative or in the negative. In this case the question whether life is meaningful would mean: do I regard a life without values that I can recognize, or without objectives that I regard as worth pursuing, as sufficiently satisfying, happy or interesting?

In this case, the question 'Is life meaningful?' can be answered, whether in the affirmative or the negative. It is therefore a meaningful question. Here again, it would matter if people were in *error* in denying that the preconditions for the attainment of certain objectives were not present; or in thinking that they would not be able to accept certain objectives or values. But for present purposes it is of no importance whether they deceive themselves, or whether they might change their views after careful consideration.

We can show that human beings take themselves to understand the question about the meaning of life, that it evidently appears to them as a meaningful question. They answer it in concrete and precise ways, for example: 'My life is meaningful because I am healthy, successful and satisfied'; or '... because I have attained the aim or aims of my life, and hope to continue to do so'; or '... because I can live for other people and help them'; or even '... because I am dying for something that is more important to me than all else'; and finally '... because I believe that there is a divine giver of meaning whose commands I am trying to follow'.

The question about the meaning of the *question* about the meaning of life, or existence, must itself be meaningful too. It is so if the question about the meaning of life is capable of being answered, in the affirmative or in the negative; if the problem with which it deals is decidable. But, in the cases mentioned so far, such decision was possible. Hence there remain only two possibilities; either we arc not, in these cases, dealing with 'the' question, the *real* question; or else those who say that the question about the meaning of life is meaningless are wrong.

Which question, then, is meant? In certain tragic situations of life, people may experience the loss of something that seemed to them to give meaning to their lives; or which, at least, seemed to be one of the preconditions of a life that they could regard as meaningful – for example, health, family, contentment and good fortune. When this happens, they often ask: 'What sense is there in my life?' And when they see others who are *not* in this unhappy position they may ask: 'What is the sense of living, when the same *could* happen to anyone?'

To such a person, what had hitherto given meaning to life may perhaps no longer appear as genuine meaning. Yet, if the loss were reversed, life might appear to him as meaningful as before; and this could be so even after he has experienced, as in a bad dream, the fragility and perilous nature of fortune and meaning.

There are, however, losses that cannot be reversed. In such a situation, the person in quest of meaning may be seeking something that would compensate for his loss. But, as long as he does this, the question about meaning is still meaningful – it can be understood and answered. For he would be able to regard his life as meaningful again if there were something, a good, whose existence would satisfy him: whether this be another person he has found, a new aim that he can regard as worthy of pursuit, or a new belief through which he can find an aim and a meaning in life.

In these 'boundary situations' of life, the afflicted, disappointed, desperate and 'lost' person seeks a meaning that is fundamentally different from every 'normal' kind of meaning. He seeks a meaning that *cannot* be lost, and that would be more valuable than anything a human being can lose; a support that would last as long as life itself. When he asks 'What is the meaning of life?', he may mean meaning in *this* sense. And now we must ask: is the question about the meaning of life, understood in this sense, meaningless? It may be held to be so, because there are no means or methods of answering the question about meaning in this case, i.e. of solving the problem it contains.

But is there such a good, not comparable with any other, and not with anything that makes the lives of human beings in general valuable and meaningful? If there is no such thing, if there cannot be such a thing, then the quest for it is condemned to failure, and we would have to give a negative answer to the question about the meaning of such questions about meaning. The assumption here, however, would be that there *cannot be* such a supremely valuable good; and this assumption should not be admitted. It would be admissible only if one could prove the existence of such a good to be impossible.

Such a good does, however, belong to people with a certain belief. This is the belief that there is a Being who knows something that human beings do not know, namely: the meaning and purpose of *every* happening, *every* event or state of affairs, whether in life or in death, experience or action. A person who has this belief will certainly not be immune from the greatest pain, desperation, misery and dissatisfaction. But, if he really believes, then no event can cause him to have lasting doubts about the meaning of life – whether his own, or life or existence in general. Nor will he be able to experience tragedy in the real sense; for tragedy in the full, radical sense exists only for those who can no longer find the meaning of life *anywhere*. The believer, however, who believes this meaning to be in the keeping of God – even if he cannot know it himself – has not lost it. Therefore someone who believes and has confidence in this way will not regard the question about the meaning of life, or his own life, as meaningless, however poor and miserable this life may be when measured by *human* standards.

Philosophers who regard the question about meaning as meaningless can do this only as people who do not believe in the existence of such a divine being – or at least they can do it only *qua* philosophers. However, whether there *is* such a being – a universal giver of meaning and supreme value – is a question that will not be answered here. But others too can regard the question of meaning, posed in this way, as meaningful, if there is something they believe in, which would compensate for every loss and which can give meaning to whatever may befall. For example, someone to whom an ideology or world-view appears more important than anything else will, to that extent, regard the question about the meaning of life as meaningful. In this respect there is no fundamental difference between him and the one who believes in the existence of a divine giver of universal meaning.

It follows that the question about the meaning of life cannot in general and *a priori* be pronounced meaningless, but only under certain conditions. It will be meaningless for someone who regards the question as being about a meaning that 'exists in itself', a so-called 'objective' meaning. For such an existence 'in itself' cannot be proved, nor can it even be understood in any real sense. Claims of this kind are therefore not to be admitted; they cannot represent the intellectual content of a sentence.

Let me sum up. No doubt the question about the meaning of life or existence must first be tested for meaningfulness. But the answer to this cannot be separated from the use of the word 'meaning', the concept of meaning, that is being used by a particular speaker. Our considerations have shown that various meanings, or types of use, of 'meaning of life' or 'meaning of existence' are current. This result is, after all, not surprising, for it is only a special case of the general need to begin by examining the relevant 'key concepts', and the use of the linguistic expressions by those who use them. Extensions of these can then be either followed or corrected; and, with supporting argument, a use of language, suitable at least for the case in question, can be introduced.

5

The Meaning of Life

Richard Taylor

The contribution by Taylor, and the next one by Nagel, are largely negative. Taylor compares the human situation with that of Sisyphus of the ancient Greek myth, who was condemned to an eternal life of meaningless activity – pushing a stone to the top of a hill, from which it would immediately roll down again. In the natural world too, according to Taylor, we have a spectacle of meaningless activity in the endless sequence of generations: 'each of these cycles, so filled with toil, is to be followed only by more of the same.' Similarly, in the case of human activity, we 'toil after goals' which are of 'transitory significance'; 'having gained one of them, we immediately set forth for the next', the latter being 'essentially more of the same'. Taylor also draws attention to a problem which might be summed up in the saying 'To travel is better than to arrive'. To have a goal to work for is satisfying; but the achievement of the goal entails that we no longer have it. Perhaps my life is given meaning by the existence in it of goal X; but this is a suicidal kind of meaning, since my efforts will be directed to an achievement which will eliminate that meaning. This problem is brought out by Taylor in an ingenious adaptation of the Sisyphus story, in which his labours lead to the construction of a beautiful and enduring temple on the top of the hill.

In spite of his negative analysis of the human condition, Taylor concludes on an optimistic note, claiming that 'the point of living is simply to be living', and that 'the meaning of life is from within us.' Such claims will not, however, satisfy those who crave for some meaning beyond that. They might be told that such demands are meaningless, for logical reasons. (For example, there is no way of evading the logical truth that when we have achieved a goal, we no longer have it.) Nevertheless they may continue dissatisfied, deploring that there are these logical restrictions on meaning and purpose.

The question whether life has any meaning is difficult to interpret, and the more one concentrates his critical faculty on it the more it seems to elude him, or to evaporate as any intelligible question. One wants to turn it aside, as a source of embarrassment, as something that, if it cannot be abolished, should at least be decently covered. And yet I think any reflective person recognizes that the question it raises is important, and that it ought to have a significant answer.

If the idea of meaningfulness is difficult to grasp in this context, so that we are unsure what sort of thing would amount to answering the question, the idea of meaninglessness is perhaps less so. If, then, we can bring before our minds a clear image of meaningless existence, then perhaps we can take a step toward coping with our original question by seeing to what extent our lives, as we actually find them, resemble that image, and draw such lessons as we are able to from the comparison.

MEANINGLESS EXISTENCE

A perfect image of meaninglessness, of the kind we are seeking, is found in the ancient myth of Sisyphus. Sisyphus, it will be remembered, betrayed divine secrets to mortals, and for this he was condemned by the gods to roll a stone to the top of a hill, the stone then immediately to roll back down, again to be pushed to the top by Sisyphus, to roll down once more, and so on again and again, *forever*. Now in this we have the picture of meaningless, pointless toil, of a meaningless existence that is absolutely *never* redeemed. It is not even redeemed by a death that, if it were to accomplish nothing more, would at least bring this idiotic cycle to a close. If we were invited to imagine Sisyphus struggling for awhile and accomplishing nothing, perhaps eventually falling from exhaustion, so that we might suppose him then eventually turning to something having some sort of promise, then the meaninglessness of that chapter of his life would not be so stark. It would be a dark and dreadful dream, from which he eventually awakens to sunlight and reality. But he does not awaken, for there is nothing for him to awaken to. His repetitive toil is his life and reality, and it goes on forever, and it is without any meaning whatever. Nothing ever comes of what he is doing, except simply, more of the same. Not by one step, nor by a thousand, nor by ten thousand does he even expiate by the smallest token the sin against the gods that led him into this fate. Nothing comes of it, nothing at all.

This ancient myth has always enchanted men, for countless meanings can be read into it. Some of the ancients apparently thought it symbolized the perpetual rising and setting of the sun, and others the repetitious crashing of the waves upon the shore. Probably the commonest interpretation is that it symbolizes man's eternal struggle and unquenchable spirit, his determination always to try once more in the face of overwhelming discouragement. This interpretation is further supported by that version of the myth according to which Sisyphus was commanded to roll the stone *over* the hill, so that it would finally roll down the other side, but was never quite able to make it.

I am not concerned with rendering or defending any interpretation of this myth, however. I have cited it only for the one element it does unmistakably contain, namely, that of a repetitious, cyclic activity that never comes to anything. We could contrive other images of this that would serve just as well, and no myth-makers are needed to supply the materials of it. Thus, we can imagine two persons transporting a stone – or even a precious gem, it does not matter – back and forth, relay style. One carries it to a near or distant point where it is received by the other; it is returned to its starting point, there to be recovered by the first, and the process is repeated over and over. Except in this relay nothing counts as winning, and nothing brings the contest to any close, each step only leads to a repetition of itself. Or we can imagine two groups of prisoners, one of them engaged in digging a prodigious hole in the ground that is no sooner finished than it is filled in again by the other group, the latter then digging a new hole that is at once filled in by the first group, and so on and on endlessly.

Now what stands out in all such pictures as oppressive and dejecting is not that the beings who enact these roles suffer any torture or pain, for it need not be assumed that they do. Nor is it that their labors are great, for they are no greater than the labors commonly undertaken by most men most of the time. According to the original myth, the stone is so large that Sisyphus never quite gets it to the top and must groan under every step, so that his enormous labor is all for nought. But this is not what appals. It is not that his great struggle comes to nothing, but that his existence itself is without meaning. Even if we suppose, for example, that the stone is but a pebble that can be carried effortlessly, or that the holes dug by the prisoners are but small ones, not the slightest meaning is introduced into their lives. The stone that Sisyphus moves to the top of the hill, whether we think of it as large or small, still rolls back every time, and the process is repeated forever. Nothing comes of it, and the work is simply pointless, That is the element of the myth that I wish to capture.

Again, it is not the fact that the labors of Sisyphus continue forever that deprives them of meaning. It is, rather, the implication of this: that they come to nothing. The image would not be changed by our supposing him to push a different stone up every time, each to roll down again. But if we supposed that these stones, instead of rolling back to their places as if they had never been moved, were assembled at the top of the hill and there incorporated, say, in a beautiful and enduring temple, then the aspect of meaninglessness would disappear. His labors would then have a point, something would come of them all, and although one could perhaps still say it was not worth it, one could not say that the life of Sisyphus was devoid of meaning altogether. Meaningfulness would at least have made an appearance, and we could see what it was.

That point will need remembering. But in the meantime, let us note another way in which the image of meaninglessness can be altered by making only a very slight change. Let us suppose that the gods, while condemning Sisyphus to the fate just described, at the same time, as an afterthought, waxed perversely merciful by implanting in him a strange and irrational impulse; namely, a compulsive impulse to roll stones. We may if we like, to make this more graphic, suppose they accomplish this by implanting in him some substance that has this effect on his character and drives. I call this perverse, because from our point of view there is clearly no reason why anyone should have a persistent and insatiable desire to do something so pointless as that. Nevertheless, suppose that is Sisyphus' condition. He has but one obsession, which is to roll stones, and it is an obsession that is only for the moment appeased by his rolling them – he no sooner gets a stone rolled to the top of the hill than he is restless to roll up another.

Now it can be seen why this little afterthought of the gods, which I called perverse, was also in fact merciful. For they have by this device managed to give Sisyphus precisely what he wants – by making him want precisely what they inflict on him. However it may appear to us, Sisyphus' fate now does not appear to him as a condemnation, but the very reverse. His one desire in life is to roll stones, and he is absolutely guaranteed its endless fulfilment. Where otherwise he might profoundly have wished surcease, and even welcomed the quiet of death to release him from endless boredom and meaninglessness, his life is now filled with mission and meaning, and he seems to himself to have been given an entry to heaven. Nor need he even fear death, for the gods have promised him an endless opportunity to indulge his single purpose, without concern or frustration. He will be able to roll stones *forever*.

What we need to mark most carefully at this point is that the picture with which we began has not really been changed in the least by adding this supposition. Exactly the same things happen as before. The only change is in Sisyphus' view of them. The picture before was the image of meaningless activity and existence. It was created precisely to be an image of that. It has not lost that meaninglessness, it has now gained not the least shred of meaningfulness. The stones still roll back as before, each phase of Sisyphus' life still exactly resembles all the others, the task is never completed, nothing comes of it, no temple ever begins to rise, and all this cycle of the same pointless thing over and over goes on forever in this picture as in the other. The *only* thing that has happened is this: Sisyphus has been reconciled to it, and indeed more, he has been led to embrace it. Not, however, by reason or persuasion, but by nothing more rational than the potency of a new substance in his veins.

THE MEANINGLESSNESS OF LIFE

I believe the foregoing provides a fairly clear content to the idea of meaninglessness and, through it, some hint of what meaningfulness, in this sense, might be. Meaninglessness is essentially endless pointlessness, and meaningfulness is therefore the opposite. Activity, and even long, drawn-out and repetitive activity, has a meaning if it has some significant culmination, some more or less lasting end that can be considered to have been the direction and purpose of the activity. But the descriptions so far also provide something else; namely, the suggestion of how an existence that is objectively meaningless, in this sense, can nevertheless acquire a meaning for him whose existence it is.

Now let us ask: Which of these pictures does life in fact resemble? And let us not begin with our own lives, for here both our prejudices and wishes are great, but with the life in general that we share with the rest of creation. We shall find, I think, that it all has a certain pattern, and that this pattern is by now easily recognized.

We can begin anywhere, only saving human existence for our last consideration. We can, for example, begin with any animal. It does not matter where we begin, because the result is going to be exactly the same.

Thus, for example, there are caves in New Zealand, deep and dark, whose floors are quiet pools and whose walls and ceilings are covered with soft light. As one gazes in wonder in the stillness of these caves it seems that the Creator has reproduced there in microcosm the heavens themselves, until one scarcely remembers the enclosing presence of the walls. As one looks more closely, however, the scene is explained. Each dot of light identifies an ugly worm, whose luminous tail is meant to attract insects from the surrounding darkness. As from time to time one of these insects draws near it becomes entangled in a sticky thread lowered by the worm, and is eaten. This goes on month after month, the blind worm lying there in the barren stillness waiting to entrap an occasional bit of nourishment that will only sustain it to another bit of nourishment until ... Until what? What great thing awaits all this long and repetitious effort and makes it worthwhile? Really nothing. The larva just transforms itself finally to a tiny winged adult that lacks even mouth parts to feed and lives only a day or two. These adults, as soon as they have mated and laid eggs, are themselves caught in the threads and are devoured by the cannibalist worms, often without having ventured into the day, the only point to their existence having now been fulfilled. This has been going on for millions of years, and to no end other than that the same meaningless cycle may continue for another millions of years.

All living things present essentially the same spectacle. The larva of a certain cicada burrows in the darkness of the earth for seventeen years, through season after season, to emerge finally into the daylight for a brief flight, lay its eggs, and die – this all to repeat itself during the next seventeen years, and so on to eternity. We have already noted, in another connection, the struggles of fish, made only that others may do the same after them and that this cycle, having no other point than itself, may never cease. Some birds span an entire side of the globe each year and then return, only to insure that others may follow the same incredibly long path again and again. One is led to wonder what the point of it all is, with what great triumph this ceaseless effort, repeating itself through millions of years, might finally culminate, and why it should go on and on for so long, accomplishing nothing, getting nowhere. But then one realizes that there is no point to it at all, that it really culminates in nothing, that each of these cycles, so filled with toil, is to be followed only by more of the same. The point of any living thing's life is, evidently, nothing but life itself.

This life of the world thus presents itself to our eyes as a vast machine, feeding on itself, running on and on forever to nothing. And we are part of that life. To be sure, we are not just the same, but the differences are not so great as we like to think; many are merely invented, and none really cancels the kind of meaninglessness that we found in Sisyphus and that we find all around, wherever anything lives. We are conscious of our activity. Our goals, whether in any significant sense we choose them or not, are things of which we are at least partly aware and can therefore in some sense appraise. More significantly, perhaps, men have a history, as other animals do not, such that each generation does not precisely resemble all those before. Still, if we can in imagination disengage our wills from our lives and disregard the deep interest each man has in his own existence, we shall find that they do not so little resemble the existence of Sisyphus. We toil after goals, most of them – indeed every single one of them – of transitory significance and, having gained one of them, we immediately set forth for the next, as if that one had never been, with this next one being essentially more of the same. Look at a busy street any day, and observe the throng going hither and thither. To what? Some office or shop, where the same things will be done today as were done yesterday, and are done now so they may be repeated tomorrow. And if we think that, unlike Sisyphus, these labors do have a point, that they culminate in something lasting and, independently of our own deep interests in them, very worthwhile, then we simply have not considered the thing closely enough. Most such effort is directed only to the establishment and perpetuation of home and family; that is, to the begetting of others who will follow in our steps to do more of the same. Each man's life thus resembles one of Sisyphus' climbs to the summit of his hill, and each day of it one of his steps; the difference is that whereas Sisyphus himself returns to push the stone up again, we leave this to our children. We at one point imagined that the labors of Sisyphus finally culminated in the creation of a temple, but for this to make any difference it had to be a temple that would at least endure, adding beauty to the world for the remainder of time. Our achievements, even though they are often beautiful, are mostly bubbles; and those that do last, like the sand-swept pyramids, soon become mere curiosities while around them the rest of mankind continues its perpetual toting of rocks, only to see them roll down. Nations are built upon the bones of their founders and pioneers, but only to decay and crumble before long, their rubble then becoming the foundation for others directed to exactly the same fate. The picture of Sisyphus is the picture of existence of the individual man, great or unknown, of nations, of the race of men, and of the very life of the world.

On a country road one sometimes comes upon the ruined hulks of a house and once extensive buildings, all in collapse and spread over with weeds. A curious eye can in imagination reconstruct from what is left a once warm and thriving life, filled with purpose. There was the hearth, where a family once talked, sang, and made plans; there were the rooms, where people loved, and babes were born to a rejoicing mother; there are the musty remains of a sofa, infested with bugs, once bought at a dear price to enhance an ever-growing comfort, beauty, and warmth. Every small piece of junk fills the mind with what once, not long ago, was utterly real, with children's voices, plans made, and enterprises embarked upon. That is how these stones of Sisyphus were rolled up, and that is how they became incorporated into a beautiful temple, and that temple is what now lies before you. Meanwhile other buildings, institutions, nations, and civilizations spring up all around, only to share the same fate before long. And if the question 'What for?' is now asked, the answer is clear: so that just this may go on forever.

The two pictures – of Sisyphus and of our own lives, if we look at them from a distance – are in outline the same and convey to the mind the same image. It is not surprising then, that men invent ways of denying it, their religions proclaiming a heaven that does not crumble, their hymnals and prayer books declaring a significance to life of which our eyes provide no hint whatever.[1] Even our philosophies portray some permanent and lasting good at which all may aim, from the changeless forms invented by Plato to the beatific vision of St Thomas and the ideals of permanence contrived by the moderns. When these fail to convince, then earthly ideals such as universal justice and brotherhood are conjured up to take their places and give meaning to man's seemingly endless pilgrimage, some final state that will be ushered in when the last obstacle is removed and the last stone pushed to the hilltop. No one believes, of course, that any such state will be final, or even wants it to be in case it means that human existence would then cease to be struggle; but in the meantime such ideas serve a very real need.

THE MEANING OF LIFE

We noted that Sisyphus' existence would have meaning if there were some point to his labors, if his efforts ever culminated in something that was not just an occasion for fresh labors of the same kind. But that is precisely the meaning it lacks. And human existence resembles his in that respect. Men do achieve things – they scale their towers and raise their stones to their hilltops – but every such accomplishment fades, providing only an occasion for renewed labors of the same kind.

But here we need to note something else that has been mentioned, but its significance not explored, and that is the state of mind and feeling with which such labors are undertaken. We noted that if Sisyphus had a keen and unappeasable desire to be doing just what he found himself doing, then, although his life would in no way be changed, it would nevertheless have a meaning for him. It would be an irrational one, no doubt, because the desire itself would be only the product of the substance in his veins, and not any that reason could discover, but a meaning nevertheless.

And would it not, in fact, be a meaning incomparably better than the other? For let us examine again the first kind of meaning it could have. Let us suppose that, without having any interest in rolling stones, as such, and finding this, in fact, a galling toil, Sisyphus did nevertheless have a deep interest in raising a temple, one that would be beautiful and lasting. And let us suppose he succeeded in this, that after ages of dreadful toil, all directed at this final result, he did at last complete his temple, such that now he could say his work was done, and he could rest and forever enjoy the result. Now what? What picture now presents itself to our minds? It is precisely the picture of infinite boredom! Of Sisyphus doing nothing ever again, but contemplating what he has already wrought and can no longer add anything to, and contemplating it for an eternity! Now in this picture we have a meaning for Sisyphus' existence, a point for his prodigious labor, because we have put it there; yet, at the same time, that which is really worthwhile seems to have slipped away entirely. Where before we were presented with the nightmare of eternal and pointless activity, we are now confronted with the hell of its eternal absence.

Our second picture, then, wherein we imagine Sisyphus to have had inflicted on him the irrational desire to be doing just what he found himself doing, should not have been dismissed so abruptly. The meaning that picture lacked was no meaning that he or anyone could crave, and the strange meaning it had was perhaps just what we were seeking.

At this point, then, we can reintroduce what has been until now, it is hoped, resolutely pushed aside in an effort to view our lives and human existence with objectivity; namely, our own wills, our deep interest in what we find ourselves doing. If we do this we find that our lives do indeed still resemble that of Sisyphus, but that the meaningfulness they thus lack is precisely the meaningfulness of infinite boredom. At the same time, the strange meaningfulness they possess is that of the inner compulsion to be doing just what we were put here to do, and to go on doing it forever. This is the nearest we may hope to get to heaven, but the redeeming side of that fact is that we do thereby avoid a genuine hell.

If the builders of a great and flourishing ancient civilization could somehow return now to see archaeologists unearthing the trivial remnants of pots and vases, a few broken statues, and such tokens of another age and greatness – they could indeed ask themselves what the point of it all was, if this is all it finally came to. Yet, it did not seem so to them then, for it was just the building, and not what was finally built, that gave their life meaning. Similarly, if the builders of the ruined home and farm that I described a short while ago could be brought back to see what is left, they would have the same feelings. What we construct in our imaginations as we look over these decayed and rusting pieces would reconstruct itself in their very memories, and certainly with unspeakable sadness. The piece of a sled at our feet would revive in them a warm Christmas. And what rich memories would there be in the broken crib? And the weed-covered remains of a fence would reproduce the scene of a great herd of livestock, so laboriously built up over so many years. What was it all worth, if this is the final result? Yet, again, it did not seem so to them through those many years of struggle and toil, and they did not imagine they were building a Gibraltar. The things to which they bent their backs day after day, realizing one by one their ephemeral plans, were precisely the things in which their wills were deeply involved, precisely the things in which their interests lay, and there was no need then to ask questions. There is no more need of them now – the day was sufficient to itself, and so was the life.

This is surely the way to look at all of life – at one's own life, and each day and moment it contains; of the life of a nation; of the species; of the life of the world; and of everything that breathes. Even the glow worms I described, whose cycles of existence over the millions of years seem so pointless when looked at by us, will seem entirely different to us if we can somehow try to view their existence from within. Their endless activity, which gets nowhere, is just what it is their will to pursue. This is its whole justification and meaning. Nor would it be any salvation to the birds who span the globe every year, back and forth, to have a home made for them in a cage with plenty of food and protection, so that they would not have to migrate any more. It would be their condemnation, for it is the doing that counts for them, and not what they hope to win by it. Flying these prodigious distances, never ending, is what it is in their veins to do, exactly as it was in Sisyphus' veins to roll stones, without end, after the gods had waxed merciful and implanted this in him.

A human being no sooner draws his first breath than he responds to the will that is in him to live. He no more asks whether it will be worthwhile, or whether anything of significance will come of it, than the worms and the birds. The point of his living is simply to be living, in the manner that it is his nature to be living. He goes through his life building his castles, each of these beginning to fade into time as the next is begun; yet, it would be no salvation to rest from all this. It would be a condemnation, and one that would in no way be redeemed were he able to gaze upon the things he has done, even if these were beautiful and absolutely permanent, as they never are. What counts is that one should be able to begin a new task, a new castle, a new bubble. It counts only because it is there to be done and he has the will to do it. The same will be the life of his children, and of theirs; and if the philosopher is apt to see in this a pattern similar to the unending cycles of the existence of Sisyphus, and to despair, then it is indeed because the meaning and point he is seeking is not there – but mercifully so. The meaning of life is from within us, it is not bestowed from without, and it far exceeds in both its beauty and permanence any heaven of which men have ever dreamed or yearned for.

NOTE

1   A popular Christian hymn, sung often at funerals and typical of many hymns, expresses this thought:

> Swift to its close ebbs out life's little day;
> Earth's joys grow dim, its glories pass away;
> Change and decay in all around I see:
> O thou who changest not, abide with me.

6

The Absurd

Thomas Nagel

Unlike Taylor, Nagel makes no attempt to reach an optimistic conclusion; his conclusion is that human life is 'absurd'. He mentions a number of familiar arguments about the insignificance of man (or individual men) when viewed in a wider context of space and time, etc. However, Nagel's argument is not that life is absurd for these reasons (he rejects 'the standard arguments for absurdity'), but that it is so because we take our lives seriously while aware *of the other point of view. The 'two inescapable viewpoints collide in us, and that is what makes life absurd. It is absurd becaues we ... continue to live with nearly undiminished seriousness in spite of' that other viewpoint. It follows from this position that the life of a being without such awareness will* not *be absurd. Thus a mouse's life, according to Nagel, is not absurd, 'because he lacks the ... self-consciousness and self-transcendence that would enable him to see that he is only a mouse'. In the passage from Taylor, by contrast, examples of animal life were put forward as paradigms of meaningless existence.*

Nagel is another writer who shows concern about the meaning of questions about the meaning of life. Is such a word as 'absurd' really applicable to life as a whole? How is the word used in ordinary discourse? Nagel gives an account, and a number of interesting examples, of the use of the 'absurd' within 'ordinary life', and claims that it can be applied, in the same sense, to life itself.

Most people feel on occasion that life is absurd, and some feel it vividly and continually. Yet the reasons usually offered in defense of this conviction are patently inadequate: they *could* not really explain why life is absurd. Why then do they provide a natural expression for the sense that it is?

I

Consider some examples. It is often remarked that nothing we do now will matter in a million years. But if that is true, then by the same token, nothing that will be the case in a million years matters now. In particular, it does not matter now that in a million years nothing we do now will matter.

Moreover, even if what we did now *were* going to matter in a million years, how could that keep our present concerns from being absurd? If their mattering now is not enough to accomplish that, how would it help if they mattered a million years from now?

Whether what we do now will matter in a million years could make the crucial difference only if its mattering in a million years depended on its mattering, period. But then to deny that whatever happens now will matter in a million years is to beg the question against its mattering, period; for in that sense one cannot know that it will not matter in a million years whether (for example) someone now is happy or miserable, without knowing that it does not matter, period.

What we say to convey the absurdity of our lives often has to do with space or time: we are tiny specks in the infinite vastness of the universe; our lives are mere instants even on a geological time scale, let alone a cosmic one; we will all be dead any minute. But of course none of these evident facts can be what *makes* life absurd, if it is absurd. For suppose we lived forever; would not a life that is absurd if it lasts seventy years be infinitely absurd if it lasted through eternity? And if our lives are absurd given our present size, why would they be any less absurd if we filled the universe (either because we were larger or because the universe was smaller)? Reflection on our minuteness and brevity appears to be intimately connected with the sense that life is meaningless; but it is not clear what the connection is.

Another inadequate argument is that because we are going to die, all chains of justification must leave off in mid-air: one studies and works to earn money to pay for clothing, housing, entertainment, food, to sustain oneself from year to year, perhaps to support a family and pursue a career – but to what final end? All of it is an elaborate journey leading nowhere. (One will also have some effect on other people's lives, but that simply reproduces the problem, for they will die too.)

There are several replies to this argument. First, life does not consist of a sequence of activities each of which has as its purpose some later member of the sequence. Chains of justification come repeatedly to an end within life, and whether the process as a whole can be justified has no bearing on the finality of these end-points. No further justification is needed to make it reasonable to take aspirin for a headache, attend an exhibit of the work of a painter one admires, or stop a child from putting his hand on a hot stove. No larger context or further purpose is needed to prevent these acts from being pointless.

Even if someone wished to supply a further justification for pursuing all the things in life that are commonly regarded as self-justifying, that justification would have to end somewhere too. If *nothing* can justify unless it is justified in terms of something outside itself, which is also justified, then an infinite regress results, and no chain of justification can be complete. Moreover, if a finite chain of reasons cannot justify anything, what could be accomplished by an infinite chain, each link of which must be justified by something outside itself?

Since justifications must come to an end somewhere, nothing is gained by denying that they end where they appear to, within life – or by trying to subsume the multiple, often trivial ordinary justifications of action under a single, controlling life scheme. We can be satisfied more easily than that. In fact, through its misrepresentation of the process of justification, the argument makes a vacuous demand. It insists that the reasons available within life are incomplete, but suggests thereby that all reasons that come to an end are incomplete. This makes it impossible to supply any reasons at all.

The standard arguments for absurdity appear therefore to fail as arguments. Yet I believe they attempt to express something that is difficult to state, but fundamentally correct.

II

In ordinary life a situation is absurd when it includes a conspicuous discrepancy between pretension or aspiration and reality: someone gives a complicated speech in support of a motion that has already been passed; a notorious criminal is made president of a major philanthropic foundation; you declare your love over the telephone to a recorded announcement; as you are being knighted, your pants fall down.

When a person finds himself in an absurd situation, he will usually attempt to change it, by modifying his aspirations, or by trying to bring reality into better accord with them, or by removing himself from the situation entirely. We are not always willing or able to extricate ourselves from a position whose absurdity has become clear to us. Nevertheless, it is usually possible to imagine some change that would remove the absurdity – whether or not we can or will implement it. The sense that life as a whole is absurd arises when we perceive, perhaps dimly, an inflated pretension or aspiration which is inseparable from the continuation of human life and which makes its absurdity inescapable, short of escape from life itself.

Many people's lives are absurd, temporarily or permanently, for conventional reasons having to do with their particular ambitions, circumstances, and personal relations. If there is a philosophical sense of absurdity, however, it must arise from the perception of something universal – some respect in which pretension and reality inevitably clash for us all. This condition is supplied, I shall argue, by the collision between the seriousness with which we take our lives and the perpetual possibility of regarding everything about which we are serious as arbitrary, or open to doubt.

We cannot live human lives without energy and attention, nor without making choices which show that we take some things more seriously than others. Yet we have always available a point of view outside the particular form of our lives, from which the seriousness appears gratuitous. These two inescapable viewpoints collide in us, and that is what makes life absurd. It is absurd because we ignore the doubts that we know cannot be settled, continuing to live with nearly undiminished seriousness in spite of them.

This analysis requires defense in two respects: first as regards the unavoidability of seriousness; second as regards the inescapability of doubt.

We take ourselves seriously whether we lead serious lives or not and whether we are concerned primarily with fame, pleasure, virtue, luxury, triumph, beauty, justice, knowledge, salvation, or mere survival. If we take other people seriously and devote ourselves to them, that only multiplies the problem. Human life is full of effort, plans, calculation, success and failure: we *pursue* our lives, with varying degrees of sloth and energy.

It would be different if we could not step back and reflect on the process, but were merely led from impulse to impulse without self-consciousness. But human beings do not act solely on impulse. They are prudent, they reflect, they weigh consequences, they ask whether what they are doing is worth while. Not only are their lives full of particular choices that hang together in larger activities with temporal structure: they also decide in the broadest terms what to pursue and what to avoid, what the priorities among their various aims should be, and what kind of people they want to be or become. Some men are faced with such choices by the large decisions they make from time to time; some merely by reflection on the course their lives are taking as the product of countless small decisions. They decide whom to marry, what profession to follow, whether to join the Country Club, or the Resistance; or they may just wonder why they go on being salesmen or academics or taxi drivers, and then stop thinking about it after a certain period of inconclusive reflection.

Although they may be motivated from act to act by those immediate needs with which life presents them, they allow the process to continue by adhering to the general system of habits and the form of life in which such motives have their place – or perhaps only by clinging to life itself. They spend enormous quantities of energy, risk, and calculation on the details. Think of how an ordinary individual sweats over his appearance, his health, his sex life, his emotional honesty, his social utility, his self-knowledge, the quality of his ties with family, colleagues, and friends, how well he does his job, whether he understands the world and what is going on in it. Leading a human life is a full-time occupation, to which everyone devotes decades of intense concern.

This fact is so obvious that it is hard to find it extraordinary and important. Each of us lives his own life – lives with himself twenty-four hours a day. What else is he supposed to do – live someone else's life? Yet humans have the special capacity to step back and survey themselves, and the lives to which they are committed, with that detached amazement which comes from watching an ant struggle up a heap of sand. Without developing the illusion that they are able to escape from their highly specific and idiosyncratic position, they can view it *sub specie aeternitatis* – and the view is at once sobering and comical.

The crucial backward step is not taken by asking for still another justification in the chain, and failing to get it. The objections to that line of attack have already been stated; justifications come to an end. But this is precisely what provides universal doubt with its object. We step back to find that the whole system of justification and criticism, which controls our choices and supports our claims to rationality, rests on responses and habits that we never question, that we should not know how to defend without circularity, and to which we shall continue to adhere even after they are called into question.

The things we do or want without reasons, and without requiring reasons – the things that define what is a reason for us and what is not – are the starting points of our skepticism. We see ourselves from outside, and all the contingency and specificity of our aims and pursuits become clear. Yet when we take this view and recognize what we do as arbitrary, it does not disengage us from life, and there lies our absurdity: not in the fact that such an external view can be taken of us, but in the fact that we ourselves can take it, without ceasing to be the persons whose ultimate concerns are so coolly regarded.

III

One may try to escape the position by seeking broader ultimate concerns, from which it is impossible to step back – the idea being that absurdity results because what we take seriously is something small and insignificant and individual. Those seeking to supply their lives with meaning usually envision a role or function in something larger than themselves. They therefore seek fulfilment in service to society, the state, the revolution, the progress of history, the advance of science, or religion and the glory of God.

But a role in some larger enterprise cannot confer significance unless that enterprise is itself significant. And its significance must come back to what we can understand, or it will not even appear to give us what we are seeking. If we learned that we were being raised to provide food for other creatures fond of human flesh, who planned to turn us into cutlets before we got too stringy – even if we learned that the human race had been developed by animal breeders precisely for this purpose – that would still not give our lives meaning, for two reasons. First, we would still be in the dark as to the significance of the lives of those other beings; second, although we might acknowledge that this culinary role would make our lives meaningful to them, it is not clear how it would make them meaningful to us.

Admittedly, the usual form of service to a higher being is different from this. One is supposed to behold and partake of the glory of God, for example, in a way in which chickens do not share in the glory of coq au vin. The same is true of service to a state, a movement, or a revolution. People can come to feel, when they are part of something bigger, that it is part of them too. They worry less about what is peculiar to themselves, but identify enough with the larger enterprise to find their role in it fulfilling.

However, any such larger purpose can be put in doubt in the same way that the aims of an individual life can be, and for the same reasons. It is as legitimate to find ultimate justification there as to find it earlier, among the details of individual life. But this does not alter the fact that justifications come to an end when we are content to have them end – when we do not find it necessary to look any further. If we can step back from the purposes of individual life and doubt their point, we can step back also from the progress of human history, or of science, or the success of a society, or the kingdom, power, and glory of God,[1] and put all these things into question in the same way. What seems to us to confer meaning, justification, significance, does so in virtue of the fact that we need no more reasons after a certain point.

What makes doubt inescapable with regard to the limited aims of individual life also makes it inescapable with regard to any larger purpose that encourages the sense that life is meaningful. Once the fundamental doubt has begun, it cannot be laid to rest.

Camus maintains in *The Myth of Sisyphus* that the absurd arises because the world fails to meet our demands for meaning. This suggests that the world might satisfy those demands if it were different. But now we can see that this is not the case. There does not appear to be any conceivable world (containing us) about which unsettlable doubts could not arise. Consequently the absurdity of our situation derives not from a collision between our expectations and the world, but from a collision within ourselves.

IV

It may be objected that the standpoint from which these doubts are supposed to be felt does not exist – that if we take the recommended backward step we will land on thin air, without any basis for judgment about the natural responses we are supposed to be surveying. If we retain our usual standards of what is important, then questions about the significance of what we are doing with our lives will be answerable in the usual way. But if we do not, then those questions can mean nothing to us, since there is no longer any content to the idea of what matters, and hence no content to the idea that nothing does.

But this objection misconceives the nature of the backward step. It is not supposed to give us an understanding of what is *really* important, so that we see by contrast that our lives are insignificant. We never, in the course of these reflections, abandon the ordinary standards that guide our lives. We merely observe them in operation, and recognize that if they are called into question we can justify them only by reference to themselves, uselessly. We adhere to them because of the way we are put together; what seems to us important or serious or valuable would not seem so if we were differently constituted.

In ordinary life, to be sure, we do not judge a situation absurd unless we have in mind some standards of seriousness, significance, or harmony with which the absurd can be contrasted. This contrast is not implied by the philosophical judgment of absurdity, and that might be thought to make the concept unsuitable for the expression of such judgments. This is not so, however, for the philosophical judgment depends on another contrast which makes it a natural extension from more ordinary cases. It departs from them only in contrasting the pretensions of life with a larger context in which *no* standards can be discovered, rather than with a context from which alternative, overriding standards may be applied.

V

In this respect, as in others, philosophical perception of the absurd resembles epistemological skepticism. In both cases the final, philosophical doubt is not contrasted with any unchallenged certainties, though it is arrived at by extrapolation from examples of doubt within the system of evidence or justification, where a contrast with other certainties *is* implied. In both cases our limitedness joins with a capacity to transcend those limitations in thought (thus seeing them as limitations, and as inescapable).

Skepticism begins when we include ourselves in the world about which we claim knowledge. We notice that certain types of evidence convince us, that we are content to allow justifications of belief to come to an end at certain points, that we feel we know many things even without knowing or having grounds for believing the denial of others which, if true, would make what we claim to know false.

For example, I know that I am looking at a piece of paper, although I have no adequate grounds to claim I know that I am not dreaming; and if I am dreaming then I am not looking at a piece of paper. Here an ordinary conception of how appearance may diverge from reality is employed to show that we take our world largely for granted; the certainty that we are not dreaming cannot be justified except circularly, in terms of those very appearances which are being put in doubt. It is somewhat far-fetched to suggest I may be dreaming; but the possibility is only illustrative. It reveals that our claims to knowledge depend on our not feeling it necessary to exclude certain incompatible alternatives, and the dreaming possibility or the total-hallucination possibility are just representatives for limitless possiblities most of which we cannot even conceive.[2]

Once we have taken the backward step to an abstract view of our whole system of beliefs, evidence, and justification, and seen that it works only, despite its pretensions, by taking the world largely for granted, we are *not* in a position to contrast all these appearances with an alternative reality. We cannot shed our ordinary responses, and if we could it would leave us with no means of conceiving a reality of any kind.

It is the same in the practical domain. We do not step outside our lives to a new vantage point from which we see what is really, objectively significant. We continue to take life largely for granted while seeing that all our decisions and certainties are possible only because there is a great deal we do not bother to rule out.

Both epistemological skepticism and a sense of the absurd can be reached via initial doubts posed within systems of evidence and justification that we accept, and can be stated without violence to our ordinary concepts. We can ask not only why we should believe there is a floor under us, but also why we should believe the evidence of our senses at all – and at some point the framable questions will have outlasted the answers. Similarly, we can ask not only why we should take aspirin, but why we should take trouble over our own comfort at all. The fact that we shall take the aspirin without waiting for an answer to this last question does not show that it is an unreal question. We shall also continue to believe there is a floor under us without waiting for an answer to the other question. In both cases it is this unsupported natural confidence that generates skeptical doubts; so it cannot be used to settle them.

Philosophical skepticism does not cause us to abandon our ordinary beliefs, but it lends them a peculiar flavor. After acknowledging that their truth is incompatible with possibilities that we have no grounds for believing do not obtain – apart from grounds in those very beliefs which we have called into question – we return to our familiar convictions with a certain irony and resignation. Unable to abandon the natural responses on which they depend, we take them back, like a spouse who has run off with someone else and then decided to return; but we regard them differently (not that the new attitude is necessarily inferior to the old, in either case).

The same situation obtains after we have put in question the seriousness with which we take our lives and human life in general and have looked at ourselves without presuppositions. We then return to our lives, as we must, but our seriousness is laced with irony. Not that irony enables us to escape the absurd. It is useless to mutter: 'Life is meaningless; life is meaningless ...' as an accompaniment to everything we do. In continuing to live and work and strive, we take ourselves seriously in action no matter what we say.

What sustains us, in belief as in action, is not reason or justification, but something more basic than these – for we go on in the same way even after we are convinced that the reasons have given out.[3] If we tried to rely entirely on reason, and pressed it hard, our lives and beliefs would collapse – a form of madness that may actually occur if the inertial force of taking the world and life for granted is somehow lost. If we lose our grip on that, reason will not give it back to us.

VI

In viewing ourselves from a perspective broader than we can occupy in the flesh, we become spectators of our own lives. We cannot do very much as pure spectators of our own lives, so we continue to lead them, and devote ourselves to what we are able at the same time to view as no more than a curiosity, like the ritual of an alien religion.

This explains why the sense of absurdity finds its natural expression in those bad arguments with which the discussion began. Reference to our small size and short lifespan and to the fact that all of mankind will eventually vanish without a trace are metaphors for the backward step which permits us to regard ourselves from without and to find the particular form of our lives curious and slightly surprising. By feigning a nebula's-eye view, we illustrate the capacity to see ourselves without presuppositions, as arbitrary, idiosyncratic, highly specific occupants of the world, one of countless possible forms of life.

Before turning to the question whether the absurdity of our lives is something to be regretted and if possible escaped, let me consider what would have to be given up in order to avoid it.

Why is the life of a mouse not absurd? The orbit of the moon is not absurd either, but that involves no strivings or aims at all. A mouse, however, has to work to stay alive. Yet he is not absurd, because he lacks the capacities for self-consciousness and self-transcendence that would enable him to see that he is only a mouse. If that *did* happen, his life would become absurd, since self-awareness would not make him cease to be a mouse and would not enable him to rise above his mousely strivings. Bringing his new-found self-consciousness with him, he would have to return to his meagre yet frantic life, full of doubts that he was unable to answer, but also full of purposes that he was unable to abandon.

Given that the transcendental step is natural to us humans, can we avoid absurdity by refusing to take that step and remaining entirely within our sublunar lives? Well, we cannot refuse consciously, for to do that we would have to be aware of the viewpoint we were refusing to adopt. The only way to avoid the relevant self-consciousness would be either never to attain it or to forget it – neither of which can be achieved by the will.

On the other hand, it is possible to expend effort on an attempt to destroy the other component of the absurd – abandoning one's earthly, individual, human life in order to identify as completely as possible with that universal viewpoint from which human life seems arbitrary and trivial. (This appears to be the ideal of certain Oriental religions.) If one succeeds, then one will not have to drag the superior awareness through a strenuous mundane life, and absurdity will be diminished.

However, insofar as this self-etiolation is the result of effort, will-power, asceticism, and so forth, it requires that one take oneself seriously as an individual – that one be willing to take considerable trouble to avoid being creaturely and absurd. Thus one may undermine the aim of unworldliness by pursuing it too vigorously. Still, if someone simply allowed his individual, animal nature to drift and respond to impulse, without making the pursuit of its needs a central conscious aim, then he might, at considerable dissociative cost, achieve a life that was less absurd than most. It would not be a meaningful life either, of course; but it would not involve the engagement of a transcendent awareness in the assiduous pursuit of mundane goals. And that is the main condition of absurdity – the dragooning of an unconvinced transcendent consciousness into the service of an immanent, limited enterprise like a human life.

VII

The final escape is suicide; but before adopting any hasty solutions, it would be wise to consider carefully whether the absurdity of our existence truly presents us with a *problem*, to which some solution must be found – a way of dealing with prima facie disaster. That is certainly the attitude with which Camus approaches the issue, and it gains support from the fact that we are all eager to escape from absurd situations on a smaller scale.

Camus – not on uniformly good grounds – rejects suicide and the other solutions he regards as escapist. What he recommends is defiance or scorn. We can salvage our dignity, he appears to believe, by shaking a fist at the world which is deaf to our pleas, and continuing to live in spite of it. This will not make our lives un-absurd, but it will lend them a certain nobility.[4]

This seems to me romantic and slightly self-pitying. Our absurdity warrants neither that much distress nor that much defiance. At the risk of falling into romanticism by a different route, I would argue that absurdity is one of the most human things about us: a manifestation of our most advanced and interesting characteristics. Like skepticism in epistemology, it is possible only because we possess a certain kind of insight – the capacity to transcend ourselves in thought.

If a sense of the absurd is a way of perceiving our true situation (even though the situation is not absurd until the perception arises), then what reason can we have to resent or escape it? Like the capacity for epistemological skepticism, it results from the ability to understand our human limitations. It need not be a matter for agony unless we make it so. Nor need it evoke a defiant contempt of fate that allows us to feel brave or proud. Such dramatics, even if carried on in private, betray a failure to appreciate the cosmic unimportance of the situation. If *sub specie aeternitatis* there is no reason to believe that anything matters, then that doesn't matter either, and we can approach our absurd lives with irony instead of heroism or despair.

NOTES

1 Cf. Robert Nozick, 'Teleology', *Mosaic*, XII, 1 (Spring 1971): 27/8.

2 I am aware that skepticism about the external world is widely thought to have been refuted, but I have remained convinced of its irrefutability since being exposed at Berkeley to Thompson Clarke's largely unpublished ideas on the subject.

3 As Hume says in a famous passage of the *Treatise*: 'Most fortunately it happens, that since reason is incapable of dispelling these clouds, nature herself suffices to that purpose, and cures me of this philosophical melancholy and delirium, either by relaxing this bent of mind, or by some avocation, and lively impression of my senses, which obliterate all these chimeras. I dine, I play a game of backgammon, I converse, and am merry with my friends; and when after three or four hours' amusement, I would return to these speculations, they appear so cold, and strain'd, and ridiculous, that I cannot find in my heart to enter into them any farther' ed. L.A. Selby-Bigge (Oxford: Clarendon, 1888). (Book 1, Part 4, Section 7; p. 269).

4 'Sisyphus, proletarian of the gods, powerless and rebellious, knows the whole extent of his wretched condition: it is what he thinks of during his descent. The lucidity that was to constitute his torture at the same time crowns his victory. There is no fate that cannot be surmounted by scorn' (*The Myth of Sisyphus*, Vintage edition, p. 90).

7

On the Meaning of Life

Moritz Schlick

The extracts that follow introduce a different note into the discussion. Nagel made the point that the predicament to which he draws attention could not conceivably be otherwise; there is no 'conceivable world (containing us)' in which such difficulties would not arise. Schlick's account of purpose, by contrast, is to some extent a matter of history and educational policy. What is wrong with human life, according to Schlick (1882–1936), is that we are too much involved with goals and purposes. He speaks of 'the curse of purposes', and sees here 'the true fall of man'. Now in one sense this is still about necessary features of human life, which could not conceivably be otherwise; for a being which had no goals or purposes, and no concept of means and ends, would not be human in the relevant sense. But Schlick's argument is largely about the 'burden of purposes' as it exists in the modern world of mass production. The modern worker, he claims, is caught in a futile circle. 'The content of [his] existence consists in the work that is needed in order to exist.' By reversing these trends of modern life, we could restore meaning to our lives. Man must try, 'in all his doings', to 'give himself up entirely to the act itself . . . The end, then, would never justify the means.' There are two areas of life which correspond to Schlick's ideal; they are youth and play. It is when we are children, he holds, that life truly has meaning; this is 'a time of play, of doing for its own sake, and hence a true bearer of the meaning of life.' Education, therefore, should be designed to preserve the playful side of man; it should 'take care that nothing of the child in man is lost as he matures'.

Not everyone is disturbed by the question, whether life has a meaning. Some – and they are not the unhappiest – have the child's mind, which has *not yet* asked about such things; others *no longer* ask, having unlearnt the question. In between are ourselves, the seekers. We cannot project ourselves back to the level of the innocent, whom life has not yet looked at with its dark mysterious eyes, and we do not care to join the weary and the blasé, who no longer believe in any meaning to existence, because they have been able to find none in their own.

A man who has failed of the goal that his youth was striving for, and found no substitute, may lament the meaninglessness of his own life; yet he still may believe in a meaning to existence generally, and think that it continues to be found where a person has reached his goals. But the man who has wrested from fate the achievement of his purposes, and then finds that his prize was not so valuable as it seemed, that he has somehow fallen prey to a deception – that man is quite blankly confronted with the question of life's value, and before him lies like a darkened wasteland the thought, not only that all things pass, but also that everything is ultimately in vain.

How are we to discover a unitary meaning, either in the perplexities of a man's lifetime, or in the stumbling progress of history itself? Existence may appear to us as a many-hued tapestry, or as a grey veil, but it is equally difficult either way to furl the billowing fabric so that its meaning becomes apparent. It all flaps past and seems to have vanished before we could render an account of it.

What is the reason for the strange contradiction, that achievement and enjoyment will not fuse into a proper meaning? Does not an inexorable law of nature appear to prevail here? Man sets himself goals, and while he is heading towards them he is buoyed up by hope, indeed, but gnawed at the same time by the pain of unsatisfied desire. Once the goal is reached, however, after the first flush of triumph has passed away, there follows inevitably a mood of desolation. A void remains, which can seemingly find an end only through the painful emergence of new longings, the setting of new goals. So the game begins anew, and existence seems doomed to be a restless swinging to and fro between pain and boredom, which ends at last in the nothingness of death. That is the celebrated line of thought which Schopenhauer made the basis of his pessimistic view of life. Is it not possible, somehow, to escape it?

We know how Nietzsche, for example, sought to conquer this pessimism. First by the flight into art: consider the world, he says, as an aesthetic phenomenon, and it is eternally vindicated! Then by the flight into knowledge: look upon life as an experiment of the knower, and the world will be to you the finest of laboratories! But Nietzsche again turned away from these standpoints; in the end, art was no longer his watchword, and nor were science, or beauty, or truth; it is hard to reduce to a brief formula what the wisest Nietzsche, the Nietzsche of *Zarathustra*, saw as the meaning of life. For if it be said that henceforth the ultimate value of life, to him, was *life itself*, that obviously says nothing clear and does not find the right expression for the deep truth which he then perceived or at least suspected. For he saw that life has no meaning, so long as it stands wholly under the domination of purposes:

Verily, it is a blessing and no blasphemy when I teach: Above all things standeth the heaven of chance, the heaven of innocence, the heaven of hazard, the heaven of sportiveness.

'Sir Hazard' – his is the most ancient title of nobility in earth: him have I restored to all things, I have saved them from the slavery of ends.

This freedom and heavenly brightness I set over all things as an azure dome, when I taught that above them and in them there willeth no 'eternal will'.[1]

In truth, we shall never find an ultimate meaning in existence, if we view it only under the aspect of purpose.

I know not, however, whether the burden of purposes has ever weighed more heavily upon mankind than at the present time. The present idolizes work. But work means goal-seeking activity, direction to a purpose. Plunge into the crowd on a bustling city street and imagine yourself stopping the passers-by, one after another, and crying to them 'Where are you off to so fast? What important business do you have?' And if, on learning the immediate goal, you were to ask further about the purpose of this goal, and again for the purpose of that purpose, you would almost always hit on the purpose after just a few steps in the sequence: maintenance of life, earning one's bread. And why maintain life? To this question you could seldom read off an intelligible answer from the information obtained.

And yet an answer has to be found. For mere living, pure existence as such, is certainly valueless; it must also have a content, and in that only can the meaning of life reside. But what actually fills up our days almost entirely is activities serving to maintain life. In other words, the content of existence consists in the work that is needed in order to exist. We are therefore moving in a circle, and in this fashion fail to arrive at a meaning for life. Nor is it any better if, in place of work itself, we direct our attention to the fruits of work. The greater part of its products is again subservient to work of some kind, and hence indirectly to the maintenance of life, and another large part is undoubtedly meaningless trash. Rathenau, if I am not mistaken, estimated this latter at one third of total production. How much would be left as meaningful? Nor, indeed, can any work-products as such ever be valuable, save insofar as they somehow fulfil and enrich life, by launching man into valuable states and activities. The state of working cannot be one of these, for by work – if we understand this concept in its philosophical generality – we simply mean any activity undertaken solely in order to realize some purpose. It is therefore the characteristic mark of work that it has its purpose outside itself, and is not performed for its own sake. The doctrine that would wish to install work as such at the centre of existence, and exalt it to life's highest meaning, is bound to be in error, because every work-activity as such is always a mere means, and receives its value only from its goals.

The core and ultimate value of life can lie only in such states as exist for their own sake and carry their satisfaction in themselves. Now such states are undoubtedly given in the pleasure-feelings which terminate the fulfilment of a volition and accompany the gratifying of a desire; but if we sought to derive the value of existence from these moments, in which life's pressure is momentarily halted, we should at once become ensnared in that argument of Schopenhauer's, which displays to us, not the meaning, but the absurdity of life.

No, life means movement and action, and if we wish to find a meaning in it we must seek for *activities* which carry their own purpose and value within them, independently of any extraneous goals; activities, therefore, which are not work, in the philosophical sense of the word. If such activities exist, then in them the seemingly divided is reconciled, means and end, action and consequences are fused into one, we have then found ends-in-themselves which are more than mere end-points of acting and resting-points of existence, and it is these alone that can take over the role of a true content to life.

There really are such activities. To be consistent, we must call them *play*, since that is the name for free, purposeless action, that is, action which in fact carries its purpose within itself. We must take the word 'play', however, in its broad, true, philosophical meaning – in a deeper sense than is commonly accorded to it in daily life. We are not thereby lending it any new or surprising meaning, but are merely repeating what was perfectly clear to at least one great mind, who apprehended the nature of the human with the eye of a poet – which is to say, in deep truth. For in his *Letters on the Aesthetic Education of Man*, Friedrich Schiller utters the following words:

For, to declare it once and for all, Man plays only when he is in the full sense of the word a man, and *he is only wholly Man when he is playing*. This proposition, which at the moment perhaps seems paradoxical, will assume great and deep significance when we have once reached the point of applying it to the twofold seriousness of duty and of destiny; it will, I promise you, support the whole fabric of aesthetic art, and the still more difficult art of living. But it is only in science that this statement is unexpected; it has long since been alive and operative in Art, and in the feeling of the Greeks, its most distinguished exponents; only they transferred to Olympus what should have been realized on earth. Guided by its truth, they caused not only the seriousness and the toil which furrow the cheeks of mortals, but also the futile pleasure that smooths the empty face, to vanish from the brows of the blessed gods, and they released those perpetually happy beings from the fetters of every aim, every duty, every care, and made idleness and indifference the enviable portion of divinity; merely a more human name for the freest and sublimest state of being.[2]

These are exalted words, which ring down from the poet's world into a care-dimmed age, and in our own world sound untimely to most ears. The poet sees a state of divine perfection among men, in which all their activities are turned into joyous play, all their working-days become holidays. Only insofar as man shares in this perfection, only in the hours when life smiles

at him without the stern frown of purpose, is he really man. And it was
sober consideration that led us to this very truth: the meaning of existence
is revealed only in play.

But doesn't this notion lead us into mere dreams, does it not loosen
every tie with reality, and have we not lost beneath our feet the solid earth
of daily life, on which we have ultimately to stay planted, since the question
of life is by nature an everyday question? In the harsh reality, especially of
the present, there seems no room for such dreams; for our age, for the
peoples of a war-racked globe, no other solution seems possible save the
word 'work', and it appears irresponsible to speak ill of it.

Yet we should not forget that the creation which the hour demands of
us is work only in the economic sense, productive activity, that is, which
leads to the engendering of values. There is, however, no irreconcilable
opposition between play in the philosophical sense and work in the economic
meaning of the term. Play, as we see it, is any activity which takes place
entirely for its own sake, independently of its effects and consequences.
There is nothing to stop these effects from being of a useful or valuable
kind. If they are, so much the better; the action still remains play, since it
already bears its own value within itself. Valuable goods may proceed from
it, just as well as from intrinsically unpleasurable activity that strives to fulfil
a purpose. Play too, in other words, can be creative; its outcome can
coincide with that of work.

This notion of creative play will be accorded a major part in the life-
philosophy of the future. If mankind is to go on existing and progressing
by way of playful activities, they will have to be creative; the necessary must
somehow be brought forth by means of them. And this is possible, since
play is not a form of doing nothing. The more activities, indeed, become
play in the philosophical sense, the more work would be accomplished in
the economic sense, and the more values would be created in human
society. Human action is work, not because it bears fruit, but only when it
proceeds from, and is governed by, the thought of its fruit.

Let us look about us: where do we find creative play? The brightest
example (which at the same time is more than a mere example), is to be
seen in the creation of the artist. His activity, the shaping of his work by
inspiration, is itself pleasure, and it is half by accident that enduring values
arise from it. The artist may have no thought, as he works, of the benefit
of these values, or even of his reward, since otherwise the act of creation
is disrupted. Not the golden chain, but the song that pours from the heart,
is the guerdon that richly rewards! So feels the poet, and so the artist. And
anyone who feels thus in what he does, *is* an artist.

Take, for example, the scientist. *Knowing*, too, is a pure play of the spirit,
the wrestling for scientific truth is an end-in-itself for him, he rejoices to
measure his powers against the riddles which reality propounds to him,

quite regardless of the benefits that may somehow accrue from this (and these, as we know, have often been the most astonishing precisely in the case of purely theoretical discoveries, whose practical utility no one could originally have guessed). The richest blessings flow from the work that is engendered as the child of its creator's happy mood, and in free play, without any anxious concern for its effects.

Not all the activity of the artist or thinker falls, of course, under the concept of creative play. The purely technical, the mere management of the material, as with the painter's colour-mixing, or the composer's setting-down of notes – all this remains, for the most part, toil and work; they are the husks and dross that often still attach to play in real life. Often, but not always; for in the process of execution the working acts involved can either become so mechanized that they hardly enter consciousness, or else develop so much charm and attractiveness that they turn into artistic play themselves.

And that is also true in the end of those actions which engender neither science nor art, but the day's necessities, and which are seemingly altogether devoid of spirit. The tilling of the fields, the weaving of fabrics, the cobbling of shoes, can all become play, and may take on the character of artistic acts. Nor is it even so uncommon for a man to take so much pleasure in such activities, that he forgets the purpose of them. Every true craftsman can experience in his own case this transformation of the means into an end-in-itself, which can take place with almost any activity, and which makes the product into a work of art. It is the joy in sheer creation, the dedication to the activity, the absorption in the movement, which transforms work into play. As we know, there is a great enchantment which almost always brings this transformation about – rhythm. To be sure, it will only work perfectly where it is not brought externally and deliberately to the activity, and artificially coupled with it, but evolves spontaneously from the nature of the action and its natural form. There are some kinds of work where this is impossible; many are of such a nature that they always remain an evil and – except, perhaps, among men entirely blunted and incapable of happiness – are invariably carried out with reluctance and distaste. With such occupations I advise a very careful scrutiny of their fruits: we shall invariably find that such mechanical, brutalizing, degrading forms of work serve ultimately to produce only trash and empty luxury. So away with them! So long, indeed, as our economy is focussed on mere increase of production, instead of on the true enrichment of life, these activities cannot diminish, and thus slavery among mankind (for these alone are true forms of slave-labour) will not be able to decline. But a civilization which maintains artificial breeding-grounds for idle trumpery by means of forced slave-labour, must eventually come to grief through its own absurdity. All that will then remain over will be simply the avocations serving to generate true culture. But in them there dwells a spirit that favours their evolution into true forms of play.

At least there is no law of nature which in any way obstructs such a development of action into an end-in-itself; basically speaking, the road lies open to the realization of Schiller's dream. The idea of a human race thus liberated from all tormenting purposes, all oppressive cares, and cheerfully dedicated to the moment, is at least not a contradictory or inconceivable idea. The individual would lead an existence, as in the profound and beautiful saying of the Bible, like the life of the lilies of the field.

The objection may be raised at this point, that such a life would represent a relapse to a lower level, to the status of plants and animals. For the latter assuredly live for the moment, their consciousness is confined to a brief present, they certainly know pain, but not care. Man, on the contrary, has the privilege of embracing long periods, whole lifetimes, in the span of his consciousness, of coexperiencing them through foresight and hindsight, and that is how he becomes the knowing, supremely self-conscious being, in which capacity he confronts all the rest of nature.

But this objection is easy to meet. Man does not have to forfeit the range of his life, his joy in the moment will not be blind and bestial, but bathed in the clearest light of consciousness. He does not escape the menace of purposes by putting his head in the sand, so as not to see the future at all; it stands before him, calmly and clearly, in the light of hope, just as the past stands behind him in the light of recollection. He can shake off the curse of purposes and liberate his vision from the blight of cares, without lessening the boon of his hopes. He still sees even the remotest consequences of his action clearly before him, and not only the real consequences, but all possible ones as well; but no specific goal stands there as an end to be necessarily attained, so that the whole road would be meaningless if it were not; every point, rather, of the whole road already has its own intrinsic meaning, like a mountain path that offers sublime views at every step and new enchantments at every turn, whether it may lead to a summit or not. The setting of certain goals is admittedly needed in order to produce the tension required for life; even playful activity is constantly setting itself tasks, most palpably in sport and competition, which still remains play so long as it does not degenerate into real fighting. But such goals are harmless, they impose no burden on life and do not dominate it; they are left aside and it does not matter if they are not achieved, since at any moment they can be replaced by others. Stretches of life that stand under the dominion of huge inexorable purposes are like riddles with an answer that we either find or fail at; but a life of play might be compared to an endless crossword puzzle, in which new words are constantly being found and connected, so that an ever larger area is progressively filled in, with no other aim but that of going on further without a halt.

The last liberation of man would be reached if in all his doings he could give himself up entirely to the act itself, inspired to his activity always by love. The end, then, would never justify the means; he might then exalt into his highest rule of action the principle: 'What is not worth doing for its own sake, don't do for anything else's sake!' All life would then be truly meaningful, down to its ultimate ramifications; to live would mean: to celebrate the festival of existence. ...

Here we can learn from the *child*. Before he has yet been caught in the net of purposes, the cares of work are unknown to him; he needs no diversion or release from the working day. And it is precisely the child that is capable of the purest joy. People everywhere are wont to sing of the happiness of youth, and this is truly more than a mere invention of the poets; youth is really not overshadowed by the dark clouds of purpose.

And with that I come to theart of what I should here like to say.

It is not in every expression of life, not in the whole breadth of it, that we are able to find a meaning – at least so long as Schiller's dream of divine perfection remains a mere dream; the meaning of the whole is concentrated and collected, rather, into a few short hours of deep, serene joy, into the hours of play. And these hours crowd thickest in *youth*. It is not only that childish games are play even in the philosophical sense of the term: it is also that later youth, which is already well acquainted with aims and purposes, and has been brought up to serve them, still does not stand entirely under their yoke, does not have its gaze fixed on them alone, is not concerned solely with attaining them, as is often the natural attitude later on. Youth, on the contrary, does not really care about purposes; if one collapses, another is quickly built up; goals are merely an invitation to rush in and fight, and this enterprising ardour is the true fulfilment of the youthful spirit. The enthusiasm of youth (it is basically what the Greeks called Eros), is devotion to the deed, not the goal. This act, this way of acting, is true play.

If it is clear in this fashion that what makes up the meaning of existence is nowhere so purely or strongly to be found as it is in youth, some notable questions and clues emerge from this. Youth, after all, is the first phase of life, and it seems incongruous that the meaning of the whole should be found only at its beginning. For according to the traditional view, life is to be regarded as a process of development, whose meaning is constantly unfolding, so that it ought to be most clearly apparent towards the end. What, then, is youth? On the received view it is the time of immaturity, in which mind and body grow, in order later to *have* grown up to their vocation; the time of learning, in which all capacities are exercised, in order to be equipped for work; even the play of youth appears from this angle as merely a preparation for the seriousness of life. It is almost always so regarded, and almost the whole of education is conducted from this point of view: it signifies a training for adulthood. Youth therefore appears as a mere means to the later purposes of life, as a necessary learning period, that would have no meaning of its own.

This view is directly opposed to the insight that we have obtained. It has seldom been remarked, what a paradox it is that the time of preparation appears as the sweetest portion of existence, while the time of fulfilment seems the most toilsome. At times, however, it has been seen. It was primarily Rousseau, and perhaps Montaigne before him, who discovered the intrinsic value of youth. He warns the educator against debasing the youth of the pupil into a mere means and sacrificing his early happiness to later proficiency; the aim should be to fill the days of youth with joy, even for their own sake. At the present day this idea has begun to make a little headway. It is a leading conception of the modern youth movement, that a young life is not only going to receive its value from the future, but bears it within itself. Youth, in fact, is not just a time of growing, learning, ripening and incompleteness, but primarily a time of play, of doing for its own sake, and hence a true bearer of the meaning of life. Anyone denying this, and regarding youth as a mere introduction and prelude to real life, commits the same error that beclouded the mediaeval view of human existence: he shifts life's centre of gravity forwards, into the future. Just as the majority of religions, discontented with earthly life, are wont to transfer the meaning of existence out of this life and into a hereafter, so man in general is inclined always to regard every state, since none of them is wholly perfect, as a mere preparation for a more perfect one.

For modern man there is little doubt that the value and aim of life must either be totally of this world, or else cannot be found at all. And if man were to run through a thousand successive lives, as the theories of transmigration maintain, this would not absolve contemporary thought from seeking in every one of these stages of existence its own special meaning, independent of what has gone before or is yet to follow. Present-day man would have no right to look upon other, metaphysical worlds, if they existed, as superior or more meaningful, and ungratefully to despise our own world by comparison. The meaning of the life that he knows can only be sought in this world, *as* he knows it.

But within life he now commits the same mistake that he committed earlier in thinking of its metaphysical continuation: from immature youth he shifts the value of life into mature adulthood; in his prime, he sees that he is still not yet ripe, that his nature and achievements are not complete, and therefore shifts the meaning of life still further on, and expects it from the peace and mellowness of old age. But on actually arriving at this peace, he then projects the meaning of existence backwards again into the days of acting and striving, and these are by then over and past recovery. And the final result is that man lets his whole life fall under the curse of purposes. It is the unceasing search into the future and concern for the future that casts its shadow over every present and clouds the joy of it.

But if life has a meaning, it must lie in the present, for only the present is real. There is no reason at all, however, why more meaning should lie in the later present, in the middle or final period of life, than in an earlier present, in the first period, known as youth. And now let us consider what 'youth' must actually mean for us in this connection. We found its true nature, not in the fact that it is a prelude and first phase of life, but rather in that it is the time of play, the time of activity for the pleasure of acting. And we recognized that all action, even the creative action of the adult, can and must, in its perfect form, take on the same character: it becomes play, self-sufficient action that acquires its value independently of the purpose.

But from this it follows that youth, in our philosophical sense, can by no means be confined to the early stages of life; it is present wherever the state of man has reached a peak, where his action has become play, where he is wholly given over to the moment and the matter in hand. We talk in such cases of youthful enthusiasm, and that is the right expression: enthusiasm is always youthful. The ardour which fires us for a cause, a deed or a man, and the ardour of youth, are one and the same fire. A man who is emotionally immersed in what he does is a youngster, a child. The great confirmation of this is genius, which is always imbued with a child-like quality. All true greatness is full of a deep innocence. The creativity of genius is the play of a child, his joy in the world is the child's pleasure in pretty things. Heraclitus of old it was who compared the creative world-spirit itself to a child at play, building things out of pebbles and bits of wood and tearing them down again. For us, therefore, the word 'youth' does not have the external meaning of a specific period of life, a particular span of years; it is a state, a way of leading one's life, which basically has nothing to do with years and the number of them.

It will now no longer be possible to misunderstand me when, as the heart of what I am moved to say, I assert the proposition that *the meaning of life is youth*.

The more youth is realized in a life, the more valuable it is, and if a person dies young, however long he may have lived, his life has had meaning. In the concept of youth, so viewed, there is an infinite abundance; an infinite abundance can be extracted from it. All values of existence can be set in relation to it. In my leisure hours I have been occupied with working out a 'Philosophy of Youth',[3] which is meant to show how every perfection whatever, in all areas of human existence, and perhaps not there alone, can be covered by the concept of youthfulness.

It was earlier the custom to group human values around three great centres: the beautiful, the good and the true. The three faculties of feeling, willing and thinking, and the three cultural areas of art, society and enquiry, were held to correspond to them. In all these triads the connection with the value of youth can easily be pointed out, by showing how at their highest level the exercise of these different faculties becomes play. As a fact, we find art and the beautiful in the pure devotion to feeling for its own sake; immersion in thinking for its own sake gives rise to knowledge and science; and so far as the good is concerned, it can be reduced to a certain harmony of human impulses, whereby willing, too, becomes a joyous game, without disagreeable struggles and hindrances due to the threatening injunctions and prohibitions imposed by purpose.

The beautiful and the theory of beauty are already by nature wide open to examination from the viewpoint attained. For we only have to utter the word 'youth' and the idea of 'beauty' arises quite spontaneously. And if we look for the link that couples the two together, we eventually light on the concept of the playful, as the harmonious and self-sufficient, to which every external purpose is foreign; and the old question of the relations of the purposive to the beautiful could thence find a simple solution. An object cannot appear beautiful without being detached from purposive connection with the necessities of life. The conditions under which such detachment occurs in reality are laws of *natural* beauty; but *art* possesses means of liberating *any* object in this fashion, and hence there is nothnig that it could not make beautiful by its depiction. It has long since become clear to us that artistic *creation* must be understood by way of the concept of play; but this is naturally true of the *enjoyment* of art as well, and above all of the meaning of the beautiful for human existence. Beauty is so much a part of the meaning of life, that without it the latter would simply be turned into absurdity. And the beautiful, the harmony of lines and colours and sounds and feelings, is the purest manifestation of play, of the mark of youth. The more youthful the art and the work of art, the greater their perfection; the more antiquated and pedantic, the more disagreeable and senseless they become.

But the highest beauty can never reside in the work of art, so long as it stands contrasted, as an artifact, to nature and life. The enjoyment of artistic beauty is play at second hand, through the medium of the work as an artificial plaything. But beauty can enter into life itself, without requiring a medium. When the beautiful form of the work of art migrates into life, we have reached the higher level of beauty, and the art of works of art, which represents a turning-away from, or (as Nietzsche calls it) a mere appendage of life, becomes superfluous. It has justly been said (by Wyneken), that 'in a perfect world, there would be no art.' And indeed, when rightly regarded, our art is but nostalgia for nature, for a better nature, and could be extinguished by a life filled with beauty. No one has proclaimed this truth more ardently than the brilliant and fertile philosopher Guyau, who died in 1888 at the age of thirty-three. For him it is merely an unwelcome and quite untypical restriction of art, to be a recreation from the struggle for existence, and a simulacrum of what moves us in real life. On the contrary, it is just the eternal affliction of the artist, that he cannot become one with the whole fullness of life, that he does not experience everything he depicts, but must sink himself in looking and portraying. The goal would be to take up beauty wholly into active life; the latter would then be stripped of that remainder of purposive work, without which, in our actual existence, no work of art comes into being ... beauty would then have secured its full share in the meaning of life, our existence would glow with the indescribable freshness of youth.

That youthfulness of life enriches it in meaning by filling it with beauty, will be readily conceded; but if I maintain that it also fills life with *goodness*, that the ethos and moral quality of life is no less intimately connected with youth and play, it will be harder to find credence. And yet this is the most important point of all. For the ethical is after all the true heart of life, and here its deepest meaning must be sought. It is, however, the general opinion, that youth, properly speaking, is beyond good and evil, that morality begins only with responsibility, and responsibility only with that seriousness which is alien to youth and the very opposite of play. The concept of *duty*, which so many philosophers place at the centre of their ethics, presupposes the concept of purpose; to obey the commands of duty means nothing else but to stand under the dominion of purposes. Could there be no truth in what such wise and excellent men have taught: that the meaning of life must be found in the performance of our duty? It is not easy to reconcile what seems such a violent conflict of views, and to discern what is wisdom, and what prejudice, in this moral doctrine of duty.

Let us recall Schiller's remark, that the principle of play as the true vocation of man will attain its deepest significance if we apply it to the seriousness of duty and destiny. What does this mean? It was Schiller who rebelled against the doctrine of Kant, whereby, of course, the moral is primarily to be found where man acts by conquering himself. For in Kant's view an action is moral only when it springs from reverence for the law of duty as its sole motive; and since in the actual man conflicting inclinations are always present, moral action means a struggle against one's own inclination, it means laborious work. Schiller was utterly and entirely right, for this account of the good is infinitely remote from the meaning that everyone is otherwise naturally accustomed to associate with the word. We do not call *him* the best man, who is obliged unceasingly to resist his own impulses and is constantly at war with his own desires; we say this, rather, of the man whose inclinations are kindly and benevolent from the start, so that he simply does not fall into doubt and self-conflict. The man who struggles with and conquers himself is perhaps the type of the *great* man, but not of the *good* one. A being whose pure will flows from his natural disposition, without reflection or hesitation or wavering, is what we call an innocent person, and innocence is always the state of greatest moral perfection. This innocence is thus by no means a kind of ignorance, but rather a kind of freedom. It belongs inseparably to youth. There is the deepest wisdom in the biblical injunction: 'Unless ye become as little children ...' Where no exertion is required, where, without fear or wavering a man does freshly from the heart what is suited to his nature, there he is simply young, however many years he may number; his will, in such a case, is a free play in which he rejoices for its own sake, without looking onward to distant goals or upward to exalted duties. He acts out of pleasure in the good deed, he is good in himself, so far as he is youthful. But so far as it costs him trouble and exertion, his soul is an elderly one.

How long will it yet take until we eradicate the great moral prejudice, that seriousness and duty are a necessary part of the concept of morality, and until the ethics of duty is superseded by a natural ethics of goodness? In current morality the ethical is distorted and sicklied o'er with age, hedged about with scruples, constrained on all sides with anxious prohibitions, robbed of its naturalness and reduced to a serious matter, which every philistine can prate about. But true virtue is joyful, it does not arise from the pressure of prohibitions and purposes, but evolves freely from willing. Child-like purity is more beautiful and perfect than heroic renunciation. Jean Paul said: 'As the eagle soars high above the highest mountains, so a right love surpasses the rugged path of duty.' But love and youth are as much akin as youth and beauty.

Thus ethical perfection can be traced back to youthfulness. Just as, in Emerson's words, age is the only real sickness, so it is also the source of all moral evil, if, from the philosophical viewpoint, we do but regard age as nothing else but subjection to the burden of purposes. From rumination about the purposes of action the badness in the moral world arises; the entry of goal-seeking into life, and involvement in the network of purposes, betokens the loss of innocence, the true fall of man. It is a deeply tragic drama to see how the freshness of youthful life is increasingly palsied by the incursion of purposes, how its relation to the human environment increasingly forfeits the character of play, and guilt becomes possible. The childish self, which at first is not clearly aware of its limits vis-à-vis the environment, gradually becomes surrounded by a boundary, beyond which the world confronts him as an enemy. I know of no more shattering feeling than the knowledge of universal 'egoism', of the adult's ruthless pursuit of goals, that is commonly apt to dawn upon a young mind when it has completed its years of schooling. The more happily gifted a person is, the later he acquires this knowledge, which in intercourse with men constrains instinctive, playful action and turns it into laborious work, with all its vicissitudes and disappointments. But he who possesses the capacity for eternal youth, whom the years cannot age, remains capable also of a joyous supreme virtue, the generous virtue that does the good laughingly and scatters its gifts freely, instead of selling them for the consciousness of duty done. . . .

Our whole culture will have to be focussed on a rejuvenation of man, rejuvenation in the philosophical sense, that all our doings become increasingly liberated from the domination of purposes, that even the actions necessary for life are turned into play. In many creatures this happens circuitously, in that youth in the purely biological sense is first extended over the whole of life, so that it turns into one long ascent which concludes at death, while the descent into old age is abolished as an unmeaning, obstructive arrangement. Such is the case with those wonderful plants, which bloom but once and then die, or with the bees, of whom the male consummates the act of mating with his death. Perhaps it can be achieved in man by a more direct route, as the sun of a brighter culture disperses the dark clouds of purpose, and the playful and youthful element, to which man is everywhere strongly disposed, emerges into the light of day.

All education should take care that nothing of the child in man is lost as he matures, that the separation of adolescence from adulthood is increasingly obliterated, so that the man remains a boy until his last years, and the woman a girl, in spite of being a mother. If we need a rule of life, let it be this: 'Preserve the spirit of youth!' For it is the meaning of life.

NOTES

1 [*Also sprach Zarathustra*, Part 3, 'Vor Sonnenaufgang'; Engl. by A. Tille, revised by M. M. Bozman, 'Before Sunrise', in *Thus Spake Zarathustra*, London 1933, p. 148.]

2 [*Über die ästhetische Erziehung des Menschen, in einer Reihe von Briefen*, 1795, no. 15; Engl. by R. Snell, *Letters on the Aesthetic Education of Man*, London 1954, p. 80.]

3 [Of the '*Philosophy of Youth*' only a fragment of the first chapter (about 25 typewritten pages) was found among Schlick's papers. Its title is 'Spiel, die Seele der Jugend' ('Play, the Soul of Youth'). The cover lists the titles of two projected further chapters: 'Schönheit, das Antlitz der Jugend' ('Beauty, the Countenance of Youth') and 'Adel, das Herz der Jugend' ('Nobility, the Heart of Youth').]

8

What is There in Horse Racing?

John Wisdom

The importance of play as against purpose is also brought out by Wisdom in his defence of horse-racing, in which he rejects the question 'What is the purpose of racing?', with its 'innuendo that if it doesn't serve a purpose it is no good and a waste of time and absurd.' Wisdom also makes a point about the frustrations of goal-seeking, as applied to the human race in general. The purpose of travel is to arrive; but if the journey (or, more generally, the achievement of a purpose) is made too easy by modern technology, then it may seem no longer worthwhile. 'Just then we are apt to realize that what we needed was not merely to be at our destination.'

I remember walking with my nurse up the village green at home. Suddenly up the road behind us a horse and light spring cart came by. It was a farmer we knew, his name was Mr Abbot; he sat on a single board, his head sunk somewhat between his shoulders, and he looked neither to left or right. His bowler rammed well down on his head was elderly, but his horse was immaculately turned out, gleaming coat, neat mane, banged tail. What I noted with anxiety was the terrific stride with which it covered the ground. Was it faster than my father's horse? And then I was a little anxious about the pony another neighbour, Mrs Russell, used to drive. She used to drive herself, her child, and the nurse to Church on Sundays. I can hear now the clamour of the church bells as she pulls up in the rectory yard. 'Nine and a half minutes this morning, Arthur,' she says as she sweeps the traces into circles and hurries the pony into a stall, for now at any moment the bells may change to that single note which means that the parson and choir are under starter's orders.

Nine and a half minutes for two and a half miles meant then the air on your face, the slight swing and lurch of the vehicle, the rasp of wheels in the mud, and the beat of the horse's hooves as, swinging round the corners of the winding lanes, you checked him a trifle before descending a steepish pitch and now again you let him go. Recently in an aeroplane I passed over the twenty miles of the Channel in about seven minutes, but we hardly seemed to move. It was excellent in its way, but was not what we meant when we used to speak of a horse that could travel.

Travel and transport: surely it is here that man has most successfully solved his difficulties. Surely here, if anywhere, he has reached his goal. And no doubt he has done a good job. And yet here, too, there appears that exasperating feature of so much success. What you gain on the roundabouts you lose on the swings. And it is not merely that: that's the trouble – it is that, in achieving what seemed the essence of what we wanted, we find the essence has eluded us; in cutting out what seemed to hinder or to be irrelevant to our satisfaction, we find that what gives contentment is more entangled with the tiresome than we had supposed. Surely when a man sets out on a journey his goal is to reach that journey's end as fast as possible, as speedily as may be. And isn't speed a matter of passing from one point to another in the minimum of time? And yet, just as we have it all laid out so that we have only to press a button to be where we want to be, just then the whole thing is apt to seem absurd. Just then we are apt to realize that what we needed was not merely to be at our destination.

This feeling of collapse and absurdity which comes over us in so many things may come over us in a small but sharp way in the simple matter of a horse race. We have won, perhaps, and the 'all right' flags are flying, but somehow the whole thing seems ridiculous. I am not pretending that this sort of dissatisfaction is always misplaced. Not at all. We may indeed have had things out of focus. But, on the other hand, the arguments by which we confirm in ourselves or spread in others such feelings of sudden contempt or depression are often muddled. And it is interesting to notice that the same arguments by which clever persons sometimes represent to us as worthless things much bigger than horse racing are also used in this smaller matter. And here, too, they are fallacious. You know how they run. They are presented in the form of questions with an innuendo. Someone asks, or perhaps one asks oneself: 'What is the purpose of it all? What is there in it? What is it but a matter of whether one horse has his head in front of another?'

These questions have a familiar and worthy ring. They may voice a useful challenge. But they need watching. Behind the words 'What is the *purpose* of racing?' lies the innuendo that if it doesn't serve a purpose it is no good and a waste of time and absurd. But the innuendo is itself absurd. For those things, such as surgical operations, or hewing coal, or what you will, which do serve a purpose, do so only because they are means to things which are worth while in themselves, worth while not because of any purpose they serve but becaue of what is in them – health and well-being before a warm fire, playing with a friend a game of draughts or ludo, if you like. With some things it is easy to realize that there is more in them than meets the eye or can be put into words – music, poetry, mathematics – though even here we have the muddled critics who ask in a complaining way: 'What purpose do they serve?' However, here we may boldly answer for we have the support of the good and the great: 'These things aren't merely means, they are part of what makes our lives worth while. With other things it is not so easy. Some things seem small, seem easy, and seem to have little in them; and then, if we give time to them, we feel bound to answer 'What is there in them?'

What is there in racing? Behind such a question is another innuendo, the innuendo that if we cannot set out in words what makes a thing worth while then it isn't worth while. But this won't do. Maybe there are no words which will do this fairly, or maybe we haven't the skill to find them. I could not say what makes 'Hamlet' a good play; perhaps I could give hints; perhaps smeone more skilled than I could do better. But, however skilled he were, I am sure that much of what makes 'Hamlet' 'Hamlet' will run between his fingers, much of it anyway. And this is not less true of small things. I could not put into words what may make a game of croquet on the rectory lawn something one remembers. One may give hints. A game of croquet may have a flavour sweet or bitter. For a game of croquet is not merely a matter of getting balls through hoops, any more than a conversation is merely a matter of getting noises out of a larynx. Both in croquet and conversation, human personality finds expression; human personalities are joined whether for good or not.

Death, Suffering and the Value of Life

9

We Have Nothing to Fear in Death

Lucretius

What is the significance of death in our lives? Is death an evil? Does it make life meaningless? Would life without death be meaningless? According to Epicurus (342–270 BC), death 'is of no concern to us; for while we exist death is not present, and when death is present, we no longer exist'. Epicurus held that there is no survival after death; and the same is true of his follower Lucretius (99–55 BC), whose arguments to show that death is not an evil are reprinted below.

If the future holds travail and anguish in store, the self must be in existence, when that time comes, in order to experience it. But from this fate we are redeemed by death, which denies existence to the self that might have suffered these tribulations. Rest assured, therefore, that we have nothing to fear in death. One who no longer is cannot suffer, or differ in any way from one who has never been born, when once this mortal life has been usurped by death the immortal.

When you find a man treating it as a grievance that after death he will either moulder in the grave or fall a prey to flames or to the jaws of predatory beasts, be sure that his utterance does not ring true. Subconsciously his heart is stabbed by a secret dread, however loudly the man himself may disavow the belief that after death he will still experience sensation. I am convinced that he does not grant the admission he professes, nor the grounds of it; he does not oust and pluck himself root and branch out of life, but all unwittingly makes something of himself linger on. When a living man confronts the thought that after death his body will be mauled by birds and beasts of prey, he is filled with self-pity. He does not banish himself from the scene nor distinguish sharply enough between himself and that abandoned carcass. He visualizes that object as himself and infects it with his own feelings as an onlooker. That is why he is aggrieved at having been created mortal. He does not see that in real death there will be no other self alive to mourn his own decease – no other self standing by to flinch at the agony he suffers lying there being mangled, or indeed being cremated. For if it is really a bad thing after death to be mauled and crunched by ravening jaws, I cannot see why it should not be disagreeable to roast in the scorching flames of a funeral pyre, or to lie embalmed in honey, stifled and stiff with cold, on the surface of a chilly slab, or to be squashed under a crushing weight of earth.

'Now it is all over. Now the happy home and the best of wives will welcome you no more, nor winsome children rush to snatch the first kiss at your coming and touch your heart with speechless joy. No chance now to further your fortune or safeguard your family. Unhappy man,' they cry, 'unhappily cheated by one treacherous day out of all the uncounted blessings of life!' But they do not go on to say: 'And now no repining for these lost joys will oppress you any more.' If they perceived this clearly with their minds and acted according to the words, they would free their breasts from a great load of grief and dread.

'Ah yes! *You* are at peace now in the sleep of death, and so you will stay to the end of time. Pain and sorrow will never touch you again. But to *us*, who stood weeping inconsolably while you were consumed to ashes on the dreadful pyre – to us no day will come that will lift the undying sorrow from our hearts.' Ask the speaker, then, what is so heart-rending about this. If something returns to sleep and peace, what reason is that for pining in inconsolable grief?

Here, again, is the way men often talk from the bottom of their hearts when they recline at a banquet, goblet in hand and brows decked with garlands: 'How all too short are these good times that come to us poor creatures! Soon they will be past and gone, and there will be no recalling them.' You would think the crowning calamity in store for them after death was to be parched and shrivelled by a tormenting thirst or oppressed by some other vain desire. But even in sleep, when mind and body alike are at rest, no one misses himself or sighs for life. If such sleep were prolonged to eternity, no longing for ourselves would trouble us. And yet the vital atoms in our limbs cannot be far removed from their sensory motions at a time when a mere jolt out of sleep enables a man to pull himself together. Death, therefore, must be regarded, so far as we are concerned, as having much less existence than sleep, if anything can have less existence than what we perceive to be nothing. For death is followed by a far greater dispersal of the seething mass of matter: once that icy breach in life has intervened, there is no more waking.

Suppose, that nature herself were suddenly to find a voice and round upon one of us in these terms: 'What is your grievance, mortal, that you give yourself up to this whining and repining? Why do you weep and wail over death? If the life you have lived till now has been a pleasant thing – if all its blessings have not leaked away like water poured into a cracked pot and run to waste unrelished – why then, you silly creature, do you not retire as a guest who has had his fill of life and take your care-free rest with a quiet mind? Or, if all your gains have been poured profitless away and life has grown distasteful, why do you seek to swell the total? The new can but turn out as badly as the old and perish as unprofitably. Why not rather make an end of life and labour? Do you expect me to invent some new contrivance for your pleasure? I tell you, there is none. All things are always the same. If your body is not yet withered with age, nor your limbs decrepit and flagging, even so there is nothing new to look forward to – not though you should outlive all living creatures, or even though you should never die at all.' What are we to answer, except that Nature's rebuttal is justified and the plea she puts forward is a true one?

But suppose it is some man of riper years who complains – some dismal greybeard who frets unconscionably at his approaching end. Would she not have every right to protest more vehemently and repulse him in stern tones? 'Away with your tears, old reprobate! Have done with your grumbling! You are withering now after tasting all the joys of life. But, because you are always pining for what is not and unappreciative of the things at hand, your life has slipped away unfulfilled and unprized. Death has stolen upon you unawares, before you are ready to retire from life's banquet filled and satisfied. Come now, put away all that is unbecoming to your years and compose your mind to make way for others. You have no choice.' I cannot question but she would have right on her side; her censure and rebuke would be well merited. The old is always thrust aside to make way for the new, and one thing must be built out of the wreck of another. There is no murky pit of Hell awaiting anyone. There is need of matter, so that later generations may arise; when they have lived out their span, they will all follow you. Bygone generations have taken your road, and those to come will take it no less. So one thing will never cease to spring from another. To none is life given in freehold; to all on lease. Look back at the eternity that passed before we were born, and mark how utterly it counts to us as nothing. This is a mirror that Nature holds up to us, in which we may see the time that shall be after we are dead. Is there anything terrifying in the sight – anything depressing – anything that is not more restful than the soundest sleep? ...

A fixed term is set to the life of mortals, and there is no way of dodging death. In any case the setting of our lives remains the same throughout, and by going on living we do not mint any new coin of pleasure. So long as the object of our craving is unattained, it seems more precious than anything besides. Once it is ours, we crave for something else. So an unquenchable thirst for life keeps us always on the gasp. There is no telling what fortune the future may bring – what chance may throw in our way, or what upshot lies in waiting. By prolonging life, we cannot subtract or whittle away one jot from the duration of our death. The time after our taking off remains constant. However many generations you may add to your store by living, there waits for you none the less the same eternal death. The time of not-being will be no less for him who made an end of life with yesterday's daylight than for him who perished many a moon and many a year before.

10

Death

Mary Mothersill

The Epicurean view has been criticized in an article by Thomas Nagel ('Death', Nous vol. IV (1970)). Nagel quoted the saying 'What you don't know can't hurt you' and claimed, contrary to it, that a person can be hurt without his knowledge – for example, by being betrayed or ridiculed behind his back. Similarly, according to Nagel, the fact that the dead person would not be aware of what he has lost ('when death is present, we no longer exist') does not entail that he is not harmed by it. And if, as Nagel believes, life is a good thing, then the person deprived of it by death has suffered a great evil and is to be pitied. This view is ridiculed by Mary Mothersill in the opening sentence of her reply to Nagel (reprinted below). However, she finally agrees with Nagel in answering 'yes' to the question whether it is bad to die; her reason being that 'every human being, except in moments of acute distress, wants to continue to live.' But to what extent is this really so? An elderly person, or someone who (rightly or wrongly) has been persuaded by arguments of the kind presented by Epicurus and Lucretius, may not care very much about continuing to live.

In considering this issue, it is important to distinguish it from two kinds of suffering associated with death. One is the suffering (pain, fear, etc.) experienced prior to death, and the other is the suffering of those left behind. The question at issue is not whether these are bad, but whether being dead is in itself an evil for the person concerned.

I

'Poor Smith! One can't help feeling sorry for him. First he loses his job; then his wife leaves him and now, to top it all off, he's dead.'

If what Nagel presents as 'the natural view of death' were indeed natural, such a remark would not strike us as odd. Death, according to Nagel, is 'a misfortune for the one who dies'. In particular, death is a deprivation and differs from the loss of a job or the loss of a wife only in being more serious. Indeed, to die is to suffer the greatest possible misfortune since that of which we are deprived by death is life, and 'life', as Nagel puts it, 'is all we have.' True enough, in a manner of speaking, and when one notices that the question Nagel attempts to answer is 'whether it is a bad thing to die', one assumes that such remarks as the preceding are a loose way of answering yes. (Certainly, if the question admits of any answer, 'yes' is more natural than 'no'.) But Nagel, one discovers, wants to be taken literally; it is his claim that Smith and every individual whose name is counted among the deceased multitudes, is unfortunate *in having died*. This calls for explanation, some new thoughts, perhaps, about the soul and immortality. Literature and religion abound in ideas of death that encourage us to think of the dead as victims of misfortune. The heroes of the *Iliad* feel pity for their fallen comrades, quite naturally, seeing that the latter themselves reappear from time to time and tell us what a wretched thing it is to be a shade. Or think of the *Divine Comedy*: Dante (the fictional narrator) is deeply affected by the sight of the torments to which the enemies of Dante (the Florentine politician) have been consigned by Dante (the poet). Philosophers as well as poets have entertained the possibility that death is a peculiar transitional phase from which one emerges – changed, to be sure, but without loss of personal identity. Plato actually defends such a thesis. William James, though he admits that the evidence in support of survival is less than compelling, holds that to believe is neither superstitious nor irrational and that the issue should be recognized as a 'live option'. Strawson is less expansive, and goes no further than to claim that the *concept* of a posthumous, disembodied, individual consciousness is not disqualified on *a priori* grounds.[1] Such a consciousness, he observes, could be sustained in existence only by its (his? her?) memories and would thus be ephemeral, fading with the passage of time to the point of eventual extinction. Strawson also gives it as his opinion that the subjective experience of such disembodied remnants would necessarily be rather drab, and life beyond the grave a lonely and cheerless affair. Strawson would do almost as well as Homer as an authority for someone who wanted to persuade us that the situation of the dead is unenviable. But Nagel will have none of it; he sets aside 'the question whether we are or might be immortal in some sense', in order to assume that 'death is the permanent and unequivocal end of our existence.' Notwithstanding that assumption, he insists that an individual's death, apart from whatever effects it may have on his survivors, is a misfortune for *him*, and that it is he who is the proper object of concern and pity. ...

What is puzzling is that, although Nagel notices and describes as a 'difficulty' the specifying of a time 'when death, if it is a misfortune, can be ascribed to its unfortuante subject', he seems not to regard the difficulty as serious. Perhaps this is because he mistakenly assumes that the issue is epistemological. Smith, being dead, does not *mind* his misfortune, but then, Nagel argues, a man who is betrayed or ridiculed by his friends behind his back is genuinely unfortunate even though he remains in a state of ignorance. The 'intelligent adult' of Nagel's most extended example, has suffered misfortune in having been reduced, as the result of brain-damage, to the state of an infant, even on the supposition that, as an infant, he is contented. Here, says Nagel, we have 'a deprivation whose severity approaches that of death'. On the general point, Nagel may be right: 'What you don't know won't hurt you', taken at face value, is false. But its falsity has no bearing on the question at issue. At a time when Smith no longer exists, there *is* no situation to which that of the brain-damaged adult can be compared, unless, indeed, the latter is himself considered to be as good as dead, in which case he is not unfortunate either. Nagel wavers on the latter point:

The intelligent adult who has been *reduced* to this condition is the subject of the misfortune. He is the one we pity, though of course he does not mind his condition – there is some doubt, in fact, whether he can be said to exist any longer.

I can see no way of making Nagel's thesis consistent with his assumptions about death and shall discuss this aspect of his argument no further. There remains the question of philosophic motivation: why would anyone *want* to maintain that a man must be judged unfortunate in *virtue* of having died? Can we not say everything we want to say about the dead without forgetting that they *are* dead? The name Smith does not drop from circulation when its bearer dies. Whatever was ever true of Smith remains true, and new truths may be discovered. Projects, associations, enterprises, on which Smith left his stamp continue; his memory may remain green; he may be first in the hearts of his countrymen; his reputation may be enhanced, his work carried on by his disciples. As to the event of Smith's death, we may say that it was premature, tragic, a loss to his friends, to the world of letters, to humanity at large. What more do we need?

Nagel speaks a good deal about the dead as the 'objects of pity'. Does he think that as such, they 'exist' in some intentional domain? But nothing so elaborate is necessary. The criteria for applying the concept of pity are relatively flexible. If it is supposed that pity for *x* entails, among other things, making efforts to alleviate the sufferings of *x*, then obviously Smith, once dead, cannot be the object of my pity. On the other hand, if it is enough that I should regret his loss, feel retrospective compassion for his sufferings, wish that I had been more sympathetic, and the like, then my pity for Smith may outlast its object. I can think of no reason to exclude the latter use. If Aristotle correctly identifies the emotions evoked by theatrical spectacles as 'pity and terror' – if we can be moved by the sorrows of the House of Atreus and by the make-believe deaths of characters we know to be mere fictions to begin with – then it seems pedantic to scruple at pity for those who once existed and now exist no more.

The constraints of grammar and logic are not, therefore, particularly onerous. We are limited in our thoughts and feelings to what Smith was or might have been; we cannot consider what he is or may become. His death is an event in our lives and perhaps a misfortune for us. It is not a misfortune for Smith since it is not an event for Smith. Death, as Wittgenstein[2] observes, is not an event of life since death is not lived through.

II

Of course, Nagel's question – 'Is it a bad thing to die?' – is itself rather mystifying. Nagel says it is a question that 'arises'. *Does* it? When does it arise? He says further that 'there is conspicuous disagreement about the matter', that some people 'think death is dreadful', while 'others have no objection to death *per se*, though they may hope that their own will be neither premature nor painful.' Who *are* these types who 'have no objection to death *per se*'? What exactly is the question on which they take sides against those who think that death is dreadful? What I think has happened is that Nagel has tried to transform a peculiar and interesting psychological phenomenon into a disputed point of theory. Perhaps this is in part deliberate; the opening quotation from Tolstoy would suggest that it is.[3] Is it not Ivan Ilyich who epitomizes those who 'have no objection to death *per se*'? It is he who finds it quite in order that Caius, being mortal, must die, but unthinkable and preposterous that he, himself, Ivan Ilyich, is going to die and, as he slowly comes to realize, die very soon. Throughout the narrative, the author reminds us that, in his ambitions, his vices, his abilities, and his tastes, Ivan Ilyich was 'unremarkable'. So, in his radical dissociation of 'I am going to die' from 'They are going to die', perhaps Ivan is Everyman. Tolstoy's insight is confirmed by observation. Consider the fortitude with which we bear the deaths even of those of our fellow men with whom we have the closest ties. Beyond that narrow circle, we are more or less indifferent. Consider how easily we are persuaded to go to war, how readily we acquiesce in the slaughter of whole populations on nothing but the thinnest of political pretexts. A contemporary ethnologist has observed that the fantasies that evolutionary theory evoked in the Victorian imagination of 'nature, red in tooth and claw', come closest to being realized in the behavior of our own distinctively murderous species. In times of peace or when not actively engaged in killing, we are surrounded on every side and all the time by dying. Those deaths are acceptable; they are simply one of the facts of life, that is to say, of *our* respective lives. We insulate ourselves as much as possible and are habitually incurious. John Donne assumes too much: our ordinary thought is 'Who cares for whom the bell tolls? At least it isn't for me.' But such indifference to the death of others by no means argues a similar complacency with respect to one's

own mortality. Montaigne has a passage which might be a commentary on
Ivan Ilyich:

We drag everything along with us.
  Whence it follows that we deem our death a weighty matter, and that it does not
take place very simply, or without the solemn consultation of the stars. ... And we
think so the more, the more highly we value ourselves. How can so much learning
be lost, with such great detriment, without special heed being taken by the fates?
Does so rare and exemplary a mind cost no more in the killing than a commonplace
and useless one? This life, which covers so many other lives, upon which so many
other lives depend, which employs so many people in its service and fills so large
a place – is it cast out of its place like that which holds by a single tie?
  No one of us feels sufficiently that he is only himself.[4]

The conjunction of callousness with self-pity that Tolstoy shows us is
very common, common enough to make me doubt that Nagel's question
could ever have any interesting general answer. Indeed, for us who believe
that the death of others is sometimes good, sometimes bad, and anyway
inevitable while at the same time believing that our own death, no matter
what the circumstances, would be an unthinkable, unparalleled disaster,
there can be no general *question* 'whether it is a bad thing to die'. It would
be a mistake, however, to think that such gross disparity in standards of
evaluation is a universal human trait or that it is somehow essential to the
human condition. If one thought so, then Tolstoy's work would not be a
Morality Play, but merely an additional case history. The poignancy of
Ivan's plight springs from his awareness that everything might have been
different and that, had he been more humane in health and prosperity, he
might now be less craven in the face of death. Gerasim, the peasant boy,
is truthful and therefore he is able to be kind. He can comfort Ivan without
insulting him because Gerasim is free of hypocrisy and can say, 'We'll all
die some day ...' without making a tacit exception in his own favor. Tolstoy
again is right to remind us that spiritual purity, whether or not preeminent
among the illiterate and poor, is a genuine virtue, and a trait that, if less
common, is no less real than Ivan's preoccupation with himself and with
false values. History and experience afford examples of men whose
sympathies extend to the feelings of those who are dying and who, perhaps
partly on that account, are themselves able to confront death without anxiety
or remorse.

III

Philosophical writing on the topic of death, if one may distinguish it from
theological writing – which presents different problems – tends to
academicism. (Why this should be so, why we find novelists and poets more
illuminating, is a question worth exploring.) Arguments and doctrines

become conventionalized, and their familiarity makes us fail to notice how extremely implausible they are. Nagel, for example, gives serious attention to an ancient sophism that purports to justify indifference to death. Indeed he presents it as an alternative – the only alternative – to his own position. (The latter, if we bracket what leads to inconsistency, I take to be just that it *is*, in general, a bad thing to die.) To this view, Nagel's imagined opponent counters with the claim that 'if one realizes that death is not an unimaginable condition of the persisting person, but a mere blank, one will see that it can have no value whatever, positive or negative.' In its Epicurean original, which Nagel paraphrases later in his paper, the point appears as follows:

Death, the most awful evil, is nothing to us, seeing that when we are, death is not come and that when death comes, we are not.[5]

In its setting and given the didactic purposes it was intended to serve, it is innocent enough. To those contemporaries for whom fear of death was augmented by anxiety about the afterlife, Epicurus is saying, 'Relax. There isn't going to *be* any afterlife.' Whether or not such advice was or is likely to be efficacious in dispelling superstitious fears, it seems sensible enough in itself. Moreover, it is to be seen as part of a set of teachings on life and death which, by comparison with many institutionalized dogmas, are enlightened and humane. The poems of Horace are the most persuasive expression of the Epicurean ideal and, in their celebration of the life of care-free retirement, give us a more intimate understanding than any formal treatise of the combination of virtues connoted by '*ataraxia*', rather thinly translated as 'equanimity'.[6]

'Death is nothing to us ...' I take to be a mild hyperbole, as conveying the thought that we, i.e., the rational Epicureans, know that we shall die but try to keep that fact in its proper perspective. The suggested inference from 'when we are, death is not come, etc.' will hardly bear looking into, but may have been intended as little more than an eristic flourish. Epicurus was not much interested in logic, believing, perhaps, that life is too short for such things.

Now it is quite another thing to take the argument as providing serious reason for thinking there is something inherently unreasonable about being afraid to die. In Nagel's version, 'Death is nothing to us ...' appears as the claim that 'Death has no value whatever, positive or negative', and this is plainly absurd. How would one manifest such a belief? By being incautious in crossing busy intersections? By thinking (Austin's example) 'The children want to learn a new game. I'll teach them Russian roulette'? It is true that a man may say and mean that he no longer cares whether he lives or dies, but his state of mind is not *ataraxia* but despair. He is not a sage, but a 'danger to himself and others'.

And what about the alleged argument? It is a textbook example of the

Fallacy of Equivocation. Either the conclusion 'Death is nothing to us ...' repeats the premise 'when we are, death is not come ...', in which case there is no inference, or else the conclusion 'Death is nothing, i.e., a matter of indifference to us' is a nonsequitur. At the very least there must be an additional premise, and it is hard to imagine a premise that would do more than elaborate the original, simple-minded pun.

And yet generation after generation of sober and rational authors, Lucretius, Cicero, Seneca, Montaigne, D'Alembert, reproduce the argument without either developing it or noting how frivolous it is. It comes up here and there in contexts quite remote from moral rhetoric. Otto Fenichel in *The Psychoanalytic Theory of Neurosis*[7] remarks that

It is questionable whether there is any such thing as a normal fear of death; actually the idea of one's own death is subjectively inconceivable and therefore probably every fear of death covers other unconscious ideas.

I shall now offer a brief statement followed by some comments of my own views on this topic. (1) The idea of one's own death is not 'subjectively inconceivable'. (2) There is such a thing as a 'normal' fear of death, and it is not only normal but rational. (3) *Ataraxia* is a genuine virtue; to preserve equanimity in misfortune or when faced by death is a trait which, in Hume's words, is 'agreeable and useful to oneself and to others'. (4) The fact that all men are mortal, coupled with the fact that to die is to cease to exist, provides no reason whatever for thinking that death, one's own or that of another, is a matter of small consequence.

(1) What is the paradox that is supposed to be connected with thoughts about one's death? What is it that is 'subjectively inconceivable'? If I believe or tacitly assume that I shall survive my death, then, given the assumption of the present argument, I believe or tacitly assume what is false.[8] Each of us believes on the best possible inductive evidence that he will die sooner or later. Since my death, like others, will be a datable event with causal antecedents, there is no reason why I should not be able to predict as well as anyone else that, on the available evidence, I shall, e.g., die two years from now, the victim of a rare tropical disease, or two minutes from now, in front of a firing squad. It is true that *I* shall be unable to confirm my prediction but that truth is as trivial as that I shall not be able to perform my own autopsy. What I know or believe about death and project in my own case has been garnered from observation and not from experience.

The predicate '*x* is dead' is asymmetrical as between first- and third-person uses. Like '*x* is unconscious', '*x* is asleep', etc., it lacks a first-person present tense, but it diverges from the latter predicates in lacking past-tense use as well. I can speak of my own death only prospectively or via subjunctives. But why should that create any logical difficulties?

(2) Fear is linked with the concept of danger, and danger with the

concept of injury. A fear may be groundless without being irrational. For example, believing falsely that Lake Superior is infested with sharks, I am fearful of swimming there. One ground, not the only one, for describing fear as 'irrational' is that it manifests itself in circumstances that the subject himself either knows or believes to be innocuous. For example, I am fearful of high places, lizards, mice, etc. Obviously there are many situations in which fear of death is entirely appropriate. For example, I believe, as it happens, truly that I have a fatal disease or am about to be shot by a firing squad. Again it is true and again trivial that I shall not be able to say after the fact either that my worst fears have been realized or that being shot is not really so bad as one had been led to believe. Nonetheless the danger is real and my fear rational. ...

I suppose that it might be said that what cannot be 'normal' is not that fear which is related to particular threatening situations, but rather a recurrent pervasive fear of death. But this is too vague to be interesting. Among emotional disorders, the phobias are distinguished fairly clearly; whether fear of death is more common or more serious than other phobic responses, I do not know, but surely there cannot be any great difficulty in recognizing it as different from ordinary fear reactions.

Perhaps the imagined difficulty has to do with specifying the phenomenal content or object of a nonspecific fear of death. How can mere nonexistence seem a threat? No doubt it cannot, but then it is not as mere nonexistence that I conceive my death. My death will have its effects and consequences as it will have its proper causes, and both the former and the latter may quite properly be objects of my present concern. What more familiar than the thought, 'Were I to die, my children would lack a parent, my friends, a friend'? If it is my dearest wish that I should finish my novel or lead my troops to victory, then, should death intervene, my dearest wish will have been frustrated. Perhaps some projects can be completed by others, but it may be that what I want is that *I* should complete them. (The simple associations that survive in the word 'deadline' can be, so to speak, read in reverse. Somebody else may do my story if I fail to get it to the printers on time, but *my* assignment will not have been completed. Death is the deadline for all my assignments. Such parallels are not dangerous once it is made clear that *no* analogy can hold between my death and any experienced event of my life. To know what it is like to hope that one will not be interrupted is to know something about (one sort of) fear of death. We may think of death (rather grandiosely) as the person from Porlock but for whose untimely visit *Kubla Khan*, or so Coleridge claimed, would have been much, much longer than it is.)

(3) Equanimity is not indifference; it is compatible with fear, perhaps even with unreasonable fear, but not with hysteria or panic.

(4) In order to make minimally respectable the inference from 'When I

die, I cease to exist' to 'My death has no value whatever, positive or negative', some further premise is required. That premise will have to be something similar to the following: 'Nothing in the universe has any value except insofar as it has benign effects on me. The only rational goals are those from the achievement of which I can hope to benefit directly.' Given such a premise, the argument has some air of plausibility. But why should anyone assume the premise? No doubt some people do, but they are like Ivan Ilyich, selfish and unenlightened (or else in some pathological sense infantile). They are the ones Montaigne has in mind in the passage beginning, 'We drag everything along with us.' The premise needed to save the argument from triviality is ambiguous in a way that permits a reversal of the conclusion. From the assumption that death is the end of existence and that nothing has value except insofar as it affects me, I may reason to the conclusion that my death, far from having 'no value, positive or negative', is the worst possible evil, the final cosmic catastrophe. Attempts to prove by demonstration that death is not to be feared are probably all equivocal in the same way, and, as practical advice, calculated to defeat their own ends. The soothing reflections recommended as an antidote to anxiety often appear to be just such as one would imagine likely to exacerbate existing fears. Montaigne describes this curious phenomenon concisely:

Philosophy orders us to have death always before our eyes, to foresee it and to reflect upon it beforehand; and then gives us rules and precautions to be provided with, that this foresight and this reflection should not pain us. Thus do physicians, who throw us into illnesses that they may have occasion to employ their drugs and their skill.[9]

In conclusion, and because I have found so much to complain of in Nagel's argument, let me try to come as close as I can to giving a straight answer to the question 'whether it is a bad thing to die'. The answer, as he claims, is 'Yes,' and the ground for the answer is that every human being, except in moments of acute distress, wants to continue to live and to postpone death. It is partly because of this truth that Nagel's question sounds rather odd. Is there some sense in which it might be 'bad to die' beyond that just indicated? Pronounced in a vacuum, 'Not only do I not want to die, but it would be a *bad thing* if I were to die' is rather pretentious. And yet, if my comments on (3) above are defensible, there are many circumstances under which the distinction would be legitimate. If, for example, we can say truly of Keats not only that his death was bad for him – and his letters are full of the sense of frustration that goes with the realization that one will not be permitted to continue – but an objective disaster, a loss to letters, a bad thing for all of us, then there is no reason why Keats could not have made the same claim on his own behalf.

If the consequences and effects of a particular death are taken as the measure of its disvalue, then we may discriminate degrees of badness and speak of ranking order. We also allow that in particular circumstances, it may be 'a good thing to die', i.e., we admit the concept of rational or justified suicide. On the other hand, if the badness of death is taken as a function simply of the subject's felt aversion to dying, there appears to be no ground for discrimination among individual cases. 'It is a bad thing for me to die' has exactly the same force and weight as 'It is a bad thing for Smith to die', given that Smith wants, as I want, to continue to live.

NOTES

1 *Individuals* (New York: Doubleday, Anchor, 1963), pp. 112 ff.
2 *Tractatus, Logico-Philosophicus* (New York: Harcourt Brace Iovanovich, 1922), p. 185.
3 [A quotation from Tolstoy's *The Death of Ivan Ilyich* appeared at the start of Nagel's paper: 'The syllogism he had learnt from Kiesewetter's logic: "Caius is a man, men are mortal, therefore Caius is mortal.", had always seemed to him correct as applied to Caius, but certainly not as applied to himself. ... What did Caius know of the smell of that striped leather ball Vanya had been so fond of?' – OH.]
4 *Essays*, Book III, Number 13, tr. Ives (New York: Heritage Press, 1946).
5 *Letter to Menoecus*, Epicurus did not invent the argument. Socrates uses something similar in the *Apology*. I do not know what the true original is, but imagine it to be much earlier, Eleatic, perhaps.
6 I have read that Epicurean doctrine had a vogue among Roman legionnaires, and that one can find soldiers' graves from Britain to Asia Minor inscribed with a standard Epicurean epitaph: 'Non fui; fui; non sum; non curo.' As epitaphs go, this one strikes me as admirable. It is witty, nonedifying and, at least to my mind, has more dignity than, e.g., an injunction to the effect that passers-by should go to Sparta and report that her citizens died at their posts.
7 *The Psychoanalytic Theory of Neurosis* (New York: Norton, 1945), p. 208.
8 I suppose one needs the further assumption that Strawson is correct in thinking that the concept of survival is logically coherent, something which seems very dubious.
9 Montaigne, *Essays*, Book III, Number 13, p. 1434.

11

Why We Should not be Biased towards the Future

Derek Parfit

The extract from Parfit should be read in the light of Lucretius' comparison of the time after death with 'the eternity that passed before we were born'. We do not regret our non-existence before death; why, then, should non-existence after death be a matter for regret? Parfit rejects this argument on the ground that, because of the pressure of natural selection, human beings are bound to be more concerned about the future than about the past. 'In giving us this bias,' he says, 'Evolution denies us the best attitude to death.' The best attitude, if we could adopt it, would indeed be to have an equal concern for past and future. Now it is true that, generally speaking, one's past and one's future are likely to contain equal proportions of good and of bad; but Parfit argues that a person endowed with the 'best attitude' could be more selective about attention to the past — dwelling more on the good things that have occurred — than he (or anyone) can afford to be about what is yet to come.

Our bias towards the future is bad for us. It would be better for us if we were like Timeless.[1] We would lose in certain ways. Thus we should not be relieved when bad things were in the past. But we should also gain. We should not be sad when good things were in the past.

The gains would outweigh the losses. One reason would be this. When we look backward, we could afford to be selective. We ought to remember some of the bad events in our lives, when this would help us to avoid repetitions. But we could allow ourselves to forget most of the bad things that have happened, while preserving by rehearsing all of our memories of the good things. It would be bad for us if we were so selective when we are looking forward. Unless we think of all the bad things that are at all likely to happen, we lose our chance of preventing them. Since we ought not to be selective when looking forward, but could afford to be when looking backward, the latter would be, on the whole, more enjoyable.

There would be other, greater gains. One would be in our attitude to ageing and to death. Let us first consider the argument with which Epicurus claimed that our future non-existence cannot be something to regret. We do not regret our past non-existence. Since this is so, why should we regret our future non-existence? If we regard one with equanimity, should we not extend this attitude to the other?

Some claim that this argument fails because, while we might live longer, it is logically impossible that we might have been born much earlier. This is not a good objection. When they learnt that the square root of two was not a rational number, the Pythagoreans regretted this. We can therefore regret truths even when it is logically impossible that these truths be false.

Epicurus's argument fails for a different reason: we are biased towards the future. Because we have this bias, the bare knowledge that we once suffered may not now disturb us. But our equanimity does not show that our past suffering was not bad. The same could be true of our past non-existence. Epicurus's argument therefore has force only for those people who lack the bias towards the future, and do not regret their past non-existence. There are no such people. So the argument has force for no one.

Though the argument fails, it may provide some consolation. If we are afraid of death, the argument shows that the object of our dread is not *our non-existence*. It is only our *future* non-existence. That we can think serenely of our past non-existence does not show that it is not something to regret. But since we do not in fact view with dread our past non-existence, we may be able to use this fact to reduce our dread, or depression, when we think about our inevitable deaths. If we often think about, and view serenely, the blackness behind us, some of this serenity may be transferred to our view of the blackness before us.

Let us now suppose that we lack the bias towards the future. We are like Timeless. We should then greatly gain in our attitude to ageing and to death. As our life passes, we should have less and less to look forward to, but more and more to look backward to. This effect will be clearer if we imagine another difference. Suppose that our lives began, not with birth and childhood, but as Adam's did. Suppose that, though we are adults, and have adult knowledge and abilities, we have only just started to exist. We lack the bias towards the future. Should we be greatly troubled by the thought that yesterday we did not exist?

This depends on how non-existence is bad. Some think that non-existence is in itself bad. But the more plausible view is that its only fault is what it causes us to lose. Suppose we take this view. We may then think it a ground for regret that our life is finite, bounded at both ends by non-existence. But, if we had just started to exist, we would not think that something bad is just behind us. Our ground for regret would merely be that we have missed much that would have been good. Suppose that I could now be much as I actually am, even though I had been born as one of the privileged few around 1700. I would then greatly regret that I was in fact born in 1942. I would far prefer to have lived through the previous two and a half centuries, having had among my friends Hume, Byron, Chekhov, Nietzsche, and Sidgwick.

In my imagined case, we are not biased towards the future, and we have just started to exist. Though we would regret the fact that we had not existed earlier, we would not be greatly troubled by the thought that only yesterday we did not exist. We would not regard this fact with the kind of dread or grief with which most actual people would regard the sudden prospect of death tomorrow. We would not have such dread or grief because, though we would have nothing good to look backward to, we would have our whole lives to look forward to.

Now suppose that our lives have nearly passed. We shall die tomorrow. If we were not biased towards the future, our reaction should mirror the one that I have just described. We should not be greatly troubled by the thought that we shall soon cease to exist, for though we now have nothing to look forward to, we have our whole lives to look backward to.

It may be objected: 'You can look backward now. But once you are dead you won't be able to look backward. And you will be dead tomorrow. So you ought to be greatly troubled.' We could answer: 'Why? It is true that after we cease to exist we shall never be able to enjoy looking backward to our lives. We now have nothing at all to look forward to, not even the pleasures of looking backward. But it was equally true that, before we began to exist, we had nothing at all to look backward to, not even the pleasures of looking forward. But that was then no reason to be greatly troubled, since we could then look forward to our whole lives. Since we can now look backward to our whole lives, why should the parallel fact – that we have nothing to look forward to – give us reason to be greatly troubled?'

This reasoning ignores those emotions which are essentially future-directed. It would not apply to those people for whom the joy in looking forward comes from making plans, or savouring alternatives. But the reasoning seems to be correct when applied to more passive types, those who take life's pleasures as they come. And, to the extent that we are like this, this reasoning shows that we would be happier if we lacked the bias towards the future. We would be much less depressed by ageing and the approach of death. If we were like Timeless, being at the end of our lives would be more like being at the beginning. At any point within our lives we could enjoy looking either backward or forward to our whole lives. ...

I believe that we ought not to be biased towards the future. This belief does not beg the question about the rationality of this bias. On any plausible moral view, it would be better if we were all happier. This is the sense in which, if we could, we ought not to be biased towards the future. In giving us this bias, Evolution denies us the best attitude to death.

NOTE

1 ['Timeless' is the name given by the author to an imaginary person described
in the preceding text, as follows: 'We can clearly describe someone who ... is
unlike us. When such a person is reminded that he once had a month of agony,
he is as much distressed as when he learns that he will later have such a month.
He is similarly neutral with respect to enjoyable events. When he is told that
he will later have some period of great enjoyment, he is pleased to learn this.
He greatly looks forward to this period. When he is reminded that he once had
just such a period, he is equally pleased. I shall call this imagined man *Timeless*'
– OH.]

12

The Vanity and Suffering of Life

Arthur Schopenhauer

Schopenhauer (1788–1860) regarded death as a 'terrible' event. But since, according to him, life itself is bad on the whole, we may 'console ourselves with death in regard to the sufferings of life, and with the sufferings of life in regard to death.' Death is also proof of the 'essential vanity' of life, which would not have 'non-being as its goal' if there were any meaning in it. However, most of this reading from Schopenhauer is taken up with arguments that human life does, indeed, contain more pain than pleasure, more suffering than happiness. He makes much of the existence of boredom in our lives, and of the human need for 'killing time'. The picture that Schopenhauer paints, of a constant alternation between pain and boredom (the pain of desire with the boredom that follows satisfaction), may be criticized as excessively simple. But that there is such a thing as boredom in human life is remarkable enough, and may seem to imply a lack of harmony in the human condition, as compared with that of wild animals. (The point would not hold so well for domestic animals.) Again, it may be said that, even if some of Schopenhauer's points are convincing in detail, there is no way of arriving at an overall balance of good and bad for something as large as life in general. But if this is so, then it must apply also to the opposite verdict – that life is, on the whole, good rather than bad. One way or another, this commonly held view is undermined by Schopenhauer's argument.

I

If the immediate and direct purpose of our life is not suffering then our existence is the most ill-adapted to its purpose in the world: for it is absurd to suppose that the endless affliction of which the world is everywhere full, and which arises out of the need and distress pertaining essentially to life, should be purposeless and purely accidental. Each individual misfortune, to be sure, seems an exceptional occurrence; but misfortune in general is the rule.

II

Just as a stream flows smoothly on as long as it encounters no obstruction, so the nature of man and animal is such that we never really notice or become conscious of what is agreeable to our will; if we are to notice something, our will has to have been thwarted, has to have experienced a shock of some kind. On the other hand, all that opposes, frustrates and resists our will, that is to say all that is unpleasant and painful, impresses itself upon us instantly, directly and with great clarity. Just as we are conscious not of the healthiness of our whole body but only of the little place where the shoe pinches, so we think not of the totality of our successful activities but of some insignificant trifle or other which continues to vex us. On this fact is founded what I have often before drawn attention to: the negativity of well-being and happiness, in antithesis to the positivity of pain.

I therefore know of no greater absurdity than that absurdity which characterizes almost all metaphysical systems: that of explaining evil as something negative. For evil is precisely that which is positive, that which makes itself palpable; and good, on the other hand, i.e. all happiness and all gratification, is that which is negative, the mere abolition of a desire and extinction of a pain.

This is also consistent with the fact that as a rule we find pleasure much less pleasurable, pain much more painful than we expected.

A quick test of the assertion that enjoyment outweighs pain in this world, or that they are at any rate balanced, would be to compare the feelings of an animal engaged in eating another with those of the animal being eaten.

III

The most effective consolation in every misfortune and every affliction is to observe others who are more unfortunate than we: and everyone can do this. But what does that say for the condition of the whole?

History shows us the life of nations and finds nothing to narrate but wars and tumults; the peaceful years appear only as occasional brief pauses and interludes. In just the same way the life of the individual is a constant struggle, and not merely a metaphorical one against want or boredom, but also an actual struggle against other people. He discovers adversaries everywhere, lives in continual conflict and dies with sword in hand.

IV

Not the least of the torments which plague our existence is the constant pressure of *time*, which never lets us so much as draw breath but pursues us all like a taskmaster with a whip. It ceases to persecute only him it has delivered over to boredom.

V

And yet, just as our body would burst asunder if the pressure of the atmosphere were removed from it, so would the arrogance of men expand, if not to the point of bursting then to that of the most unbridled folly, indeed madness, if the pressure of want, toil, calamity and frustration were removed from their life. One can even say that we *require* at all times a certain quantity of care or sorrow or want, as a ship requires ballast, in order to keep on a straight course.

Work, worry, toil and trouble are indeed the lot of almost all men their whole life long. And yet if every desire were satisfied as soon as it arose how would men occupy their lives, how would they pass the time? Imagine this race transported to a Utopia where everything grows of its own accord and turkeys fly around ready-roasted, where lovers find one another without any delay and keep one another without any difficulty: in such a place some men would die of boredom or hang themselves, some would fight and kill one another, and thus they would create for themselves more suffering than nature inflicts on them as it is. Thus for a race such as this no stage, no form of existence is suitable other than the one it already possesses.

VI

Since, as we recalled above, pleasure and well-being is negative and suffering positive, the happiness of a given life is not to be measured according to the joys and pleasures it contains but according to the absence of the positive element, the absence of suffering. This being so, however, the lot of the animals appears more endurable than that of man. Let us look at both a little more closely.

However varied the forms may be which human happiness and misery assume, inciting man to seek the one and flee from the other, the material basis of them all is physical pleasure or physical pain. This basis is very narrow: it consists of health, food, protection from wet and cold, and sexual gratification; or the lack of these things. Man has, consequently, no larger share of real physical pleasure than the animals have, except perhaps to the extent that his more highly charged nervous system intensifies every sensation of pleasure – as it also does every sensation of pain. Yet how much stronger are the emotions aroused in him than those aroused in the animals! how incomparably more profound and vehement are his passions! – and all to achieve exactly the same result in the end: health, food, covering, etc.

This arises first and foremost because with him everything is powerfully intensified by thinking about absent and future things, and this is in fact the origin of care, fear and hope, which, once they have been aroused, make a far stronger impression on men than do actual present pleasures or sufferings, to which the animal is limited. For, since it lacks the faculty of reflection, joys and sorrows cannot accumulate in the animal as they do in man through memory and anticipation. With the animal, present suffering, even if repeated countless times, remains what it was the first time: it cannot sum itself up. Hence the enviable composure and unconcern which characterizes the animal. With man, on the other hand, there evolves out of those elements of pleasure and suffering which he has in common with the animal an intensification of his sensations of happiness and misery which can lead to momentary transports which may sometimes even prove fatal, or to suicidal despair. More closely considered, what happens is this: he deliberately intensifies his needs, which are originally scarcely harder to satisfy than those of the animal, so as to intensify his pleasure: hence luxury, confectionery, tobacco, opium, alcoholic drinks, finery and all that pertains to them. To these is then added, also as a result of reflection, a source of pleasure, and consequently of suffering, available to him alone and one which preoccupies him beyond all measure, indeed more than all the rest put together: ambition and the sense of honour and shame – in plain words, what he thinks others think of him. This, in a thousand, often curious shapes then becomes the goal of all those endeavours of his which go beyond physical pleasure or pain. He excels the animal in his capacity for enjoying intellectual pleasures, to be sure, and these are available to him in many degrees, from the simplest jesting and conversation up to the highest achievements of the mind; but as a counterweight to this, on the side of suffering stands boredom, which is unknown to the animals at least in the state of nature and is only very slightly perceptible in the very cleverest domesticated ones, while to man it has become a veritable scourge. Want and boredom are indeed the twin poles of human life. Finally it remains to be mentioned that with man sexual gratification is tied to a very obstinate selectivity which is sometimes intensified into a more or less passionate love. Thus sexuality becomes for man a source of brief pleasure and protracted suffering.

It is indeed remarkable how, through the mere addition of thought, which the animal lacks, there should have been erected on the same narrow basis of pain and pleasure that the animal possesses so vast and lofty a structure of human happiness and misery, and man should be subjected to such vehement emotions, passions and convulsions that their impress can be read in enduring lines on his face; while all the time and in reality he is concerned only with the very same things which the animal too attains, and attains with an incomparably smaller expenditure of emotion. Through all this, however, the measure of suffering increases in man far more than the enjoyment, and it is very greatly enhanced specifically by the fact that he actually *knows* of death, while the animal only instinctively flees it without actually knowing of it and therefore without ever really having it in view, which man does all the time. ...

That human life must be some kind of mistake is sufficiently proved by the simple observation that man is a compound of needs which are hard to satisfy; that their satisfaction achieves nothing but a painless condition in which he is only given over to boredom; and that boredom is a direct proof that existence is in itself valueless, for boredom is nothing other than the sensation of the emptiness of existence. For if life, in the desire for which our essence and existence consists, possessed in itself a positive value and real content, there would be no such thing as boredom: mere existence would fulfil and satisfy us. As things are, we take no pleasure in existence except when we are striving after something – in which case distance and difficulties make our goal look as if it would satisfy us (an illusion which fades when we reach it) – or when engaged in purely intellectual activity, in which case we are really stepping out of life so as to regard it from outside, like spectators at a play. Even sensual pleasure itself consists in a continual striving and ceases as soon as its goal is reached. Whenever we are not involved in one or other of these things but directed back to existence itself we are overtaken by its worthlessness and vanity and this is the sensation called boredom.

That the most perfect manifestation of the will to live represented by the human organism, with its incomparably ingenious and complicated machinery, must crumble to dust and its whole essence and all its striving be palpably given over at last to annihilation – this is nature's unambiguous declaration that all the striving of this will is essentially vain. If it were something possessing value in itself, something which ought unconditionally to exist, it would not have non-being as its goal. ...

In the plant there is as yet no sensibility, and hence no pain. A certain very small degree of both dwells in the lowest animals, in infusoria and radiata; even in insects the capacity to feel and suffer is still limited. It first appears in a high degree with the complete nervous system of the vertebrate animals, and in an ever higher degree, the more intelligence is developed. Therefore, in proportion as knowledge attains to distinctness, consciousness is enhanced, pain also increases, and consequently reaches its highest degree in man; and all the more, the more distinctly he knows, and the more intelligent he is. The person in whom genius is to be found suffers most of all. In this sense, namely in reference to the degree of knowledge generally, not

to mere abstract knowledge, I understand and here use that saying in Ecclesiastes: *Qui auget scientiam, auget et dolorem.*[1] This precise relation between the degree of consciousness and that of suffering has been beautifully expressed in perceptive and visible delineation in a drawing by Tischbein, that philosophical painter or painting philosopher. The upper half of his drawing represents women from whom their children are being snatched away, and who by different groupings and attitudes express in many ways deep maternal pain, anguish, and despair. The lower half of the drawing shows, in exactly the same order and grouping, sheep whose lambs are being taken from them. In the lower half of the drawing an animal analogy corresponds to each human head, to each human attitude, in the upper half. We thus see clearly how the pain possible in the dull animal consciousness is related to the violent grief that becomes possible only through distinctness of knowledge, through clearness of consciousness.
...

The basis of all willing, however, is need, lack, and hence pain, and by its very nature and origin it is therefore destined to pain. If, on the other hand, it lacks objects of willing, because it is at once deprived of them again by too easy a satisfaction, a fearful emptiness and boredom come over it; in other words, its being and its existence itself become an intolerable burden for it. Hence its life swings like a pendulum to and fro between pain and boredom,and these two are in fact its ultimate constituents. This has been expressed very quaintly by saying that, after man had placed all pains and torments in hell, there was nothing left for heaven but boredom.

But the constant striving, which constitutes the inner nature of every phenomenon of the will, obtains at the higher grades of objectification its first and most universal foundation from the fact that the will here appears as a living body with the iron command to nourish it. What gives force to this command is just that this body is nothing but the objectified will-to-live itself. Man, as the most complete objectification of this will, is accordingly the most necessitous of all beings. He is concrete willing and needing through and through; he is a concretion of a thousand wants and needs. With these he stands on the earth, left to his own devices, in uncertainty about everything except his own need and misery. Accordingly, care for the maintenance of this existence, in the face of demands that are so heavy and proclaim themselves anew every day, occupies, as a rule, the whole of human life. With this is directly connected the second demand, that for the propagation of the race. At the same time dangers of the most varied kinds threaten him from all sides, and to escape from them calls for constant vigilance. With cautious step and anxious glance around he pursues his path, for a thousand accidents and a thousand enemies lie in wait for him. Thus he went in the savage state, and thus he goes in civilized life; there is no security for him:

Qualibus in tenebris vitae, quantisque periclis
Degitur hocc' aevi, quodcunque est![2]

Lucretius, ii, 15.

The life of the great majority is only a constant struggle for this same existence, with the certainty of ultimately losing it. What enables them to endure this wearisome battle is not so much the love of life as the fear of death, which nevertheless stands in the background as inevitable, and which may come on the scene at any moment. Life itself is a sea full of rocks and whirlpools that man avoids with the greatest caution and care, although he knows that, even when he succeeds with all his efforts and ingenuity in struggling through, at every step he comes near to the greatest, the total, the inevitable and irremediable shipwreck, indeed even steers right on to it, namely death. This is the final goal of the wearisome voyage, and is worse for him than all the rocks that he has avoided.

Now it is at once well worth noting that, on the one hand, the sufferings and afflictions of life can easily grow to such an extent that even death, in the flight from which the whole life consists, becomes desirable, and a man voluntarily hastens to it. Again, on the other hand, it is worth noting that, as soon as want and suffering give man a relaxation, boredom is at once so near that he necessarily requires diversion and amusement. The striving after existence is what occupies all living things, and keeps them in motion. When existence is assured to them, they do not know what to do with it. Therefore the second thing that sets them in motion is the effort to get rid of the burden of existence, to make it no longer felt, 'to kill time', in other words, to escape from boredom. Accordingly we see that almost all men, secure from want and cares, are now a burden to themselves, after having finally cast off all other burdens. They regard as a gain every hour that is got through, and hence every deduction from that very life, whose maintenance as long as possible has till then been the object of all their efforts. Boredom is anything but an evil to be thought of lightly; ultimately it depicts on the countenance real despair. It causes beings who love one another as little as men do, to seek one another so much, and thus becomes the source of sociability. From political prudence public measures are taken against it everywhere, as against other universal calamities, since this evil, like its opposite extreme, famine, can drive people to the greatest excesses and anarchy; the people need *panem et circenses*. The strict penitentiary system of Philadelphia makes mere boredom an instrument of punishment through loneliness and idleness. It is so terrible an instrument, that it has brought convicts to suicide. Just as need and want are the constant scourge of the people, so is boredom that of the world of fashion. In middle-class life boredom is represented by the Sunday, just as want is represented by the six weekdays.

Now absolutely every human life continues to flow on between willing and attainment. Of its nature the wish is pain; attainment quickly begets satiety. The goal was only apparent; possession takes away its charm. The wish, the need, appears again on the scene under a new form; if it does not, then dreariness, emptiness, and boredom follow, the struggle against which is just as painful as is that against want. For desire and satisfaction to follow each other at not too short and not too long intervals, reduces the suffering occasioned by both to the smallest amount, and constitutes the happiest life. What might otherwise be called the finest part of life, its purest joy, just because it lifts us out of real existence, and transforms us into disinterested spectators of it, is pure knowledge which remains foreign to all willing, pleasure in the beautiful, genuine delight in art. But because this requires rare talents, it is granted only to extremely few, and even to those only as a fleeting dream. Then again higher intellectual power makes those very few susceptible to much greater sufferings than duller men can ever feel. Moreover, it makes them feel lonely among beings that are noticeably different from them, and in this way also matters are made even. But purely intellectual pleasures are not accessible to the vast majority of men. They are almost wholly incapable of the pleasure to be found in pure knowledge; they are entirely given over to willing. Therefore, if anything is to win their sympathy, to be *interesting* to them, it must (and this is to be found already in the meaning of the word) in some way excite their *will*, even if it be only through a remote relation to it which is merely within the bounds of possibility. The will must never be left entirely out of question, since their existence lies far more in willing than in knowing; action and reaction are their only element. The naïve expressions of this quality can be seen in trifles and everyday phenomena; thus, for example, they write their names up at places worth seeing which they visit, in order thus to react on, to affect the place, since it does not affect them. Further, they cannot easily just contemplate a rare and strange animal, but must excite it, tease it, play with it, just to experience action and reaction. But this need for exciting the will shows itself particularly in the invention and maintenance of card-playing, which is in the truest sense an expression of the wretched side of humanity. ...

Depressing as this discussion is, I will, however, draw attention in passing to one aspect of it from which a consolation can be derived, and perhaps even a stoical indifference to our own present ills may be attained. For our impatience at these arises for the most part from the fact that we recognize them as accidental, as brought about by a chain of causes that might easily be different. We are not usually distressed at evils that are inescapably necessary and quite universal, for example, the necessity of old age and death, and of many daily inconveniences. It is rather a consideration of the accidental nature of the circumstances that have brought suffering precisely on us which gives this suffering its sting. Now we have recognized that pain as such is inevitable and essential to life; that nothing but the mere form in which it manifests itself depends on chance; that therefore our present suffering fills a place which without it would be at once occupied by some other suffering which the one now present excludes; and that, accordingly, fate can affect us little in what is essential. If such a reflection were to become a living conviction, it might produce a considerable degree of stoical equanimity, and greatly reduce our anxious concern about our own welfare. But such a powerful control of the faculty of reason over directly felt suffering is seldom or never found in fact.

Moreover, through this consideration of the inevitability of pain, of the supplanting of one pain by another, of the dragging in of a fresh pain by the departure of the preceding one, we might be led to the paradoxical but not absurd hypothesis that in every individual the measure of the pain essential to him has been determined once for all by his nature, a measure that could not remain empty or be filled to excess, however much the form of the suffering might change. Accordingly, his suffering and well-being would not be determined at all from without, but only by that measure, that disposition, which might in fact through the physical condition experience some increase and decrease at different times, but which on the whole would remain the same, and would be nothing but what is called his temperament. More accurately, this is called the degree in which he might be ευχολοζ or δυσχολοζ, as Plato puts it in the first book of the *Republic*, in other words, of an easy or difficult nature. In support of this hypothesis is the well-known experience that great sufferings render lesser ones quite incapable of being felt, and conversely, that in the absence of great sufferings even the smallest vexations and annoyances torment us, and put us in a bad mood. But experience also teaches us that if a great misfortune, at the mere thought of which we shuddered, has now actually happened, our frame of mind remains on the whole much the same as soon as we have overcome the first pain. Conversely, experience also teaches us that, after the appearance of a long-desired happiness, we do not feel ourselves on the whole and permanently much better off or more comfortable than before. Only the moment of appearance of these changes moves us with unusual strength, as deep distress or shouts of joy; but both of these soon disappear, because they rested on illusion. For they do not spring from the immediately present pleasure or pain, but only from the opening up of a new future that is anticipated in them. Only by pain or pleasure borrowing from the future could they be heightened so abnormally, and consequently not for any length of time. The following remarks may be put in evidence in support of the hypothesis we advanced, by which, in knowing as well as in feeling suffering or well-being, a very large part would be subjective and determined *a priori*. Human cheerfulness or dejection is obviously not determined by external circumstances, by wealth or position, for we come across at least as many cheerful faces among the poor as among the rich. Further, the motives that induce suicide are so very different, that we cannot mention any misfortune which would be great enough to bring it about in any character with a high degree of probability, and few that would be so small that those like them would not at some time have caused it. Now although the degree of our cheerfulness or sadness is not at all times the same, yet in consequence of this view we shall attribute it not to the change of external circumstances, but to that of the internal state, the physical condition. For when an actual, though always only temporary, enhancement of our cheerfulness takes place, even to the extent of joy, it usually appears without any external occasion. It is true that we often see our pain result only from a definite external relation, and that we are visibly oppressed and saddened merely by this. We then believe that, if only this were removed, the greatest contentment would necessarily ensue. But this is a delusion. The measure of our pain and our well-being is, on the whole, subjectively determined for each point of time according to our hypothesis; and in reference to this, that external motive for sadness is only what a blister is for the body, to which are drawn all the bad humours that would otherwise be spread throughout it. The pain to be found in our nature for this period of time, which therefore cannot be shaken off, would be distributed at a hundred points were it not for that definite external cause of our suffering. It would appear in the form of a hundred little annoyances and worries over things we now entirely overlook, because our capacity for pain is already filled up by that principal evil that has concentrated at a point all the suffering otherwise dispersed. In keeping with this is also the observation that, if a great and pressing care is finally lifted from our breast by a fortunate issue, another immediately takes its place. The whole material of this already existed previously, yet it could not enter consciousness as care, because the consciousness had no capacity left for it. This material for care, therefore, remained merely as a dark and unobserved misty form on the extreme horizon of consciousness. But now as there is room, this ready material at once comes forward and occupies the throne of the reigning care of the day (πρυτανεύουσα). If so far as its matter is concerned it is very much lighter than the material of the care that has vanished, it knows how to blow itself out, so that it apparently equals it in size, and thus, as the chief care of the day, completely fills the throne. . . .

All satisfaction, or what is commonly called happiness, is really and essentially always *negative* only, and never positive. It is not a gratification which comes to us originally and of itself, but it must always be the satisfaction of a wish. For desire, that is to say, want, is the precedent condition of every pleasure; but with the satisfaction, the desire and therefore the pleasure cease; and so the satisfaction or gratification can never be more than deliverance from a pain, from a want. Such is not only every actual and evident suffering, but also every desire whose importunity disturbs our peace, and indeed even the deadening boredom that makes existence a burden to us. But it is so difficult to attain and carry through anything; difficulties and troubles without end oppose every plan, and at every step obstacles are heaped up. But when everything is finally overcome and attained, nothing can ever be gained but deliverance from some suffering or desire; consequently, we are only in the same position as we were before this suffering or desire appeared. What is immediately given to us is always only the want, i.e., the pain. The satisfaction and pleasure can be known only indirectly by remembering the preceding suffering and privation that ceased on their entry. Hence it comes about that we are in no way aware of the blessings and advantages we actually possess; we do not value them, but simply imagine that they must be so, for they make us happy only negatively by preventing suffering. Only after we have lost them do we become sensible of their value, for the want, the privation, the suffering is what is positive, and proclaims itself immediately. Thus also we are pleased at remembering need, sickness, want, and so on which have been overcome, because such remembrance is the only means of enjoying present blessings. It is also undeniable that in this respect, and from this standpoint of egoism, which is the form of the will-to-live, the sight or description of another's sufferings affords us satisfaction and pleasure, just as Lucretius beautifully and frankly expresses it at the beginning of his second book:

> *Suave, mari magno, turbantibus aequora ventis,*
> *E terra magnum alterius spectare laborem:*
> *Non, quia vexari quemquam est jucunda voluptas;*
> *Sed, quibus ipse malis careas, quia cernere suave est.*[3]

Yet later on we shall see that this kind of pleasure, through knowledge of our own well-being obtained in this way, lies very near the source of real, positive wickedness.

In art, especially in poetry, that true mirror of the real nature of the world and of life, we also find evidence of the fact that all happiness is only of a negative, not a positive nature, and that for this reason it cannot be lasting satisfaction and gratification, but always delivers us only from a pain or want that must be followed either by a new pain or by languor, empty longing, and boredom. Every epic or dramatic poem can always present to us only a strife, an effort, and a struggle for happiness, never enduring and complete happiness itself. It conducts its heroes to their goal through a thousand difficulties and dangers; as soon as the goal is reached, it quickly lets the curtain fall. For there would be nothing left for it but to show that the glittering goal, in which the hero imagined he could find happiness, had merely mocked him, and that he was no better after its attainment than before. Since a genuine, lasting happiness is not possible, it cannot be a subject of art. It is true that the real purpose of the idyll is the description of such a happiness, but we also see that the idyll as such cannot endure. In the hands of the poet it always becomes an epic, and is then only a very insignificant epic made up of trifling sorrows, trifling joys, and trifling efforts; this is the commonest case. Or it becomes a merely descriptive poem, depicting the beauty of nature, in other words, really pure, will-free knowing, which is of course the only pure happiness which is not preceded either by suffering or need, or yet followed by repentance, suffering, emptiness, or satiety. This happiness, however, cannot fill the whole of life, but only moments of it. What we see in poetry we find again in music, in the melodies of which we again recognize the universally expressed, innermost story of the will conscious of itself, the most secret living, longing, suffering, and enjoying, the ebb and flow of the human heart. Melody is always a deviation from the keynote through a thousand crotchety wanderings up to the most painful discord. After this, it at last finds the keynote again, which expresses the satisfaction and composure of the will, but with which nothing more can then be done, and the continuation of which would be only a wearisome and meaningless monotony corresponding to boredom. ...

We feel pain, but not painlessness; care, but not freedom from care; fear, but not safety and security. We feel the desire as we feel hunger and thirst; but as soon as it has been satisfied, it is like the mouthful of food which has been taken, and which ceases to exist for our feelings the moment it is swallowed. We painfully feel the loss of pleasures and enjoyments, as soon as they fail to appear; but when pains cease even after being present for a long time, their absence is not directly felt, but at most they are thought of intentionally by means of reflection. For only pain and want can be felt positively; and therefore they proclaim themselves; well-being, on the contrary, is merely negative. Therefore, we do not become conscious of the three greatest blessings of life as such, namely health, youth, and freedom, as long as we possess them, but only after we have lost them; for they too are negations. We notice that certain days of our life were happy only after they have made room for unhappy ones. In proportion as enjoyments and pleasures increase, susceptibility to them decreases; that to which we are accustomed is no longer felt as a pleasure. But in precisely this way is the susceptibility to suffering increased; for the cessation of that to which we are accustomed is felt painfully. Thus the measure of what is necessary increases through possession, and thereby the capacity to feel pain. The hours pass the more quickly the more pleasantly they are spent, and the more slowly the more painfully they are spent, since pain, not pleasure, is the positive thing, whose presence makes itself felt. In just the same way we become conscious of time when we are bored, not when we are amused. Both cases prove that our existence is happiest when we perceive it least; from this it follows that it would be better not to have it. Great and animated delight can be positively conceived only as the consequence of great misery that has preceded it; for nothing can be added to a state of permanent contentment except some amusement or even the satisfaction of vanity.

NOTES

1 'He that increaseth knowledge increaseth sorrow.' [Ecclesiastes, i, 18 – Tr.]
2 'In what gloom of existence, in what great perils, this life is spent as long as it endures!' [Tr.]
3 'It is a pleasure to stand on the seashore when the tempestuous winds whip up the sea, and to behold the great toils another is enduring. Not that it pleases us to watch another being tormented, but that it is a joy to us to observe evils from which we ourselves are free.' [*De Rerum Natura*, II. 1 *seqq*. – Tr.]

13

Murder
and
A World without Human Beings

G. E. Moore

The question whether life is, on the whole, good or bad has a bearing, not only on the alleged badness of death, but also on the question of killing. The 'sanctity of life' is commonly regarded as a fundamental (perhaps the most fundamental) principle of morality. On this view, the unlawful taking of life is the worst of all crimes, and the death penalty the worst penalty of all. This view is sometimes grounded on the premise that life is the highest of all the goods we possess. But, as we saw in the reading from Schopenhauer, this premise is, at least, open to challenge. G. E. Moore (1873–1958), from whom the next reading is taken, had an open mind on the question, and this affected his views about the wrongness of murder. The committing of individual murders is wrong, he argues, because of its effect on those left behind. But what about 'universal murder' – the extinction of the whole human race? To prove that this is wrong, we would need to 'disprove the main contention of pessimism – namely that the existence of human life is on the whole an evil.'

Murder

The general disutility of murder can only be proved, provided the majority of the human race will certainly persist in existing. In order to prove that murder, if it were so universally adopted as to cause the speedy extermination of the race, would not be good as a means, we should have to disprove the main contention of pessimism – namely that the existence of human life is on the whole an evil. And the view of pessmism, however strongly we may be convinced of its truth or falsehood, is one which never has been either proved or refuted conclusively. That universal murder would not be a good thing at this moment can therefore not be proved. But, as a matter of fact, we can and do assume with certainty that, even if a few people are willing to murder, most people will not be willing. When, therefore, we say that murder is in general to be avoided, we only mean that it is so, so long as the majority of mankind will certainly not agree to it, but will persist in living. And that, under these circumstances, it is generally wrong for any single person to commit murder seems capable of proof. For, since there is in any case no hope of exterminating the race, the only effects which we have to consider are those which the action will have upon the increase of the goods and the diminution of the evils of human life. Where the best is not attainable (assuming extermination to be the best) one alternative may still be better than another. And, apart from the immediate evils which murder generally produces, the fact that, if it were a common practice, the feeling of insecurity, thus caused, would absorb much time, which might be spent to better purpose, is perhaps conclusive against it. So long as men desire to live as strongly as they do, and so long as it is certain that they will continue to do so, anything which hinders them from devoting their energy to the attainment of positive goods, seems plainly bad as a means. And the general practice of murder, falling so far short of universality as it certainly must in all known conditions of society, seems certainly to be a hindrance of this kind.

A World without Human Beings

'No one', says Prof. Sidgwick, 'would consider it rational to aim at the production of beauty in external nature, apart from any possible contemplation of it by human beings.'[1] Well, I may say at once, that I, for one, do consider this rational; and let us see if I cannot get any one to agree with me. Consider what this admission really means. It entitles us to put the following case. Let us imagine one world exceedingly beautiful. Imagine it as beautiful as you can; put into it whatever on this earth you most admire – mountains, rivers, the sea; trees, and sunsets, stars and moon. Imagine these all combined in the most exquisite proportions, so that no one thing jars against another, but each contributes to increase the beauty of the whole. And then imagine the ugliest world you can possible conceive. Imagine it simply one heap of filth, containing everything that is most disgusting to us, for whatever reason, and the whole, as far as may be, without one redeeming feature. Such a pair of worlds we are entitled to compare: they fall within Prof. Sidgwick's meaning, and the comparison is highly relevant to it. The only thing we are not entitled to imagine is that any human being ever has or ever, by any possibility, *can*, live in either, can ever see and enjoy the beauty of the one or hate the foulness of the other. Well, even so, supposing them quite apart from any posisble contemplation by human beings; still, is it irrational to hold that it is better that the beautiful world should exist, than the one which is ugly? Would it not be well, in any case, to do what we could to produce it rather than the other? Certainly I cannot help thinking that it would; and I hope that some may agree with me in this extreme instance. The instance is extreme. It is highly improbable, not to say, impossible, we should ever have such a choice before us. In any actual choice we should have to consider the possible effects of our action upon conscious beings, and among these possible effects there are always some, I think, which ought to be preferred to the existence of mere beauty. But this only means that in our present state, in which but a very small portion of the good is attainable, the pursuit of beauty for its own sake must always be postponed to the pursuit of some greater good, which is equally attainable. But it is enough for my purpose, if it be admitted that, *supposing* no greater good were at all attainable, then beauty must in itself be regarded as a greater good than ugliness; if it be admitted that, in that case, we should not be left without any reason for preferring one course of action to another, we should not be left without any duty whatever, but that it would then be our positive duty to make the world more beautiful, so far as we were able, since nothing better than beauty could then result from our efforts. If this be once admitted, if in any imaginable case you do admit that the existence of a more beautiful thing is better in itself than that of one more ugly, quite apart from its effects on any human feeling, then Prof. Sidgwick's principle has broken down. Then we shall have to include in our ultimate end something beyond the limits of human existence. I admit, of course, that our beautiful world would be better still, if there were human beings in it to contemplate and enjoy its beauty. But that admission makes nothing against my point. If it be once admitted that the beautiful world *in itself* is better than the ugly, then it follows, that however many beings may enjoy it, and however much better their enjoyment may be than it is itself, yet its mere existence adds *something* to the goodness of the whole: it is not only a means to our end, but also itself a part thereof. ...

By far the most valuable things, which we know or can imagine, are certain states of consciousness, which may be roughly described as the pleasures of human intercourse and the enjoyment of beautiful objects. No one, probably, who has asked himself the question, has ever doubted that personal affection and the appreciation of what is beautiful in Art or Nature, are good in themselves; nor, if we consider strictly what things are worth having *purely for their own sakes*, does it appear probable that any one will think that anything else has *nearly* so great a value as the things which are included under these two heads. I have myself urged that the mere existence of what is beautiful does appear to have *some* intrinsic value; but I regard it as indubitable that Prof. Sidgwick was so far right, in the view there discussed, that such mere existence of what is beautiful has value, so small as to be negligible, in comparison with that which attaches to the *consciousness* of beauty. This simple truth may, indeed, be said to be universally recognized. What has *not* been recognized is that it is the ultimate and fundamental truth of Moral Philosophy. That it is only for the sake of these things – in order that as much of them as possible may at some time exist – that any one can be justified in performing any public or private duty; that they are the *raison d'être* of virtue; that it is they – these complex wholes *themselves*, and not any constituent or characteristic of them – that form the rational ultimate end of human action and the sole criterion of social progress: these appear to be truths which have been generally overlooked.

NOTE

1 [Henry Sidgwick, *The Methods of Ethics* (Macmillan, 1967), p. 114 – OH.]

14

The Sanctity of Life

Jonathan Glover

The question 'Why is killing wrong?' provides the starting-point of the next reading. Glover considers what it is about life that is 'intrinsically valuable', and introduces 'the concept of a "life worth living".' He will 'assume', he says, 'that, where someone's life is worth living, this is a good reason for holding that it would be ... wrong to kill him'; though he is not prepared to say 'what sorts of things do make life worth living'. If life is, on the whole, good (or 'worthwhile'), and if this is the reason for the value that is placed on it, then certain questions arise about the value of life in general. Thus, 'Should we attach any value to the creation of extra people whose lives are worth living?' Glover answers that we should (assuming this could be done without causing problems of overpopulation). This would have the curious consequence that – other things being equal – the world must be a better place now than it was, say, in the year 1000, merely because it contains so many more people, and presumably more whose lives are 'worth living'. Glover also raises the question (corresponding to Moore's 'universal murder') whether it would 'have mattered if the human race had become sterile thousands of years ago', and again offers an affirmative answer. He admits, however, that he has 'no argument to convince' those who take a different view of the matter.

Most of us think it is wrong to kill people. Some think it is wrong in all circumstances, while others think that in special circumstances (say, in a just war or in self-defence) some killing may be justified. But even those who do not think killing is always wrong normally think that a special justification is needed. The assumption is that killing can at best only be justified to avoid a greater evil.

It is not obvious to many people what the answer is to the question 'Why is killing wrong?' It is not clear whether the wrongness of killing should be treated as a kind of moral axiom, or whether it can be explained by appealing to some more fundamental principle or set of principles. One very common view is that some principle of the sanctity of life has to be included among the ultimate principles of any acceptable moral system. ...

'BEING ALIVE IS INTRINSICALLY VALUABLE'

Someone who thinks that taking life is intrinsically wrong may explain this by saying that the state of being alive is itself intrinsically valuable. This claim barely rises to the level of an argument for the sanctity of life, for it simply asserts that there is value in what the taking of life takes away.

Against such a view, cases are sometimes cited of people who are either very miserable or in great pain, without any hope of cure. Might such people not be better off dead? But this could be admitted without giving up the view that life is intrinsically valuable. We could say that life has value, but that not being desperately miserable can have even more value.

I have no way of refuting someone who holds that being alive, even though unconscious, is intrinsically valuable. But it is a view that will seem unattractive to those of us who, in our own case, see a life of permanent coma as in no way preferable to death. From the subjective point of view, there is nothing to choose between the two. Schopenhauer saw this clearly when he said of the destruction of the body:

But actually we feel this destruction only in the evils of illness or of old age; on the other hand, for the *subject*, death itself consists merely in the moment when consciousness vanishes, since the activity of the brain ceases. The extension of the stoppage to all the other parts of the organism which follows this is really already an event after death. Therefore, in a subjective respect, death concerns only consciousness.[1]

Those of us who think that the direct objections to killing have to do with death considered from the standpoint of the person killed will find it natural to regard life as being of value only as a necessary condition of consciousness. For permanently comatose existence is subjectively indistinguishable from death, and unlikely often to be thought intrinsically preferable to it by people thinking of their own future.

'BEING CONSCIOUS IS INTRINSICALLY VALUABLE'

The believer in the sanctity of life may accept that being alive is only of instrumental value and say that it is consciousness that is intrinsically valuable. In making this claim, he still differs from someone who only values consciousness because it is necessary for happiness. Before we can assess this belief in the intrinsic value of being conscious, it is necessary to distinguish between two different ways in which we may talk about consciousness. Sometimes we talk about 'mere' consciousness and sometimes we talk about what might be called 'a high level of consciousness'.

'Mere' consciousness consists simply in awareness or the having of experience. When I am awake, I am aware of my environment. I have a stream of consciousness that comes abruptly to a halt if I faint or fades out when I go to sleep (until I have dreams). There are large philosophical problems about the meaning of claims of this kind, which need not be discussed here. I shall assume that we all at some level understand what it is to have experiences, or a stream of consciousness.

But this use of 'consciousness' should be distinguished from another, perhaps metaphorical, use of the word. We sometimes say that men are at a higher level of consciousness than animals, or else that few, if any, peasants are likely to have as highly developed a consciousness as Proust. It is not clear exactly what these claims come to, nor that the comparison between men and animals is of the same sort as the comparison between peasants and Proust. But perhaps what underlies such comparisons is an attempt to talk about a person's experiences in terms of the extent to which they are rich, varied, complex or subtle, or the extent to which they involve emotional responses, as well as various kinds of awareness. Again, it is not necessary to discuss here the analysis of the meaning of these claims. It is enough if it is clear that to place value on 'mere' consciousness is different from valuing it for its richness and variety. I shall assume that the claim that being conscious is intrinsically good is a claim about 'mere' consciousness, rather than about a high level of consciousness.

If one is sceptical about the intrinsic value of 'mere' consciousness, as against that of a high level of consciousness, it is hard to see what consideration can be mentioned in its favour. The advocate of this view might ask us to perform a thought experiment of a kind that G. E. Moore would perhaps have liked. We might be asked to imagine two universes, identical except that one contained a being aware of its environment and the other did not. It may be suggested that the universe containing the conscious being would be intrinsically better.

But such a thought experiment seems unconvincing. There is the familiar difficulty that, confronted with a choice so abstract and remote, it may be hard to feel any preference at all. And, since we are dealing with 'mere' consciousness rather than with a high level of consciousness, it is necessary to postulate that the conscious being has no emotional responses. It cannot be pleased or sorry or in pain; it cannot be interested or bored; it is merely aware of its environment. Views may well differ here, but, if I could be brought to take part in this thought experiment at all, I should probably express indifference between the two universes. The only grounds I might have for preferring the universe with the conscious being would be some hope that it might evolve into some more interesting level of consciousness. But to choose on these grounds is not to assign any intrinsic value to 'mere' consciousness.

The belief that the sole reason why it is directly wrong to take human life is the intrinsic value of 'mere' consciousness runs into a problem concerning animals. Many of us place a special value on human life as against animal life. Yet animals, or at least the higher ones, seem no less aware of their surroundings than we are. Suppose there is a flood and I am faced with the choice of either saving a man's life or else saving the life of a cow. Even if all side-effects were left out of account, failure to save the man seems worse than failure to save the cow. The person who believes that the sanctity of life rests solely on the value of 'mere' consciousness is faced with a dilemma. Either he must accept that the life of the cow and the life of the man are in themselves of equal value, or he must give reasons for thinking that cows are less conscious than men or else not conscious at all.

It is hard to defend the view that, while I have good grounds for thinking that other people are conscious, I do not have adequate reasons for thinking that animals are conscious. Humans and animals in many ways respond similarly to their surroundings. Humans have abilities that other animals do not, such as the ability to speak or to do highly abstract reasoning, but it is not only in virtue of these abilities that we say people are conscious. And there is no neurophysiological evidence that suggests that humans alone can have experiences.

The alternative claim is that animals are less conscious than we are. The view that 'mere' consciousness is a matter of degree is attractive when considered in relation to animals. The philosophical literature about our knowledge of other minds is strikingly silent and unhelpful about the animal boundaries of consciousness. How far back down the evolutionary scale does consciousness extend? What kind and degree of complexity must a nervous system exhibit to be the vehicle of experiences? What kind and degree of complexity of behaviour counts as the manifestation of consciousness? At least with our present ignorance of the physiological basis of human consciousness, any clear-cut boundaries of consciousness, drawn between one kind of animal and another, have an air of arbitrariness. For this reason it is attractive to suggest that consciousness is a matter of degree, not stopping abruptly, but fading away slowly as one descends the evolutionary scale.

But the belief that 'mere' consciousness is a matter of degree is obscure as well as attractive. Is it even an intelligible view?

There are two ways in which talk of degrees of consciousness can be made clearer. One is by explaining it in terms of the presence or absence of whole 'dimensions' of consciousness. This is the way in which a blind man is less conscious of his environment than a normal man. (Though, if his other senses have developed unusual acuity, he will in other respects be more conscious than a normal man.) But if a lower degree of consciousness consists either in the absence of a whole dimension such as sight, or in senses with lower acuity than those of men, it is not plausible to say that animals are all less conscious than we are. Dogs seem to have all the dimensions of consciousness that we do. It is true that they often see less well, but on the other hand their sense of smell is better than ours. If the sanctity of life were solely dependent on degree of consciousness interpreted this way, we often could not justify giving human life priority over animal life. We might also be committed to giving the life of a normal dog priority over the life of a blind man.

The other way in which we talk of degrees of 'mere' consciousness comes up in such contexts as waking up and falling asleep. There is a sleepy state in which we can be unaware of words that are softly spoken, but aware of any noise that is loud or sharp. But this again fails to separate men from animals. For animals are often alert in a way that is quite unlike the drowsiness of a man not fully awake.

Whether or not 'mere' consciousness fades away lower down on the evolutionary scale (and the idea of a sharp boundary *does* seem implausible), there seems at least no reason to regard the 'higher' animals as less aware of the environment than ourselves. (It is not being suggested that animals are only at the level of 'mere' consciousness, though no doubt they are less far above it than most of us.) If the whole basis of the ban on killing were the intrinsic value of mere consciousness, killing higher animals would be as bad as killing humans.

It would be possible to continue to hold mere consciousness to be of intrinsic value, and either to supplement this principle with others or else to abandon the priority given to human life. But when the principle is distinguished from different ones that would place a value on higher levels of consciousness, it has so little intuitive appeal that we may suspect its attractiveness to depend on the distinction not being made. If, in your own case, you would opt for a state never rising above mere consciousness, in preference to death, have you purged the illegitimate assumption that you would take an interest in what you would be aware of?

'BEING HUMAN IS INTRINSICALLY VALUABLE'

It is worth mentioning that the objection to taking human life should not rest on what is sometimes called 'speciesism': human life being treated as having a special priority over animal life *simply* because it is human. The analogy is with racism, in its purest form, according to which people of a certain race ought to be treated differently *simply* because of their membership of that race, without any argument referring to special features of that race being given. This is objectionable partly because of its moral arbitrariness: unless some relevant empirical characteristics can be cited, there can be no argument for such discrimination. Those concerned to reform our treatment of animals point out that speciesism exhibits the same arbitrariness. It is not in itself sufficient argument for treating a creature less well to say simply that it is not a member of our species. An adequate justification must cite relevant differences between the species. We still have the question of what features of a life are of intrinsic value.

THE CONCEPT OF A 'LIFE WORTH LIVING'

I have suggested that, in destroying life or mere consciousness, we are not destroying anything intrinsically valuable. These states only matter because they are necessary for other things that matter in themselves. If a list could be made of all the things that are valuable for their own sake, these things wold be the ingredients of a 'life worth living'.

One objection to the idea of judging that a life is worth living is that this seems to imply the possibility of comparing being alive and being dead. And, as Wittgenstein said, 'Death is not an event in life: we do not live to experience death.'

But we can have a preference for being alive over being dead, or for being conscious over being unconscious, without needing to make any 'comparisons' between these states. We prefer to be anaesthetized for a painful operation; queuing for a bus in the rain at midnight, we wish we were at home asleep; but for the most part we prefer to be awake and experience our life as it goes by. These preferences do not depend on any view about 'what it is like' being unconscious, and our preference for life does not depend on beliefs about 'what it is like' being dead. It is rather that we treat being dead or unconscious as nothing, and then decide whether a stretch of experience is better or worse than nothing. And this claim, that life of a certain sort is better than nothing, is an expression of our preference.

Any list of the ingredients of a worth-while life would obviously be disputable. Most people might agree on many items, but many others could be endlessly argued over. It might be agreed that a happy life is worth living, but people do not agree on what happiness is. And some things that make life worth living may only debatably be to do with happiness. (Aristotle:[2] 'And so they tell us that Anaxagoras answered a man who was raising problems of this sort and asking why one should choose rather to be born than not – "for the sake of viewing the heavens and the whole order of the universe".')

A life worth living should not be confused with a morally virtuous life. Moral virtues such as honesty or a sense of fairness can belong to someone whose life is relatively bleak and empty. Music may enrich someone's life, or the death of a friend impoverish it, without him growing more or less virtuous.

I shall not try to say what sorts of things do make life worth living.

(Temporary loss of a sense of the absurd led me to try to do so. But, apart from the disputability of any such list, I found that the ideal life suggested always sounded ridiculous.) I shall assume that a life worth living has more to it than mere consciousness. It should be possible to explain the wrongness of killing partly in terms of the destruction of a life worth living, without presupposing more than minimal agreement as to exactly what makes life worth-while.

I shall assume that, where someone's life is worth living, this is a good reason for holding that it would be directly wrong to kill him. This is what can be extracted from the doctrine of the sanctity of life by someone who accepts the criticisms made here of that view. If life is worth preserving only because it is the vehicle for consciousness, and consciousness is of value only because it is necessary for something else, then that 'something else' is the heart of this particular objection to killing. It is what is meant by a 'life worth living' or a 'worth-while life'.

The idea of dividing people's lives into ones that are worth living and ones that are not is likely to seem both presumptuous and dangerous. As well as seeming to indicate an arrogant willingness to pass godlike judgements on other people's lives, it may remind people of the Nazi policy of killing patients in mental hospitals. But there is really nothing godlike in such a judgement. It is not a moral judgement we are making, if we think that someone's life is so empty and unhappy as to be not worth living. It results from an attempt (obviously an extremely fallible one) to see his life from his own point of view and to see what he gets out of it. It must also be stressed that no suggestion is being made that it automatically becomes right to kill people whose lives we think are not worth living. It is only being argued that, if someone's life is worth living, this is *one* reason why it is directly wrong to kill him.

IS THE DESIRE TO LIVE THE CRITERION OF A WORTH-WHILE LIFE?

It might be thought that a conclusive test of whether or not someone's life is worth living is whether or not he wants to go on living. The attractiveness of this idea comes partly from the fact that the question whether someone has a worth-while life involves thinking from his point of view, rather than thinking of his contribution to the lives of other people.

This proposal would commit us to believing that a person cannot want to end his life if it is worth living, and that he cannot want to prolong his life where it is not worth living. But these beliefs are both doubtful. In a passing mood of depression, someone who normally gets a lot out of life may want to kill himself. And someone who thinks he will go to hell may wish to prolong his present life, however miserable he is. The frying pan may be worse than nothing but better than the fire. And some people, while not believing in hell, simply fear death. They may wish they had never been born, but still not want to die.

For these reasons, someone's own desire to live or die is not a conclusive indication of whether or not he has a life worth living. And, equally obviously, with people who clearly do have lives worth living, the relative strength of their desires to live is not a reliable indicator of how worthwhile they find their lives. Someone whose hopes are often disappointed may cling to life as tenaciously as the happiest person in the world.

If we are to make these judgements, we cannot escape appealing to our own independent beliefs about what sorts of things enrich or impoverish people's lives. But, when this has been said, it should be emphasized that, when the question arises whether someone's life is worth living at all, his own views will normally be evidence of an overwhelmingly powerful kind. Our assessments of what other people get out of their lives are so fallible that only a monster of self-confidence would feel no qualms about correcting the judgement of the person whose life is in question.

LENGTH OF LIFE

The upshot of this discussion is that one reason why it is wrong to kill is that it is wrong to destroy a life which is worth living.

This can be seen in a slightly different perspective when we remember that we must all die one day, so that killing and life-saving are interventions that alter length of life by bringing forward or postponing the date of death. An extreme statement of this perspective is to be found in St Augustine's *City of God*:

There is no one, it goes without saying, who is not nearer to death this year than he was last year, nearer tomorrow than today, today than yesterday, who will not by and by be nearer than he is at the moment, or is not nearer at the present time than he was a little while ago. Any space of time that we live through leaves us with so much less time to live, and the remainder decreases with every passing day; so that the whole of our lifetime is nothing but a race towards death, in which no one is allowed the slightest pause or any slackening of the pace. All are driven on at the same speed, and hurried along the same road to the same goal. The man whose life was short passed his days as swiftly as the longer-lived; moments of equal length rushed by for both of them at equal speed, though one was farther than the other from the goal to which both were hastening at the same rate.

The objection to killing made here is that it is wrong to shorten a worthwhile life. Why is a longer-lasting worth-while life a better thing than an equally worth-while but briefer life? Some people, thinking about their own lives, consider length of life very desirable, while others consider the number of years they have is of no importance at all, the quality of their lives being all that matters.

There is an argument (echoed in Sartre's short story *Le Mur*) used by Marcus Aurelius in support of the view that length of life is unimportant:

If a god were to tell you 'Tomorrow, or at least the day after, you will be dead', you would not, unless the most abject of men, be greatly solicitous whether it was to be the later day rather than the morrow, for what is the difference between them? In the same way, do not reckon it of great moment whether it will come years and years hence, or tomorrow.[3]

This argument is unconvincing. From the fact that some small differences are below the threshold of mattering to us, it does not follow that all differences are insignificant. If someone steals all your money except either a penny or twopence, you will not mind much which he has left you with. It does not follow that the difference between riches and poverty is trivial.

There are at least two good reasons why a longer life can be thought better than a short one. One is that the quality of life is not altogether independent of its length: many plans and projects would not be worth undertaking without a good chance of time for their fulfilment. The other reason is that, other things being equal, more of a good thing is always better than less of it. This does not entail such absurd consequences as that an enjoyable play gets better as it gets longer, without limit. The point of the phrase 'other things being equal' is to allow for waning of interest and for the claims of other activities. So, unless life begins to pall, it is not in any way unreasonable to want more of it and to place a value on the prolonging of other people's worth-while lives.

This suggests an answer to a traditional scepticism about whether people are harmed by being killed. This scepticism is stated in its most extreme form by Socrates in the *Apology*: 'Now if there is no consciousness, but only a dreamless sleep, death must be a marvellous gain.' There is clearly some exaggeration here. Death is not a dreamless sleep, but something we can treat as on a par with it. There is the doubtful suggestion that people would normally prefer a dreamless sleep to their waking lives. But, stripped of these exaggerations, there remains the valid point that being dead is not a state we experience, and so cannot be unpleasant. It was this that led Lucretius to think that the fear of death was confused:

If the future holds travail and anguish in store, the self must be in existence, when that time comes, in order to experience it. But from this fate we are redeemed by death, which denies existence to the self that might have suffered these tribulations.

He reinforced this by a comparison with the time before birth:

Look back at the eternity that passed before we were born, and mark how utterly it counts to us as nothing. This is a mirror that nature holds up to us, in which we may see the time that shall be after we are dead. Is there anything terrifying in the sight – anything depressing ...?[4]

Lucretius is right that being dead is not itself a misfortune, but this does not show that it is irrational to want not to die, nor that killing someone does him no harm. For, while I will not be miserable when dead, I am happy while alive, and it is not confused to want more of a good thing rather than less of it.

Bernard Williams has suggested that a reply to Lucretius of this kind does not commit us to wanting to be immortal.[5] He argues that immortality is either inconceivable or terrible. Either desires and satisfactions change so much that it is not clear that the immortal person will still be *me*, or else they are limited by my character and will start to seem pointlessly boring: 'A man at arms can get cramp from standing too long at his post, but sentry-duty can after all be necessary. But the threat of monotony in eternal activities could not be dealt with in that way, by regarding immortal boredom as an unavoidable ache derived from standing ceaselessly at one's post.' It is true that the reply to Lucretius does not commit us to desiring immortality. But I am not convinced that someone with a fairly constant character *need* eventually become intolerably bored, so long as they can watch the world continue to unfold and go on asking new questions and thinking, and so long as there are other people to share their feelings and thoughts with. Given the company of the right people, I would be glad of the chance to sample a few million years and see how it went. ...

EXTRA HAPPY PEOPLE

Should we attach any value to the creation of extra people whose lives are worth living?

One reason for utilitarians, and for all of us whose idea of a life worth living is bound up with some kinds of mental state, to answer 'yes', is that the mental states resulting from an act of conception are very like the mental states that would be eliminated by killing someone. It has been pointed out that the mental-state utilitarian will not license killing on the strength of the argument that dead people will not know that their desire to live has been over-ridden. This is because of the experiences the person will have if not killed, including his experience of the continuing fulfilment of his preference for being alive. But a similar argument can be used to support the creation of a person who will be glad he was born.

Another reason has to do with the continuance of the human race. Suppose we could take a drug which would render us infertile, but make us so happy that we would not mind being childless. Would it be wrong for everyone now alive to take it, ensuring that we would be the last generation? Would it have mattered if the human race had become sterile thousands of years ago? Some people are indifferent to either of these possibilities, and I have no argument to convince them. But other people, including me, think that to end the human race would be about the worst thing it would be possible to do. This is because of a belief in the intrinsic value of there existing in the future at least some people with worth-while lives. And, if we reject any kind of time bias, it is hard to see the case for valuing extra people spread out across future time that would not also place some value on extra people contemporary with us.

These reasons seem to me good ones for thinking that, *other things being equal*, the more people with worth-while lives there are the better. This is likely to arouse feelings of horror in many people, for reasons related to our reluctance to accept the total view. We may think of an exhausted mother of eight children feeling obliged to have still more. Or we may think of starvation, shortages and overcrowding caused by over-population.

In practice, the disastrous side-effects of people feeling obliged to have children they do not want, and of having too large a population for the world's resources, together with the more problematic happiness of children not really wanted, will normally heavily outweigh the view that, if other things were equal, the more happy people there are the better. Even if we adopted the total view, it seems likely that in many cases the addition to the population of extra people with worth-while lives would often not even increase the total happiness.

It may be said that, even if in practice the total view is often innocuous for these reasons, it is still at least theoretically possible that a larger population at a very low level could have greater total happiness than a smaller population at a much higher level. If so, many people, including me, will be very reluctant to adopt the total view. But the concession that, other things being equal, there is value in extra happy people need not commit us to a simple policy of maximizing happiness. It would do so only if our way of deciding what is desirable were the kind of crude multiplication suggested by the total view. But there is no need for this. It is open to us to say that *one* thing we value is total happiness as obtained by computing numbers at different levels of happiness (though this rather abstract conception itself puts strain on our assumptions of rough measurability) without simply adopting the total view. For we may decide that we value people's lives having various qualities (which would put them high on the scale of 'worth-while life') and that the absence of these qualities cannot be compensated for by any numbers of extra worth-while lives without them. There is some analogy with common attitudes to what is valued within a single life. I enjoy eating fish and chips, but no number of extra hours eating fish and chips will compensate me for being deprived of the ability to read. (This is not to say that there are things whose value cannot be compared: it is rather to say that the ability to read is of *greater* value to me than any amount of fish and chips.)

So we can think that extra people with lives worth living are in themselves a good thing, without having to allow that there is always *some* number of such people whose existence outweighs any particular impoverishment of life.

NOTES

1 A. Schopenhauer: *The World as Will and Representation*, translated by E. J. F. Payne, New York, 1969, Book 4, section 54.
2 *Eudemian Ethics*, 1216 s. 11.
3 Marcus Aurelius: *Meditations*, translated by M. Staniforth, Harmondsworth, 1964.
4 Lucretius: *The Nature of the Universe*, translated by R. E. Latham, Harmondsworth, 1951.
5 Bernard Williams: 'The Makropulos Case', in *Problems of the Self*, Cambridge, 1973.

15

What is Wrong with Killing People?

R. E. Ewin

In 'What is Wrong with Killing People?' R. E. Ewin rejects several of the reasons that have been or may be brought forward in support of the prohibition against killing. He concludes, however (drawing on arguments from Hobbes), that this prohibition can be defended as a 'minimum condition' of the existence of society, in the same sort of way as the existence of promise-keeping. It may be questioned, however, whether the prohibition against killing is of special *importance (commensurate with the 'sanctity' of life) in the preservation of society. In a society in which the desire and occasion for killing were rare, other conditions and prohibitions might be regarded as more important.*

Qualifications are needed to make the point a tight one, but it seems quite plain that it is wrong to kill people. What is not so plain is *why* it is wrong to kill people, especially when one considers that the person killed will not be around to suffer the consequences afterwards. He does not suffer as a consequence of death, and he need not suffer even while dying. His friends, relatives, and dependents might suffer, but that does not seem to be enough to solve the problem; it is, in the Common Moral Consciousness, just as wrong to kill somebody who has no friends, relatives, or dependents. To think of the wrongness of killing somebody in terms of whether or not it will upset somebody else is to miss completely the somewhat obscure point. The Common Moral Consciousness is quite clear that the reason why it is wrong to kill somebody has something to do with him, not with his mother or maiden aunt.

Utilitarianism will not do the job of explaining why it is wrong to kill somebody. The most commonly used of the traditional points against Utilitarianism is that it subjugates the interests of the individual to those of the majority – which could, in the appropriate circumstances, commit a Utilitarian to the view that the execution of an innocent man chosen at random was justified. Negative Utilitarianism, the tenets of which require us to minimize pain rather than to maximize pleasure, has even more radical consequences: as has been pointed out,[1] it would require us to kill people painlessly. It does not simply require us to do it painlessly if we must kill people; it requires us to kill people if we *can* do it painlessly. Killing somebody just like that, not in time of war, self-defence, or judicial execution, is ungenerous, unmerciful, cruel, and perhaps arrogant, but none of those words explains what is wrong with it; there is a good deal more to it than that. Nor is the word 'unjust' one that immediately springs to mind. We could simply intuit the wrongness of killings, but that would not get us far and would leave us with problems in our accounts of moral argument, moral education and theory of knowledge. It is not simply that the consequences of everybody's killing somebody would be unpleasant, either, and it is not that my killing somebody is contrary to the point of an institution required for the performance of the act.

I have asked a few people of my acquaintance what is wrong with killing people, and have received a small range of replies each of which is fairly obviously inadequate. It may be true that killing somebody shows insufficient respect for persons, but there is more to it than that; killing somebody is not, as this answer suggests, morally on a par with spitting in his eye. If I kill somebody then my act is, indeed, unrectifiable, but that does not make it wrong; all that unrectifiability can do is to make something that was wrong anyway into something worse. It is not so obviously true that killing somebody restricts his freedom of action, since he would no longer be around to have any freedom of action, but, even overlooking that problem, killing somebody does more than breaking his leg or locking him up, either of which would involve restricting his freedom of action. Locking somebody up unrectifiably would be more serious, but still the feeling persists that killing him would be wrong in a different way, whether or not it would be worse. Locking somebody up for a long time involves preventing his doing what he wants to do, frustrating him, and perhaps eventually driving him insane; in short, it involves inflicting upon him a good deal of unpleasure. Killing somebody does not thus involve the infliction of unpleasure, or, at least, it need not; the death itself may be painless, and after that the person killed suffers neither pleasure nor unpleasure. Killing somebody may involve denying him equality of rights with me, but it need not; I may be quite prepared to die myself, but it is still wrong for me to kill anybody else. No matter what I plan to do, the lives of others should not depend upon my whim. Even if I do not plan to kill myself immediately after killing somebody else, and thus do, in some way, deny my victim equality of rights with me, my killing him is not morally the same as my drinking beer while denying him the right to do so, or cursing around the house and then upbraiding my son for doing the same thing. It may be said that killing is simply more serious, but why? It is not more serious simply in being a denial of equality of rights, and if the point is that the right to live is more important than the right to drink or curse, then nothing is settled: one aspect of the problem from which I began is the problem why the right to live is more important. It is quite clear that when I kill somebody I deny his legal rights, but, at least at first glance, that is a far cry from showing that I deny his moral rights, and to show that I have acted illegally is not to show that I have acted immorally. The legal requirement or prohibition of an act does not, unfortunately, entail its moral requirement or prohibition, nor vice versa; hence arguments about marijuana, abortion, conscription, and so on.

So I want to reject all the answers suggested so far, at least in the simplistic forms in which they have been suggested. That there is something in some of what has been said, though, should emerge as we go on.

Moral philosophers, when they do take specific examples, tend to take them from a fairly restricted range and tend to choose them in terms of how well they illustrate a theory. Perhaps they also feel that there is no point in trying to explain something quite as obvious as the wrongness of murder. There are certainly some grounds for saying that explanation should be, not of the obvious, but in terms of it. Unfortunately, very few that I have read have tried to explain the wrongness of killing, and those accounts that have been given are usually notable for their implausibility. In some cases one need only read the account to reject it; argument seems hardly to be necessary. The wrongness of murder is explained by G. E. Moore, for example,[2] basically in terms of the fact that murder's becoming a common practice would promote a general feeling of insecurity which would take up time that could be spent to better purpose. Tiddleywinks' becoming a common practice would similarly take up time that could be spent to better purpose. Moore did not leave it at that: it was only occasional murder that he thought he had shown to be wrong; a policy of universal murder is a different thing altogether, and Moore did not think that he could similarly show that to be wrong. He wrote:

the general disutility of murder can only be proved, provided the majority of the human race will certainly persist in existing. In order to prove that murder, if it were so universally adopted as to cause the speedy extermination of the race, would not be good as a means, we should have to disprove the main contention of pessimism – namely that the existence of human life is on the whole an evil. And the view of pessimism, however strongly we may be convinced of its truth or falsehood, is one which never has been either proved or refuted conclusively. That universal murder would not be a good thing at this moment can therefore not be proved.[3]

There is a logical mistake involved in asking whether murder is wrong either as a universal policy or as an occasional pastime; we can intuitively see that murder is wrong because that is what the word 'murder' means. This problem, as it arises in the passage that I have just quoted, can be removed simply by substituting the word 'kill' for the word 'murder'. The problem that arises then is that not all killing is regarded as wrong, and it would be false to say, without my earlier remark about qualifications, that it is quite certain that killing people is wrong. There are various conditions more or less commonly accepted as making it not wrong to kill somebody: I may kill somebody if he threatens to kill me and killing him is my only means of defending myself; I may kill somebody if the leader of my society announces that we are in a state of war with the other person's society; I may kill somebody if he is my slave or a member of another tribe or has passed the age of 65; I may kill somebody if he has committed such crimes as to be declared an outlaw; or I may kill somebody if he is in great and unrelievable pain. Each of these conditions is more or less widely accepted in this society or another as making killing permissible, so one cannot reasonably say simply that it is quite certain that killing people is wrong whether or not it is clear why killing people is wrong. But certainly some cases of killing people are wrong, and in working out just what makes these cases wrong we ought also to be working out just what conditions make killings permissible. The task which I have set myself, that of explaining what is wrong with killing people, can also be regarded as the task of explicating the concept of murder, and Moore's use of the word 'murder' in saying that a policy of universal murder may be a good thing does not show that his argument necessarily involves a self-contradiction even though his expression of it might.

Nevertheless, the relationship between the concepts of kiling and murder explains why we have a feeling, not simply of uneasiness about Moore's argument, but of blank rejection. Moore, it seems, has simply missed the point if he makes his judgment of killing in terms of its utility. The devil may have his due, and if I choose to lead a less pleasant life than I could, or one providing me with fewer goods than I might have, then, nobody, one is inclined to say, has the right to stop me. Murder is wrong in itself, and the fact that we have formed such a concept or added such a word to our moral vocabulary suggests that, in the Common Moral Consciousness, those acts of killing which are wrong are regarded as being wrong in themselves, not merely as being disutilitarian. When one man wantonly kills another, not in self-defence or anything like that, but, say, simply because he enjoys killing people, we have no need to wait for the consequences before judging the act to be a murder and therein wrong; as remarked earlier, the reactions of the victim's mother or maiden aunt have nothing to do with the morality of killing. Were euthanasia legal in the society, a man might make an appointment with his doctor to be killed and thus put out of unbearable pain, but if somebody knowing nothing of this were to break in and shoot him, anticipating the doctor out of the sheer joy of killing, then that act would be a murder and wrong even though it had the same consequences as an act to which no objection would have been raised. We have no need to wait for the consequences before we judge a killing to be murder and thus wrong; the consequences may be good or bad, but either way they are incidental to the morality of the act. A child-murderer's pointing out the high probability of his victim's growing up to be another Hitler has not justified his act though he might have shown that, incidentally, it had done the rest of us a good turn.

If I do not immediately comment on this, I shall no doubt be accused of begging the question. Why are the consequences incidental? To rule them out of consideration by saying that they are incidental, it might be objected, begs the question by building in a moral judgment.

Now, I did not say simply that the consequences are incidental to the act; I said that they are incidental to the *morality* of the act. Whether they are incidental or not depends on how the act is described. If it is described simply as killing, then the consequences may not be incidental to the act: they may be exactly what the killer was aiming at, in which case they are anything but incidental. But the morality of his act does not depend on his having killed, it depends on his having murdered. To put it another way, his act is not wrong *in that it is a killing*, it is wrong *in that it is a murder*. So his act is morally assessed in terms of murder, and so far as the morality of his act is concerned it comes under the description of murder and not simply under the description of killing. At this stage we can say, roughly, that a murder is done if one man intentionally kills another and if none of the conditions defeating a claim of murder are present – the killing was not done in self-defence, nor was it done in time of war, and so on. These conditions do not refer to the consequences, they refer to the intention, knowledge, and mental state of the killer. We can apply the concept of murder without reference to the consequences after death, so the consequences after death are incidental to the act's being a murder.

But what, it might be asked, if people believed that consequences did affect the morality of killing? Perhaps none of the defeating conditions do refer to consequences, but why should we not introduce a new one that does?

That's the way the world is, that's the way our concepts are; that's where we have to start from. If the world were different (even if only in that people held different beliefs from those they do hold), then our concepts would be different. If *everybody really* believed that when we die we go to heaven – all those grapes, on a hot day there are half a dozen comely angels to fan us, the English never win a test match and there is no tax on beer – if everybody really believed that then, whether or not their beliefs were true, we probably would not have a concept of murder at all. Our morality and the moral concepts we have would be different. Our concepts are the way they are because the world is the way it is and because people believe, want and need what they do believe, want, and need. That is where we have to start from, so that is where I do start from.

None of this is meant to imply that the concept of murder is always easy to apply or that it in no way has any connection with the future tense. That is why there is still equivocation about the child-killer if he can really prove that his victim would turn out to be another Hitler; one really feels uneasy about taking either side in the dispute, which is to say that the concept is difficult to apply in such cases. But what gives rise to the equivocation is not the consequences of the killing, as I have already tried to show. What gives rise to the equivocation is the intention of the agent, which is a different thing. That he did spare us another Hitler is irrelevant; that he intended to do so is not. His intentions, though not the consequences of his act, affect whether or not he has committed a murder; whether his intentions were realized is incidental. If his intention does defeat a claim of murder (as has been argued is the case in assassinations), then it is irrelevant that another Hitler turns up anyway, so that the killer has not spared us that after all.

So, if an act of killing is wrong, it is wrong in itself and not because of its consequences. For the same reason, the distinction Moore draws between universal murder as a policy and murder as a spare-time hobby is of no moral significance. An individual case of murder is wrong in itself, i.e., wrong in that it is murder; if a policy of universal murder is introduced, the only change made in the situation is that we have a lot more individual cases of murder each of which is wrong in itself. Murders are judged one by one; the number of them has no effect on the wrongness of each. Introducing a policy of universal action can have special effects: introducing a policy of universally doing what we say we will do after uttering the words 'I promise' changes the situation by creating a new institution, that of promising. But introducing a policy of universal murder creates no such new institution and does not relevantly change the situation. Obedience to the rule, 'Always murder', does not even partly constitute a practice; it simply collects a number of individual cases each of which remains what it would have been without the policy: wrong in itself.

There is an argument that might be constructed along lines similar to something that Moore wrote elsewhere, though I have no wish to father the argument on to his moral philosophy. The argument goes like this: I am more certain of the truth of the claim that there is a hand before my face than I could be of any statement used as a premiss in an argument to prove or disprove it.[4] A similar claim about killing might be well calculated to evoke a sympathetic reaction, especially if one considers that philosophers have presented so many different moral theories purporting to provide arguments supporting such claims as that killing is wrong, as to make the mind reel. Universal agreement about the theories has yet to be reached, but rejection of the claim that killing is wrong has been very rare indeed. Perhaps the reason for this is the one suggested by Moore's proof of an external world: I am more certain of the truth of the claim that killing is wrong than I could be of any statement used as a premiss in an argument to prove or disprove it. My initial feeling of uneasiness about such a claim might be explained by a story. Moore's argument took several different examples in his different presentations of it: I am more certain that there is a hand before my face, that I am writing, that I am seated at my desk, that there is a skylight above my head. The argument in the last of these forms, so the story goes, was used by Moore in a lecture in America when, unfortunately, there was no skylight above his head; there was only a patch of light reflected from a window in the wall.

The analogue of Moore's external-world argument was suggested to me by another which I find difficult to pin down with certainty but which I have come across in conversation. It is a sort of paradigm-case argument which could be used in discussion of murder, and I think that there are traces of it in the writings of Anscombe and Geach. If somebody questioned the wrongness of killing people then, according to this argument, we should simply reply in some such terms as these: 'Anybody who doesn't realize that it is wrong to kill people does not understand what morality is; he has a debased conscience, and I have no desire to argue with him.' Compare what Anscombe says: '... if someone really thinks, *in advance*, that it is open to question whether such an action as procuring the judicial execution of the innocent should be quite excluded from consideration – I do not want to argue with him; he shows a corrupt mind.'[5] It is not clear to me that Anscombe's remark is to be taken as a straightforward example of the paradigm-case argument as I am setting it up for killing, since she is, in that paper, frying bigger, or at least more general, fish, but I think that what she says must be at least closely related to the paradigm-case argument. To take over the form of an argument that she uses elsewhere in that paper, judicial execution of the innocent may be a paradigm case of murder; anybody denying that it is murder may be simply pretending that he does not know what the word 'murder' means. To say that, though, does not explain why murder is the concept that it is or *what* concept it is. What she says does not finish the matter, and does not make it *philosophically* improper to pretend that it is an open question whether innocent men ought to be judicially executed. So pretending, we might work out why they ought not to be executed and thus learn something about the concept of murder. I should add, lest it seem that I am attacking Anscombe where I am not, that she does not claim that such a pretence is philosophically improper; she claims that regarding the killing of the innocent as a possible course of action is *morally* improper, and that any philosophical theory of morals implying that it should be regarded as a possible course of action is to be dismissed. I have no wish to disagree with her on either count.

Be it Anscombe's argument, one related to it, or even one completely unrelated to it, the paradigm-case argument that I have described is one that could be used to argue about killing people. 'Killing people is a paradigm of wrongness; if you fail to recognize that killing people is wrong then you have a corrupt mind and no understanding of what morality is.' This, no doubt, is significantly different from the analogue of Moore's external-world argument, but they share the rejection of the idea that argument is possible, or, anyway, appropriate. This is a dubious, and indeed dangerous, claim about anything to do with morality. For a start, one should be ready to explain to the confused masses why the judicial execution of an innocent scapegoat is not preferable to the death of millions; one should, it is true, also be ready to persuade them of the point, which might be a different matter. Also, the list of conditions which are more or less widely accepted in different societies as defeating a claim of murder needs to be considered; if they are not completely arbitrary (and if murder is a moral concept, then they are not), then they stand in some rational relationship to the concept of murder, and that relationship will help to explain why killing is wrong when it is wrong. So argument about the wrongness of such cases of killing is possible. At least: argument is possible to justify the claim that such cases of killings are wrong. If one is stuck with a borderline case in an argument about a condition purporting to defeat a claim of murder, as one might be in some cases of provocation or of crimes of passion, then argument will clearly be appropriate.

If we take up specifically the external-world analogue, the first point to be made should perhaps be that there is a difference between 'I am certain …' and 'It is certain …', a point that I tried to make briefly with my reference to Moore's skylight. To say that it is certain that such-and-such is to say something like that such-and-such is necessarily true. To say that I am certain that such-and-such, on the other hand, is just to say that such-and-such seems obvious to me, or that I am very deeply convinced of it. But, unfortunately, as we all learnt at our first-year tutor's knee, our being very deeply convinced of something proves nothing but our own existence. In morals, especially, what one person is firmly convinced of another may firmly disbelieve, and what everybody is firmly convinced of at one time everybody may firmly disbelieve at another. It was once quite firmly believed that slavery was a social system required by justice because slaves were naturally inferior beings, and the belief was shared by even the slaves – or so I'm told. A contrary belief would be fairly widely held today. It was once generally and firmly held that women ought to be subject to their husbands and ought not to have equal rights with men, but things have now changed to the extent that the Women's Liberation Movement has to be taken less as a claim for justice than as a claim to have not only the moon but jam on it as well. There is surely some test for right and wrong in such cases. People changed their minds for reasons; we can, anyway, give some reasons for adverse judgment on the former belief in each of the examples I have cited.

Even if it is obvious that we should not kill people, and even if we are all quite firmly convinced of that, it would not follow that there are no *reasons* for judging killing to be wrong. From finding explanations for the obvious in the physical goings-on around us we gain all sorts of advantages in terms of theories which enable us to predict or explain all sorts of less obvious things.

That does not dispose of all the force of the external-world argument, but what remains does so because that argument can be taken as a version of the paradigm-case argument that I sketched earlier. The point of that argument, in this context, is that it attempts to give grounds for doing away with claims for justification. 'This is red; it's a paradigm case of redness; nothing can or need be done to justify that claim.' How far will the argument go in the moral case? The idea of a paradigm-case argument being applied to killing has some initial plausibility. One reason for its plausibility is simply that it does seem obvious that killing is wrong but not at all obvious *why* it is wrong. Another reason is that moral education often seems to be carried out in terms of paradigms: we are told that pulling pussy's tail is naughty, or at another level, not to hit little sister, though perhaps the word 'education' ought to appear in scare quotes if such activities are said to be part of moral education. So the argument has some initial plausibility, but in view of the second reason I gave for that it ought to be said that the paradigm-case argument is not a theory of learning or concept-formation though it might rest on one in some way. It is an argument purporting to show that certain claims can be justified or refuted in a certain way; I may learn mathematics by means of coloured blocks, but that does not make green blocks a paradigm of threeness or allow me to operate mathematical paradigm-case arguments on colours. To operate the paradigm-case argument on murder, we should first have to show that we could learn the concept of murder only by ostension, or something of the sort, and that one could not gain the concept of wrongness without reference specifically to cases of killing. If I can gain the concept without reference to cases of killing, then I could, on the assumptions made by the paradigm-case argument, significantly ask whether killing people is wrong; a different sort of argument would be needed to show that it is wrong.

Suppose I look at a letter-box and say 'This is red.' If I am idiot enough to say that, somebody else may be idiot enough to ask me to justify my claim. What can I say if he does? 'I see it, and conditions of observation are normal; what more do you want?' This at least looks like a perfectly reasonable rejection of a request for justification. But morality is supposed to be rational; if viciousness does not tie up with reasons for not performing vicious acts, we are stuck with problems about what has been called the action-guiding nature of moral judgments; morality is commonly conceived of as providing and/or assessing reasons for action, whether or not those reasons actually motivate anybody in the situation. If moral concepts are actually taught in terms of paradigms of movements and not in terms of reasons, then they do not carry the implications we thought they did. If the claim is not simply that it is obvious *that* killing is wrong, but also that it is obvious *why* killing is wrong, that's fine (though false), but it does not mean that there are no reasons or that we should not give the reasons.

Hobbes thought that murder was a species of injustice, though, as I commented earlier, this is not a word that naturally leaps to mind in connection with killing. He thought that it was unjust partly because he gave a somewhat idiosyncratic account of justice: '... when a Covenant is made, then to break it is *Unjust*: And the definition of INJUSTICE is no other than *the not Performance of Covenant*. And whatsoever is not Unjust, is *Just*.'[6] Hobbes's account of justice was straightforwardly in terms of contract; it is unjust to break a contract, just (though perhaps cruel, arrogant, etc.) to do anything which does not involve breaking a contract. In entering social life, each of us has made a contract with each other member of the society not to kill him, in return for which the other members of the society have contracted not to kill us. There are qualifications of detail, and interesting ones, to be added to this, but that will do for the moment. Each of us has contracted not to kill, so killing is an infringement of contract and therefore unjust. The rest of what I have to say will be an attempt to show that Hobbes has the central points of the matter right.

Sometimes it does make a difference whether everybody else does the same, a point that Hume made in discussion of what he called the artificial virtues. An act which is, if taken by itself, in no way wrong, can become wrong if it is at variance with a general practice. My act of concluding soon after saying 'I promise that I will conclude soon' has no particular moral value unless there is a practice or institution of promising, which requires a fairly high incidence of other people's doing what they say they will do after uttering the words 'I promise'. If there were no such practice, I could decide to do something *like* introducing it for myself: I could make sure that whenever I preceded a remark about my future behaviour with the (puzzling to other people) words 'I promise', I went on to do whatever I had said I would do; should I fail to do so, I might subject myself to all sorts of hardship. But that does not by itself introduce a practice of promising; it imposes no obligation on me, and it makes my act neither right if I do what I 'promised' to do nor wrong if I fail to do so. Promising is a practice, and depends on fairly wide acceptance of the rule that we ought to do what we say we will do after uttering the words 'I promise'. The fairly wide acceptance of the rule affects the morality of what I do after saying 'I promise' (and then essaying some remark about my future

behaviour) in a way in which the general acceptance of a rule against
kicking dogs does not affect the morality of kicking dogs. If kicking dogs
is wrong, then it is wrong no matter how many people fail to recognize the
fact. But we cannot sensibly say that, if promise-breaking is wrong, it is
wrong no matter how many people fail to recognize the fact; if enough
people fail to recognize the fact, then promise-breaking becomes impossible.
The rule that we ought to do what we promise to do, unlike the rule that
we ought not to kick dogs, does not only serve as a standard against which
to judge people's behaviour in a moral situation; it is one of the constituents
of the moral situation.

The situation is similar with respect to driving on the left. Isolated
instances of driving on the left have no moral value unless there is a practice
of driving on the left. There is no 'natural' morality with respect to such
activities apart from the practice; if all Americans are immoral, it is not
because they drive on the right. It is important to notice here that part of
what a practice is, is the acceptance of a rule as a rule, so that the rule
can properly be said to be a *constituent* of the morality of the situation. The
point is worth making in discussion of this example because it might well
seem that, in the case of driving on the left, all that we need is consistency,
and that the acceptance of a rule requiring driving on the left is entirely
beside the logical point in that it is relevant only because it produces that
consistency. People might or might not drive on the left because they accept
a rule requiring them to do so; we do not need to know *why* they do it in
order to know *that* their doing it results in fewer accidents than there would
be if 50% of the people drove on one side of the road and 50% on the
other. It is important that acceptance of the rule produces such consistency,
but it has more logical consequences than that; without the rule there is
no practice. Unless there is a rule requiring driving on the left, a man who
drives on the right, though he may be doing something unusual, is doing
nothing wrong. An obligation to drive on the left is not generated simply
by most people's doing it any more than an obligation to see 'Zabriskie
Point' is generated simply by most people's doing it; to have the obligation
we must have acceptance of a rule requiring that people drive on the left.
A man who drives on the right then does wrong because his act is not in
accordance with that rule; but the rule does not describe the morality of
the act, it creates it.

The example of driving on the left is mildly odd in a way worth noting.
How does the morality of a practice work? To ask the question in terms
of a particular case, why should I keep my promises? If everybody else
subjects himself to a rule requiring that he keep his promises even in cases
in which it is to his immediate disadvantage to do so, does so to my benefit,
and does so on the understanding that I will do the same (an understanding
I give whenever I buy into the institution by using the words, 'I promise'

in the relevant circumstances), then it is only just that I should so subject myself, too. (I note, in parenthesis, to forestall one objection, that this shows only why I should keep my promises and not why I should make any.) This is a case of what has been called commutative obligation, which rests on commutative justice, and it is fairly clear that it is at least part of the point that Hobbes was getting at when he gave his apparently eccentric account of justice. If I join in a practice and willingly accept the benefits of other people's restricting their behaviour in the ways that the practice requires, then I am under an obligation similarly to restrict my behaviour.[7] To accept the benefits and refuse to contribute my mite is to fail to fulfil an obligation and is unjust. The case of driving on the left is mildly odd because I cannot gain the benefits accruing from others' subscribing to that practice unless I fit in with it; taking the benefits and refusing to fit in is simply ruled out. My driving on the right when everybody else drives on the left is letting myself in for trouble. That does not make driving on the left relevantly different from keeping promises, though. If I drive on the right when others drive on the left, it is not simply bad for me in that I will run into other people, it is bad for other people in that they will run into me. I am not the only one who suffers; others will suffer, too, and it is because they will suffer that there is an obligation.

If I do not drive on the left then I do not reap any benefit from having others do so, it is true. If I do not reap any benefit, whence the obligation? The driving-on-the-left rule is one of a set, and I gain from others' fitting in with the set; commutative obligation can arise with respect to a set of rules just as well as with respect to one particular rule. None of this is to deny that a practice could itself be so unjust as to outweigh any obligation *prima facie* imposed by commutative justice.

How would killing stand if people actually lived in their natural condition as Hobbes describes it – that is, not simply in a society that lacked a state or any established form of government, but in a world in which the contest always went to the stronger and men killed whenever it suited their interests to do so? In such a situation, with no co-operation between men, we would not have even a society; if, as is often said, morality is man-made in terms of his society, then there will be no morality in the natural condition and men will be free to do what they will. Hobbes has often been interpreted as making just such a claim as this. Specifically with respect to killing (but also, I think, generally), it is an eminently plausible position. If other men killed freely whenever it served their interests to do so, thus placing me in constant fear of death at their hands, it seems that it would not be wrong for me to kill also; indeed, I might be foolish not to forestall them by killing. Intuitively, it does seem clear that the fact that everybody else killed in this way would be relevant to the morality of my killing. (I shall suggest below that the point is not merely intuitive, at this level anyway.)

If Hobbes is right, as his position has so far been described, the prohibition on killing people is of the same logical sort as the prohibition on promise-breaking; the rule against killing people is a constitutive, not merely descriptive, rule of morality, and there is no obligation to refrain from killing people unless the rule is generally accepted. Actually, for reasons I will explain later, I think that Hobbes saw more than this, whether or not he said more. His theory as set out so far explains quite a bit about killing. We enter the social contract primarily to protect our lives, and secondarily to make them more enjoyable by making us more secure in our possessions and so on. The points come in that order because we cannot have the enjoyment without having the life. One condition releasing me from the obligation not to kill somebody else, it follows, is that he is trying to kill me; he is then failing to keep his side of the bargain and thus releases me from mine. I promised not to kill him provided that I was given security of my own life, and that condition is not being met. The same holds true of the enemy in time of war. If life begins at forty and ceases to be enjoyable at sixty-five, it might be written into the contract, or be one of the established practices of a society, that out of respect for the aged we shall put them to death when they reach that age. Hobbes's theory, as it stands, gives an explanation why murder is prohibited, why there are defeating conditions to a claim of murder, why the defeating conditions are what they are, and why they can vary from one society to another (the contracts that were signed differed in details). It also explains why murder, though wrong for reasons of the same logical sort as promise-breaking, is a matter of greater import than is promise-breaking: protection of our lives was the primary reason for our making the contract, and gaining more good things to make life more enjoyable, which promising does, was secondary. These are requirements that any satisfactory answer to the question 'What is wrong with killing people?' would have to meet. If we do not want to be caught up with the signing of contracts and the requirement that people once did live in their Hobbesian natural condition before the contract was signed, the whole thing can quickly be rewritten in terms of commutative obligation and the established practices in societies as they are. The talk of our reasons for signing the contract can be translated into talk of the benefits we gain from living in a society rather than a Hobbesian natural condition, and talk about primary and secondary reasons can be translated, with the same argument, into talk about the relative importance of the benefits that we gain.

Hobbes's theory as so far described looks fairly neat, but there is an inadequacy in it, and one of which he was aware, whether or not he dealt with it satisfactorily.

THE RIGHT OF NATURE, which Writers commonly call *Jus Naturale*, is the Liberty each man hath, to use his own power, as he will himselfe, for the preservation of his own Nature; that is to say, of his own Life; and consequently, of doing anything, which in his own Judgement, and Reason, hee shall conceive to be the aptest means thereunto.[8]

In this passage, Hobbes places limitations on the right of nature; in the natural condition, where others kill whenever it serves their interests to do so, I still cannot do just as I please. He summarizes the point in his second Law of Nature: '*By all means we can, to defend our selves*',[9] and emphasizes the restrictions on our freedom in the first: '*Seek Peace, and follow it.*'[10] In a natural condition where others kill whenever it serves their interests to do so, it is permissible for me to forestall an attempt to kill me by killing whoever would make the attempt; to do so is to kill in self-defence, and in Hobbes's natural condition would be the only way of defending myself short of living as a hermit. The fact that everybody else kills does affect the morality of killing that I do; it means that the defeating condition of self-defence can be invoked far more often. Even in the natural condition, no matter how others may behave, it is not permissible for me to kill for the sheer joy of it. Even in the natural condition there is a prohibition on killing, so the Hobbesian account given so far is inadequate. The reason why killing for sheer pleasure is ruled out, I think, is that the man who does that is not apt to become a social being.

It is not clear that people in a Hobbesian natural condition could have moral concepts; if each man is at war with all others so that there is no community, it is not clear that 'people' in a natural condition would have any concepts above those that the lower animals have. Looking at the natural condition with the concepts that we have, though, we can see that the man who has no desire to kill for pleasure and who is fit to become a social being is a man who has a virtue. *In* a natural condition, perhaps, no moral distinctions could be drawn, but they can be drawn when we talk *about* the natural condition. (In a natural condition the virtue of a man fit to become a social being might not be recognized, but the quality of character that he has is a virtue in that situation because it makes it possible to leave that situation.

Killing is wrong when and because it is murder, which is a species of injustice. If it is asked why we have a concept of murder and why wanton killing is wrong even in a natural condition, the answer is that we could not have a society without a concept of murder. In Hart's terminology,[11] killing is contrary to natural law, i.e., a minimum condition for the existence of a society is that there be some prohibition on killing. If people were never tempted to kill each other we should have no need of a concept of murder, but people are so tempted. If people were not so vulnerable there might be less need for restrictions on killing; but we are vulnerable. If people killed promiscuously and we had no security against their doing so, we should have to be prepared to forestall them by killing in our turn (and it would need to be the first turn), so that we should be back in our natural condition. The minimum condition that must be met by people if they are to co-operate with each other is that they should not kill each other. To have a society is, amongst other things, to have a concept of murder and thus a prohibition on killing. We ought not to kill because, being members of society, we have a concept of murder and thus recognize an obligation not to kill. To have a concept of murder, or to have the word 'murder' in the language, is to have *general* acceptance of an obligation not to kill; in that respect, it is similar to promising. An individual man might know what 'murder' meant but not recognize the obligation. If he asks 'Why should I not kill people?' he is asking for reasons of self-interest or something of the sort; he is not asking about the morality of killing.

That explains why there is a prohibition on killing or why we have a concept of murder. Why the prohibition and the concept take the form they do, what conditions defeat a claim of murder, is to be explained by reference to commutative obligation and the established practices of a society.

NOTES

1   R. N. Smart, 'Negative Utilitarianism', *Mind*, 1958.
2   *Principia Ethica*, Cambridge paperback, 1959, pp. 156–7.
3   Ibid., p. 156.
4   See G. E. Moore, 'Proof of an External World', in *Philosophical Papers* (London, 1959), pp. 146–7.
5   'Modern Moral Philosophy', in *The Is/Ought Question*, ed. W. D. Hudson (London, 1969), p. 192.
6   *Leviathan*, ch. 15, Everyman ed., p. 74.
7   Cf. H. L. A. Hart, 'Are There Any Natural Rights?', *Philosophical Review*, 1955.
8   Hobbes, *Leviathan*, ch. XIV, Everyman ed., p. 66.
9   Ibid., p. 67.
10 Ibid., p. 67.
11 See *The Concept of Law* (Oxford, 1961), pp. 189–95.

16

A Covenant for the Ark?

Peter Singer

The second extract from Moore raised in a dramatic way the role of human consciousness in the assignment of value to things. If there were no human beings, could it still be the case that one kind of world were better than another? Glover, having put forward a similar thought-experiment, objects that 'with a choice so abstract and remote, it may be hard to feel any preference at all.' A more concrete expression of the problem is provided in the lecture by Singer, who recounts the case of a recent Australian election, in which such a question actually played an important role. The question was whether to proceed with the exploitation of a river for electricity, with a resulting destruction of wild habitats. The interest of the case (for Singer's and for our purpose) lay in the fact that the river is situated in a remote area, unlikely to be visited by anyone. Singer points out that those who opposed the scheme did not want the area preserved because they might get pleasure from it some day; they wanted it, he says, 'saved for its own sake'. Such views are widely held nowadays, and the same is true of 'animal rights', the main subject of the lecture. But can they be defended against sceptics? According to Singer, there is need for 'humility on the part of our species' in our dealings with the natural world. Now humility, like other virtues and vices that are sometimes cited in this connection, is primarily an attitude between human individuals; and it is not clear that it can be extended to relations between one species and another (the human species as against the rest). Similarly, we often hear about 'the greed of man' in this context; but there is no such person as 'man'. (Singer's argument should also be compared with Mill's forthright rejection of nature as an object of moral value, at the end of section three.)

In Australia we have just had a general election. As in Britain, our economy is going backwards and unemployment is at record levels. Yet perhaps the most talked about campaign issue, and one that certainly contributed to the defeat of Malcolm Fraser's government, had nothing to do with the recession: it was the proposed damming of the Franklin river, in Tasmania's south-west wilderness. Not more than a handful of the electors are ever likely to see the Franklin, except on their television screens. To get to the dam site you have to walk through some of the most rugged country in the world. Indeed, if even a quarter of the people now telling opinion pollsters that they oppose the damming of the Franklin river were actually to go there, one of the prime arguments for preserving the area – its untouched state – would be destroyed. That may sound ironical. It is not meant to be. While many Australians want the Franklin river saved, very few want it saved so that they can go and enjoy it. Most of them want it saved *for its own sake*; not as a means to further their own interests, or even to further the interests of the community as a whole. They want the dam stopped because they think the wilderness of south-west Tasmania has value in itself.

The movement for wilderness preservation is part of something still more significant: an expansion of our moral horizons beyond our own species. This expansion underlies not only the growing consciousness of the importance of nature preservation but also the sudden appearance of an entirely new phenomenon: the struggle for animal liberation. I want to examine this phenomenon, and what it means for our understanding of ethics.

Although there were one or two 19th-century thinkers who asserted that animals have rights, the serious political movement in this direction is very young, dating back no more than five or six years. It's quite distinct from the efforts of the more traditional organizations, such as the RSPCA, to stop people treating animals cruelly. But even these traditional concerns are relatively recent when seen in the perspective of 3,000 years of Western civilization.

Concern for animal suffering can be found in Hindu thought, and the Buddhist idea of compassion is a universal one, extending to animals as well as humans; but our Western traditions are very different. *Our* intellectual roots lie in Ancient Greece and in the Judaeo-Christian tradition. Neither is kind to those not of our species.

In the conflict between rival schools of thought in Ancient Greece, it was the school of Aristotle that eventually became dominant. Aristotle held the view that nature is a hierarchy in which those with less reasoning ability exist for the sake of those with more reasoning ability. Thus plants, he said, exist for the sake of animals, and animals for the sake of man, to provide him with food and clothing.

Nowadays we've rejected Aristotle's idea that less rational human beings exist in order to serve more rational humans; but we still retain some of the corresponding attitude to non-human animals. It's buttressed by the other great intellectual tradition of the West – a tradition in which the following words stand as a foundation for everything else:

And God said, Let us make man in our image, after our likeness: and let them have dominion over the fish of the sea, and over the fowl of the air, and over the earth, and over every creeping thing that creepeth upon the earth.

So God created man in his own image ...
And God blessed them, and God said unto them, Be fruitful, and multiply, and replenish the earth, and subdue it; and have dominion over the fish of the sea, and over the fowl of the air, and over every living thing that moveth upon the earth.

Here is a myth to make human beings feel their supremacy and their power. Man alone is made in the image of God. Man alone is given dominion over all the animals, and told to subdue the earth. Accordingly, mainstream Christianity, for its first 1,800 years, put non-human animals outside its sphere of concern. On this issue the key figures in early Christianity were unequivocal. Paul scornfully rejected the thought that God might care about the welfare of oxen, and the incident of the Gadarene swine, in which Jesus is described as sending devils into a herd of pigs and making them drown themselves in the sea, is explained by Augustine as intended to teach us that we have no duties towards animals. This interpretation was accepted by Thomas Aquinas, who stated that the only possible objection to cruelty to animals was that it might lead to cruelty to humans – according to Aquinas, there was nothing wrong in itself with making animals suffer.

This became the official view of the Roman Catholic Church to such good – or bad – effect that as late as the middle of the 19th century, Pope Pius IX refused permission for the founding of a society for the prevention of cruelty to animals in Rome, on the grounds that to grant permission would imply that human beings have duties to the lower creatures.

Even in England, which has a reputation for being dotty about animals, the first efforts to obtain legal protection for members of other species were made only 180 years ago. They were greeted with derision. *The Times* was so lacking in appreciation of the idea that the suffering of animals ought to be prevented that it attacked proposed legislaton that would stop the 'sport' of bull-baiting. Said that august newspaper: 'Whatever meddles with the private personal disposition of man's time or property is tyranny.' Animals, clearly, were just property.

Even when the first anti-cruelty law did get on the statute books it was built on the assumption that the interests of non-human animals deserve protection only when serious human interests are not at stake. Animals remained very clearly 'lower creatures' – their interests must be sacrificed to our own in the event of conflict.

One could assert that to have rights one must be a member of the human race, and that is all there is to it. But if we can get away with taking that as a moral axiom, the racist can with equal logical force make it his axiom that to have rights you have to be a member of the Caucasian race, and that is all there is to that. Conversely, once we agree that race is not, in itself, morally significant, how can species be? Some 200 years ago, Jeremy Bentham put it like this:

The day *may* come when the rest of the animal creation may acquire those rights which never could have been withholden from them but by the hand of tyranny. The French have already discovered that the blackness of the skin is no reason why a human being should be abandoned without redress to the caprice of a tormentor. It may one day come to be recognized that the number of the legs, the villosity of the skin, or the termination of the *os sacrum* are reasons equally insufficient for abandoning a sensitive being to the same fate.

Some of you might say: 'It's not because we're members of the human species that we're justified in overriding the interests of other animals; it's because we're rational and they're not.' Or others might say it's because we are autonomous beings or because we have a sense of justice. All these, and more, have been invoked to justify us in sacrificing their interests to ours.

One way of replying would be to consider whether non-human animals really do lack these allegedly important characteristics. The more we learn of non-human animals, particularly chimpanzees, but also many other species, the less able we are to defend the claim that we humans are unique because we're the only ones capable of reasoning, or capable of autonomous action, or capable of the use of language, or possessing a sense of justice. But I shall not go into this reply here, because it would do nothing for the many species of animals who couldn't be said to meet whatever test was being proposed.

There is a much shorter way of replying. Consider the passage I was quoting from Bentham, for he anticipated the objection. After dismissing the ideas that number of legs, roughness of skin or fine details of bone formation should 'trace the insuperable line' between those who have moral standing and those who do not, Bentham goes on to ask what else might mark this boundary:

Is it the faculty of reason, or perhaps the faculty of discourse? But a full-grown horse or dog is beyond comparison a more rational, as well as a more conversable animal, than an infant of a day or week or even a month, old. But suppose they were otherwise, what would it avail? The question is not Can they *reason*? Can they *talk*? but Can they *suffer*?

Bentham is clearly right. Whatever test we propose as a means of separating human from non-human animals, it's plain that if all non-human animals are going to fail it, some humans will fail as well. Infants are neither rational, nor autonomous, nor language-using, nor possessing a sense of justice. Are they therefore to be treated like non-human animals, to be fattened for the table, if we should fancy the taste of their flesh, or to be used to find out if some new hair shampoo will blister human eyeballs?

Ah, but infants, though not rational, autonomous, or able to talk, still have the potential to become like us adult humans; so the defender of human supremacy will reply to Bentham. The relevance of potential is another complicated argument that I shall avoid, by the stratagem of focusing your attention on another class of humans who would fail this test: they are humans unfortunate enough to have been born with irreparable brain damage, so severe that they'll never be able to reason, or talk, or do any of the other things that are often said to distinguish us from non-human animals. The fact that we don't use them as means to our ends indicates that we don't really see decisive moral significance in rationality, or autonomy, or language, or a sense of justice, or any of the other criteria said to distinguish us from other animals.

This is speciesism, pure and simple, and as indefensible as the most blatant racism. There is no ethical basis for elevating membership of one particular species into a morally crucial characteristic. From an ethical point of view, we all stand on an equal footing – whether we stand on two feet, or four, or none at all. That is the crux of the philosophy of the animal liberation movement; but to forestall misunderstanding I'd better say something immediately about this notion of equality. It does *not* mean that animals have all the same rights as you and I have. They don't have the rights to vote, to free speech, to freedom of religion. Animal liberationists do not minimize the obvious differences between most members of our species and members of other species.

Here is an example. Suppose we decided to perform lethal scientific experiments on normal adult humans, kidnapped at random from public parks for this purpose. Soon, every adult who entered a park would become fearful of being kidnapped for experimentation. The resultant terror would be a form of suffering additional to whatever pain was involved in the experiment itself. The same experiments carried out on non-human animals would cause less suffering overall, for the non-human animals would not have the same anticipatory dread. This does not mean, I hasten to add, that it is all right to experiment on animals as we please; but only that if the experiment *is* to be done at all, there is *some* reason, compatible with the equal consideration of interests, for preferring to use non-human animals rather than normal adult humans.

There's one point that needs to be added to this example. Nothing in it depends on the fact that the normal adult humans are members of our species. It is their capacity for knowledge of what *may* happen to them that's crucial. If it were not normal adults, but rather severely brain-damaged humans, then they would be in the same position as non-human animals at a similar mental level.

The moral significance of taking life is more complex still. There is furious controversy about the circumstances in which it is legitimate to kill human beings, so it's no wonder that it should be difficult to decide whether non-human animals have any rights to life. Here I would say, once again, that species in itself cannot make a difference. If it's wrong to take the life of a severely brain-damaged, abandoned human infant, it must be equally wrong to take the life of a dog or a pig at a comparable mental level.

But perhaps it is *not* wrong to take the life of such a brain-damaged human infant – after all, many people think such infants should be allowed to die, and an infant 'allowed to die' ends up just as dead as one that is killed. Indeed, one could easily argue that our readiness to put a hopelessly ill non-human animal out of its misery is the one and only respect in which we treat animals better than we treat people.

The influence of the Judaeo-Christian insistence on the godlike nature of human beings is nowhere more apparent than in the standard Western doctrine of the sanctity of human life: a doctrine that puts the life of the most hopelessly and irreparably brain-damaged human – the kind whose level of awareness is not under-estimated by the term 'human vegetable' – above the life of a chimpanzee. The sole reason for this strange set of priorities is, of course, the fact that the chimpanzee is not a member of our species, and the human vegetable is biologically human. This doctrine is now starting to be eroded by the acceptance of abortion, which is the killing of a being that is indisputably a member of the human species, and by the questioning of the value of applying all the power of modern medical technology to saving human life in all cases.

I think we will emerge from the present decade with a significantly different attitude to the sanctity of human life, an attitude which considers the quality of the life at stake, rather than the simple matter of whether the life is or is not that of a member of the species *Homo sapiens*. Once this happens, we shall be ready to take a much broader view of the wrongness of killing, one in which the capacities of the being in question play a central role. Such a view will not discriminate on the basis of species alone, but it will still make distinctions between the seriousness of killing beings with the mental capacities of normal human adults and killing beings who do not possess, and never have possessed, these mental capacities. It isn't a bias in favour of our own species that leads us to think that there's greater moral significance in taking the life of a normal human than, for example, that of a pig. To give just one reason for this distinction, a normal human has hopes and plans for the future: to take the life of a normal human is therefore to cut off these plans, and prevent them ever being fulfilled. Pigs, I expect, do not have as clear a conception of themselves as beings with a past and a future. Consequently, to kill a pig is not to prevent the fulfilment of any plans, or at least not of any long-range future plans. This does not, I stress, mean that it is all right, or morally trivial, to kill pigs. If pigs are capable of enjoying their lives, as I believe they are, we do better when we let them continue to live than when we needlessly end their lives. All I am saying is that when we needlessly end the life of a pig, we're not doing something *as* bad as when we needlessly end the life of a normal human adult.

The animal liberation movement, therefore, is *not* saying that all lives are of equal worth, or that all interests of humans and other animals are to be given equal weight, no matter what those interests may be. It is saying that where animals and humans do have similar interests – we might take the interest in avoiding physical pain as an example, for it's an interest that humans clearly share with other animals – those interests are to be counted equally, with no automatic discount just because one of the beings is not human. A simple point, no doubt, but nevertheless part of a far-reaching ethical revolution.

The ethical revolution is the culmination of a long line of ethical development. I cannot do better than quote the words of that splendid 19th-century historian of ideas, W. E. H. Lecky. In his *History of European Morals*, Lecky wrote:

At one time the benevolent affections embrace merely the family, soon the circle expanding includes first a class, then a nation, then a coalition of nations, then all humanity, and finally, its influence is felt in the dealings of man with the animal world.

Lecky has anticipated what the animal liberationists are now saying. In an earlier stage of our development, most human groups held to a tribal ethic. Members of the tribe were protected, but people of other tribes could be robbed or killed as one pleased. Gradually, the circle of protection expanded, but as recently as 150 years ago, we didn't include blacks. So African human beings could be captured, shipped to America and sold. In Australia, white settlers regarded the Aborigines as pests and hunted them down, much as kangaroos are hunted down today. Just as we've progressed beyond the blatantly racist ethic of the era of slavery and colonialism, so we must now progress beyond the speciesist ethic of the era of factory farming, of animals as mere research tools, of whaling, seal-hunting, kangaroo slaughter, and the destruction of wilderness. We must take the final step in expanding the circle of ethics.

An attractive idea, you might say, but a little naive. Lecky's idea of the expanding circle of benevolence is typically 19th-century in its optimistic vision of moral progress. The Victorians expected that as we became more educated we would also become more civilized and morally better. Was not that optimism shattered in the trenches of France between 1914 and 1918? How can anyone attempt to revive it, in the century that witnessed Auschwitz?

I shall not attempt to carry out any kind of moral calculus of the crimes of this century, as compared with the crimes of previous centuries. Technology has made mass slaughter easier, so one cannot assess moral progress by the numbers of innocents slain. In any case, the kind of moral progress I have in mind is to be judged by the most advanced conceptions of ethics, not by the atrocities of evil dictators. At this advanced level, there has been progress. The officially accepted standards of ethics, as embodied in political rhetoric, constitutional statements of rights, United Nations declarations, and so on, are more all-encompassing than the officially accepted standards of any previous period in the history of the West.

Perhaps progress at this elevated level is of less practical relevance than progress at the level of actual behaviour; but advanced ethical ideas eventually influence the practices of the whole community. Racial prejudice still disadvantages blacks, but these disadvantages are slight compared with what whites did to blacks before the acceptance of the moral ideal of human equality. To extend this ideal of equal consideration of interests to all creatures would not stop all human abuse, any more than declarations of human equality have stopped racial prejudice; but the long-term effects for other species would be immense.

A more sophisticated objection to the idea of moral progress comes from our knowledge of evolution. In its simplest version, this objection asserts that nature is always red in tooth and claw, and any species that survives does so by eliminating any other species that threaten its interests. So while the idea of the expanding circle makes sense until the circle is broad enough for us to work co-operatively for the sake of our whole species, any extension beyond this point would be unnatural and, in evolutionary terms, would make us less fit for survival. This objection can be refuted by a deeper understanding of evolution.

In recent years, scientists working in evolutionary theory have ceased to describe evolution as simply a competition between different species. The real basis of selection, many of them now say, is not the species, nor some smaller group, but the individual, or even the gene.

Consider a gene, or a cluster of genes, that led an animal to behave altruistically – for example, to give warning signals when a predator is near, at the cost of drawing upon itself the attention of the predator. That kind of behaviour might benefit the species as a whole; but it would reduce the breeding prospects of the altruistic individual. So there is a conflict between the *value to the species* of having warnings given when predators are around; and the *loss to the individual* who gives the warnings and is at greater risk of being taken by the predator. In this conflict between the interests of the individual and the interests of the species, it's the interests of the individual that will predominate, from an evolutionary point of view.

So the theory that altruism exists because it benefits the *species* has been undermined. If the idea of extending the circle of ethics beyond our own species is condemned as unrealistic on the grounds that it runs counter to the thrust of evolution, then the more limited extension of the circle to include all human beings must be equally unrealistic.

Why, then, does altruism occur at all? The standard sociobiological answer is that whatever altruism does exist is either altruism towards kin or altruism towards those who can reciprocate. Altruism towards kin can be explained by the fact that we share genes with our kin. Therefore genes which lead individuals to favour their children, siblings and cousins will be more likely to survive and increase their representation in future generations. So altruism within families can be fitted comfortably into evolutionary theory. The other form of altruism the sociobiologists are prepared to allow is reciprocal altruism: 'You scratch my back and I'll scratch yours.' Such behaviour evolves because in the long run it pays off.

If this was all there was to ethics, out would go many of our most cherished ethical views. To expect the affluent to give aid to the weaker, poorer nations would be contrary to evolutionary theory; so would a concern for unrelated weaker members of our own community who aren't likely to be able to do much for us in return for any good we do for them. Among these weaker groups would be the poor, the elderly, the very young and the mentally feeble – in other words, precisely those groups we usually think of as requiring our special attention.

Fortunately, we don't have to accept the grim view of ethics that seems to be implied by evolutionary theory. For a start, the theory doesn't square with the most plausible view of human behaviour. As I was preparing this lecture, the worst bushfire for more than 40 years struck my home state of Victoria, killing 46 people and leaving thousands homeless. Many of the dead were volunteer firefighters, some of whom had travelled miles from their own towns to fight the fires that threatened other people. After the fires, too, there was an extraordinary response to an appeal to help the homeless survivors. Hundreds of caravans, many stocked with food, were driven to refuge centres and left on indefinite loan to whoever needed them most. One 19-year-old girl gave $A2,000 which she'd been saving for an overseas trip, saying that the bushfire victims needed it more than she did.

Of course, one can always try to explain away such behaviour as somehow not altruistic at all – American sociobiologist Edward Wilson tries to explain away the altruism of Mother Teresa by suggesting that she helps the destitute of Calcutta only because she expects to be rewarded in the afterlife for the good deeds she does on earth. I don't find such explanations convincing. Nor am I impressed by those who say that people who seem to be behaving altruistically are really selfish, because they get some inner pleasure from the knowledge that they're helping others. If people who get pleasure from helping others are selfish, what we need is more of this kind of selfish altruism and less of the ordinary kind of selfish selfishness.

Outside the limited horizons of sociobiology there are alternative explanations for the existence of altruism. One is that our capacity for ethical action beyond the bounds of kin and reciprocity is linked to our ability to reason. Sociobiologists might reply that our ability to reason is also the result of evolution. Indeed it is. Any creature capable of reasoning has an immense advantage in many situations where survival is at stake. But this need not mean that the use of reason is limited to survival or other self-interested ends. The capacity to reason is special because it can lead us to places we did not expect to go. Beginning to reason is like stepping on to an esclator that leads upward and out of sight. Once we take the first step, the distance to be travelled is independent of our will and we cannot know in advance where it is going to end.

Maybe the same kind of thing can occur in ethics. The crux of ethics is the ability to detach oneself from one's own standpoint and take an impartial perspective. This is impossible for a creature that lacks all reasoning ability; but once we can discuss moral issues, it becomes impossible entirely to avoid seeing a situation as others see it.

I am only one among others, and their interests ought to count as mine do. But who are 'the others'? With that question we return to the themes with which I began. When I see myself as one among others, the relevant point of the comparison is that others also have feelings, can suffer or be happy. Any being capable of feeling anything, whether pain or pleasure, or any kind of conscious preference or aversion should therefore be included. This would include, as a minimum, mammals and birds, most probably all vertebrate species and quite possibly – and here it becomes more difficult to know – some invertebrates as well.

We reach the same conclusion by analysing the principle of doing unto others as you would have them do unto you. If we ask how far this principle extends, it extends as far as the intelligibility of asking myself: 'How would I like that done to me if I were that being, with the sensitivity and preferences that being has?'

Well, how far does the intelligibility of this question extend? As long as a being has conscious preferences, the question makes some sense. If I know that a being will feel pain if operated on without an anaesthetic, then I know enough to say that, if I were that being, I would not like to be operated on without an anaesthetic. This may sound anthropomorphic, but we should beware of the unthinking use of that expression as a term of abuse. To imagine oneself in the situation of another creature is likely to lead to error when one naively assumes that some other creature must have all the same feelings as a human being; it's entirely proper when it draws on the best available information about the nature of that creature and what it's likely to experience. To form an opinion as to what a pig or a whale or a fish is experiencing is certainly not easy, but at the same time we shouldn't give up the task as hopeless. Where speech is lacking, we can still use other kinds of evidence: observations of behaviour, and also knowledge of the nature of the brain and nervous system of the animal in question. This may not be enough to produce certainty, but it does mean that we're not merely guessing. That we do not need speech to appreciate the feelings of a creature we really know well is something to which every dog owner – indeed every parent – can attest.

Equal consideration for animals will mean some sacrifice on our part. We'll have to think again about our diet, with its heavy reliance on animal products, especially those from factory farms. This could, however, turn out to be a blessing in disguise from the point of view of our own health, the ecology of our environment and the world food problem. We'll also have to reassess the whole issue of animal experimentation. Scientists have recently become more aware of the threat to their current practices posed by the animal liberation movement. They've been telling the public how crucial all this experimentation is to the progress of medical research. Without entering into the debate about the truth of that claim, I shall just remark that, unless these scientists take into account the costs to the animals they experiment upon, they've not even begun to make out a moral case for continued experimentation. Let me give you one example. An American drug company is developing vaccine against a strain of hepatitis known as hepatitis B. This is a common form of the disease, affecting hundreds of millions of people around the world. The snag is that the United States drug regulations required the vaccine to be tested on animals before it is used on humans – and the only animal known to suffer from hepatitis B is the chimpanzee. To obtain a large enough breeding colony of chimps, it would be necessary to import a considerable number of them from Africa – and as many as five wild chimpanzees may die for every one that is landed alive in the United States. Is the benefit to humans sufficient to override the loss to chimpanzees? The numbers involved might lead you to say that it was; and in fact the testing is now going on. But is there really no alternative route to the manufacture of the vaccine that did not require animal testing?

Such alternatives may not always be available. But the correct strategy, however, is to look for them. If we think of other animals as expendable tools, we shall not see that there is any dilemma at all, and we will not look for ways around the problem. If we don't have ready access to experimental animals, our whole style of thought will be different, and who knows what we shall find?

For instance, how many of you noticed the obvious contradiction that I just uttered, when I said that hundreds of millions of people suffer from hepatitis B, and then immediately went on to say that the only animal known to suffer from the disease is the chimpanzee? Has the possibility of obtaining human volunteers been explored? Could there not be adequate safeguards to make this a viable possibility?

Before I leave this topic, let me make it plain that I am not saying that *no* animal should *ever* be used in *any* experiment. I *am* saying that the interests of the animal must always be given its full weight within the moral calculus.

In Sweden, a carefully designed committee system, including outsiders as well as scientists, now assesses proposed experiments. Like the hospital ethics committees which now consider proposals for research on humans, this is the sort of mechanism which could ensure that the interests of animals get the consideration they deserve.

We are now witnessing the first stirrings of a momentous new stage in our moral thinking. Will this new stage also be the final stage in the expansion of ethics? Or is something still left out? Recall the opposition to the destruction of wilderness which I spoke of at the beginning of this talk. Certainly one could oppose the damming of the Franklin river because of the destruction of the habitat of the animals that dwell there; but is this the whole story?

Many of those trying to stop the dam would deny it. The wilderness movement all over the world is striving to make us acknowledge that there is inherent value in nature itself, in trees and rocks and rivers and mountains. It is striving for an expansion of the circle of ethics beyond those beings that have some minimal degree of consciousness, and thus beyond the point at which I can put myself in the position of some other being and say: 'If I were that being, with the capacities it has, I would not like that done to me.' For I take it that a river, no matter how wild and free flowing, has no consciousness and there is no sense at all in claiming that it would not like to be dammed. Similarly, a mountain could not mind being quarried, or even a tree have a conscious preference for not being felled.

Perhaps the best that can be said about the preservation of wilderness – apart from the value of the wilderness for the sentient creatures that live in it or will pass through it – is that respect for wilderness is a sign of much needed humility on the part of our species. When we clear the bush, dam the rivers and push freeways across the countryside, we're thinking of ourselves and our mastery of nature. When we stop doing these things we can appreciate the complex living world that existed long before we did and still gets along very nicely without us. Only then can we see ourselves in perspective, not as the source of everything that is of value, but as beings who exist alongside a myriad of different forms of life, and do not possess any inherent right to dominion over them.

SECTION THREE

Nature and Society

17

The Tree of Knowledge

Genesis

The last reading, from Singer, also provides an introduction to section three, which is about the value of nature as opposed to the creations of man. One of the main questions here will be whether human beings were not better off in their original 'state of nature' than in the social or civilized state. A vivid expression of this problem appears in the following reading, from Genesis. *There must have been a time when human beings – like other animals – had no concept of right and wrong; no language in which moral distinctions could be made. But having eaten 'of the tree of the knowledge of good and evil', they find themselves not only with new knowledge, but with new kinds of problems, such as could not occur among animals. That* nakedness *should be the first of these, according to the story, is of special interest. The 'unnatural' quality of human feelings and human problems is well illustrated by this example, and by the corresponding feeling of* shame, *whose importance in our scheme of moral concepts is often overlooked.*

The Lord God took the man and put him in the garden of Eden to till it and keep it. And the Lord God commanded the man, saying, 'You may freely eat of every tree of the garden; but of the tree of the knowledge of good and evil you shall not eat, for in the day that you eat of it you shall die.'

Now the serpent was more subtle than any other wild creature that the Lord God had made. He said to the woman, 'Did God say, "You shall not eat of any tree of the garden"?' And the woman said to the serpent, 'We may eat of the fruit of the trees of the garden; but God said, "You shall not eat of the fruit of the tree which is in the midst of the garden, neither shall you touch it, lest you die."' But the serpent said to the woman, 'You will not die. For God knows that when you eat of it your eyes will be opened, and you will be like God, knowing good and evil.' So when the woman saw that the tree was good for food, and that it was a delight to the eyes, and that the tree was to be desired to make one wise, she took of its fruit and ate; and she also gave some to her husband, and he ate. Then the eyes of both were opened, and they knew that they were naked;

and they sewed fig leaves together and made themselves aprons.

And they heard the sound of the Lord God walking in the garden in the cool of the day, and the man and his wife hid themselves from the presence of the Lord God among the trees of the garden. But the Lord God called to the man, and said to him, 'Where are you?' And he said, 'I heard the sound of thee in the garden, and I was afraid, because I was naked; and I hid myself.' He said, 'Who told you that you were naked? Have you eaten of the tree of which I commanded you not to eat?' The man said, 'The woman whom thou gavest to be with me, she gave me fruit of the tree, and I ate.' Then the Lord God said to the woman, 'What is this that you have done?' The woman said, 'The serpent beguiled me, and I ate.' The Lord God said to the serpent,

'Because you have done this,
cursed are you above all cattle,
and above all wild animals;
upon your belly you shall go,
and dust you shall eat
all the days of your life.
I will put enmity between you and the woman,
and between your seed and her seed;
he shall bruise your head,
and you shall bruise his heel.'

To the woman he said,
'I will greatly multiply your pain in childbearing;
in pain you shall bring forth children,
yet your desire shall be for your husband,
and he shall rule over you.'

And to Adam he said,
'Because you have listened to the voice of your wife,
and have eaten of the tree of which I commanded you,
"You shall not eat of it",
cursed is the ground because of you;
in toil you shall eat of it all the days of your life;
thorns and thistles it shall bring forth to you;
and you shall eat the plants of the field.
In the sweat of your face you shall eat bread
till you return to the ground,
for out of it you were taken;
you are dust,
and to dust you shall return.'

18

The Origin of Inequality

Jean-Jacques Rousseau

The following extracts from Rousseau's Discourse *are chosen especially for the light they throw on the origin of the 'factitious passions' (such as shame). Rousseau (1712–78) describes how, once humanity had arrived at a certain stage, there would necessarily arise situations in which rivalry and emulation would make their appearance. Men would acquire a new set of motives and emotions, unknown in the animal world (and in the original human 'state of nature'). As distinct from the original motive of self-preservation (amour de soi), they would embark on a new set of self-regarding motives (amour-propre), including vanity, honour, reputation, deception, revenge and contempt; and from these would spring the enslavement of man by man, and other woes of the human condition as we know it today. The savage, according to Rousseau, is self-sufficient; whereas civilized man 'only knows how to live in the opinion of others'. He is an 'artificial' creature, having renounced the harmony of the natural state, and is at odds with himself and his fellows.*

The value of Rousseau's writings (here and elsewhere) is sometimes underestimated, because he seems to indulge in fanciful speculation about the remote past and about the life of primitive people ('savages') existing today; and many of his statements are anyway known to be false. But a more profitable way of reading Rousseau is to treat his stories not as claims about what actually happened on particular occasions in the remote past, but as examples of the kind *of events that must have occurred, in the transformation of man from the original state to that in which we find him today. Given the possession of language and the association of people in groups, certain kinds of situations are bound to arise, and these will lead inevitably to the new 'artificial' motives and passions that Rousseau regards as crucial to the transformation. Although Rousseau is not clear on this point, it might be argued that the emergence of* language *is the crucial factor. Some of Wittgenstein's remarks about animals may usefully be borne in mind in this connection; for example his question 'Why can't a dog simulate pain? Is he too honest?' (L. Wittgenstein,* Philosophical Investigations, *Blackwell, 1958, I/ 259).*

In the remarkable final passage, Rousseau addresses himself to the question 'What, then, is to be done?' Having given a negative answer to the question whether man is happier in the civilized state, what does he propose to do about it? This (unlike the rest of the reading) is a confusing passage, but the upshot is that Rousseau himself is not prepared to retire from society and return to nature. This may seem rather a let-down; but we must remember that the argument has been, not merely about the external conditions of nature, but about the nature of ourselves. To achieve the 'return to nature', Rousseau would have to divest himself of his nature as a social being, unlearning what he learned from the tree of knowledge; and this he cannot do.

It appears, at first view, that men in a state of nature, having no moral relations or determinate obligations one with another, could not be either good or bad, virtuous or vicious; unless we take these terms in a physical sense, and call, in an individual, those qualities vices which may be injurious to his preservation, and those virtues which contribute to it; in which case, he would have to be accounted most virtuous, who put least check on the pure impulses of nature. But without deviating from the ordinary sense of the words, it will be proper to suspend the judgment we might be led to form on such a state, and be on our guard against our prejudices, till we have weighed the matter in the scales of impartiality, and seen whether virtues or vices preponderate among civilized men: and whether their virtues do them more good than their vices do harm; till we have discoverd whether the progress of the sciences sufficiently indemnifies them for the mischiefs they do one another, in proportion as they are better informed of the good they ought to do; or whether they would not be, on the whole, in a much happier condition if they had nothing to fear or to hope from any one, than as they are, subjected to universal dependence, and obliged to take everything from those who engage to give them nothing in return.

Above all, let us not conclude, with Hobbes, that because man has no idea of goodness, he must be naturally wicked; that he is vicious because he does not know virtue; that he always refuses to do his fellow-creatures services which he does not think they have a right to demand; or that by virtue of the right he justly claims to all he needs, he foolishly imagines himself the sole proprietor of the whole universe. Hobbes had seen clearly the defects of all the modern definitions of natural right: but the consequences which he deduces from his own show that he understands it in an equally false sense. In reasoning on the principles he lays down, he ought to have said that the state of nature, being that in which the care for our own preservation is the least prejudicial to that of others, was consequently the best calculated to promote peace, and the most suitable for mankind. He does say the exact opposite, in consequence of having improperly admitted, as a part of savage man's care for self-preservation, the gratification of a multitude of passions which are the work of society, and have made laws necessary. A bad man, he says, is a robust child. But it remains to be proved whether man in a state of nature is this robust child: and, should we grant that he is, what would he infer? Why truly, that if this man, when robust and strong, were dependent on others as he is when feeble, there is no extravagance he would not be guilty of; that he would beat his mother when she was too slow in giving him her breast; that he would strangle one of his younger brothers, if he should be troublesome to him, or bite the leg of another, if he put him to any inconvenience. But that man in the state of nature is both strong and dependent involves two contrary suppositions. Man is weak when he is dependent, and is his own master before he comes to be strong. Hobbes did not reflect that the same cause, which prevents a savage from making use of his reason, as our jurists hold, prevents him also from abusing his faculties, as Hobbes himself allows: so that it may be justly said that savages are not bad merely because they do not know what it is to be good: for it is neither the development of the understanding nor the restraint of law that hinders them from doing ill; but the peacefulness of their passions, and their ignorance of vice: *tanto plus in illis proficit vitiorum ignoratio, quam in bis cognitio virtutis.*[1] There is another principle which has escaped Hobbes; which, having been bestowed on mankind, to moderate, on certain occasions, the impetuosity of *amour-propre* or, before its birth, the desire of self-preservation, tempers the ardour with which he pursues his own welfare, by an innate repugnance at seeing a fellow-creature suffer.[2] I think I need not fear contradiction in holding man to be possessed of the only natural virtue, which could not be denied him by the most violent detractor of human virtue. I am speaking of compassion, which is a disposition suitable to creatures so weak and subject to so many evils as we certainly are: by so much the more universal and useful to mankind, as it comes before any kind of reflection; and at the same time so natural, that the very brutes themselves sometimes give evident proofs of it. ...

With passions so little active, and so good a curb, men, being rather wild than wicked, and more intent to guard themselves against the mischief that might be done them, than to do mischief to others, were by no means subject to very perilous dissensions. They maintained no kind of intercourse with one another, and were consequently strangers to vanity, deference, esteem, and contempt; they had not the least idea of 'mine' and 'thine', and no true conception of justice; they looked upon every violence to which they were subjected, rather as an injury that might easily be repaired than as a crime that ought to be punished; and they never thought of taking revenge, unless perhaps mechanically and on the spot, as a dog will sometimes bite the stone which is thrown at him. Their quarrels therefore would seldom have very bloody consequences; for the subject of them would be merely the question of subsistence. ...

Let us conclude then that man in a state of nature, wandering up and down the forests, without industry, without speech, and without home, an equal stranger to war and to all ties, neither standing in need of his fellow-creatures nor having any desire to hurt them, and perhaps even not distinguishing them one from another; let us conclude that, being self-sufficient and subject to so few passions, he could have no feelings or knowledge but such as befitted his situation; that he felt only his actual necessities, and disregarded everything he did not think himself immediately concerned to notice, and that his understanding made no greater progress than his vanity. If by accident he made any discovery, he was the less able to communicate it to others, as he did not know even his own children. Every art would necessarily perish with its inventor, where there was no kind of education among men, and generations succeeded generations without the least advance; when, all setting out from the same point, centuries must have elapsed in the barbarism of the first ages; when the race was already old, and man remained a child.

If I have expatiated at such length on this supposed primitive state, it is because I had so many ancient errors and inveterate prejudices to eradicate, and therefore thought it incumbent on me to dig down to their very root, and show, by means of a true picture of the state of nature, how far even the natural inequalities of mankind are from having that reality and influence which modern writers suppose.

It is in fact easy to see that many of the differences between men which are ascribed to nature stem rather from habit and the diverse modes of life of men in society. Thus a robust or delicate constitution, and the strength or weakness attaching to it, are more frequently the effects of a hardy or effeminate method of education than of the original endowment of the body. It is the same with the powers of the mind; for education not only makes a difference between such as are cultured and such as are not, but even increases the differences which exist among the former, in proportion to their respective degrees of culture: as the distance between a giant and a dwarf on the same road increases with every step they take. If we compare the prodigious diversity, which obtains in the education and manner of life of the various orders of men in the state of society, with the uniformity and simplicity of animal and savage life, in which every one lives on the same kind of food and in exactly the same manner, and does exactly the same things, it is easy to conceive how much less the difference between man and man must be in a state of nature than in a state of society, and how greatly the natural inequality of mankind must be increased by the inequalities of social institutions.

But even if nature really affected, in the distribution of her gifts, that partiality which is imputed to her, what advantage would the greatest of her favourites derive from it, to the detriment of others, in a state that admits of hardly any kind of relation between them? Where there is no love, of what advantage is beauty? Of what use is wit to those who do not converse, or cunning to those who have no business with others? I hear it constantly repeated that, in such a state, the strong would oppress the weak; but what is here meant by oppression? Some, it is said, would violently domineer over others, who would groan under a servile submission to their caprices. This indeed is exactly what I observe to be the case among us; but I do not see how it can be inferred of men in a state of nature, who could not easily be brought to conceive what we mean by dominion and servitude. One man, it is true, might seize the fruits which another had gathered, the game he had killed, or the cave he had chosen for shelter; but how would he ever be able to exact obedience, and what ties of dependence could there be among men without possessions? If, for instance, I am driven from one tree, I can go to the next; if I am disturbed in one place, what hinders me from going to another? Again, should I happen to meet with a man so much stronger than myself, and at the same time so depraved, so indolent, and so barbarous, as to compel me to provide for his sustenance while he himself remains idle; he must take care not to have his eyes off me for a single moment; he must bind me fast before he goes to sleep, or I shall certainly either knock him on the head or make my escape. That is to say, he must in such a case voluntarily expose himself to much greater trouble than he seeks to avoid, or can give me. After all this, let him be off his guard ever so little; let him but turn his head aside at any sudden noise, and I shall be instantly twenty paces off, lost in the forest, and, my fetters burst asunder, he would never see me again.

Without my expatiating thus uselessly on these details, everyone must see that as the bonds of servitude are formed merely by the mutual dependence of men on one another and the reciprocal needs that unite them, it is impossible to make any man a slave, unless he be first reduced to a situation in which he cannot do without the help of others: and, since such a situation does not exist in a state of nature, every one is there his own master, and the law of the strongest is of no effect. ...

Men, who have up to now been roving in the woods, by taking to a more settled manner of life, come gradually together, form separate bodies, and at length in every country arises a distinct nation, united in character and manners, not by regulations or laws but by uniformity of life and food, and the common influence of climate. Permanent neighbourhood could not fail to produce, in time, some connection between different families. Among young people of opposite sexes, living in neighbouring huts, the transient commerce required by nature soon led, through mutual intercourse, to another kind not less agreeable, and more permanent. Men began now to take the difference between objects into account, and to make comparisons; they acquired imperceptibly the ideas of beauty and merit, which soon gave rise to feelings of preference. In consequence of seeing each other often, they could not do without seeing each other constantly. A tender and pleasant feeling insinuated itself into their souls, and the least opposition turned it into an impetuous fury: with love arose jealousy; discord triumphed, and human blood was sacrificed to the gentlest of all passions.

As ideas and feelings succeeded one another, and heart and head were brought into play, men continued to lay aside their original wildness; their private connections became every day more intimate as their limits extended. They accustomed themselves to assemble before their huts round a large tree; singing and dancing, the true offspring of love and leisure, became the amusement, or rather the occupation, of men and women thus assembled together with nothing else to do. Each one began to consider the rest, and to wish to be considered in turn; and thus a value came to be attached to public esteem. Whoever sang or danced best, whoever was the handsomest, the strongest, the most dexterous, or the most eloquent, came to be of most consideration; and this was the first step towards inequality, and at the same time towards vice. From these first distinctions arose on the one side vanity and contempt and on the other shame and envy: and the fermentation caused by these new leavens ended by producing combinations fatal to innocence and happiness.

As soon as men began to value one another, and the idea of consideration had got a footing in the mind, every one put in his claim to it, and it became impossible to refuse it to any with impunity. Hence arose the first obligations of civility even among savages; and every intended injury became an affront; because, besides the hurt which might result from it, the party injured was certain to find in it a contempt for his person, which was often more insupportable than the hurt itself. . . .

It now became the interest of men to appear what they really were not. To be and to seem became two totally different things; and from this distinction sprang insolent pomp and cheating trickery, with all the numerous vices that go in their train. On the other hand, free and independent as men were before, they were now, in consequence of a multiplicity of new wants, brought into subjection, as it were, to all nature, and particularly to one another; and each became in some degree a slave even in becoming the master of other men: if rich, they stood in need of the service of others; if poor, of their assistance; and even a middle condition did not enable them to do without one another. Man must now, therefore, have been perpetually employed in getting others to interest themselves in his lot, and in making them, apparently at least, if not really, find their advantage in promoting his own. Thus he must have been sly and artful in his behaviour to some, and imperious and cruel to others; being under a kind of necessity to ill-use all the persons of whom he stood in need, when he could not frighten them into compliance, and did not judge it his interest to be useful to them. Insatiable ambition, the thirst of raising their respective fortunes, not so much from real want as from the desire to surpass others, inspired all men with a vile propensity to injure one another, and with a secret jealousy, which is the more dangerous, as it puts on the mask of benevolence, to carry its point with greater security. In a word, there arose rivalry and competition on the one hand, and conflicting interests on the other, together with a secret desire on both of profiting at the expense of others. All these evils were the first effects of property, and the inseparable attendants of growing inequality. ...

The original man having vanished by degrees, society offers to us only an assembly of artificial men and factitious passions, which are the work of all these new relations, and without any real foundation in nature. We are taught nothing on this subject, by reflection, that is not entirely confirmed by observation. The savage and the civilized man differ so much in the bottom of their hearts and in their inclinations, that what constitutes the supreme happiness of one would reduce the other to despair. The former breathes only peace and liberty; he desires only to live and be free from labour; even the *ataraxia* of the Stoic falls far short of his profound indifference to every other object. Civilized man, on the other hand, is always moving, sweating, toiling, and racking his brains to find still more laborious occupations: he goes on in drudgery to his last moment, and even seeks death to put himself in a position to live, or renounces life to acquire immortality. He pays his court to men in power, whom he hates, and to the wealthy, whom he despises; he stops at nothing to have the honour of serving them; he is not ashamed to value himself on his own meanness and their protection; and, proud of his slavery, he speaks with disdain of those, who have not the honour of sharing it. What a sight would the perplexing and envied labours of a European minister of State present to the eyes of a Caribbean! How many cruel deaths would not this indolent savage prefer to the horrors of such a life, which is seldom even sweetened by the pleasure of doing good! But, for him to see into the motives of all this solicitude the words 'power' and 'reputation' would have to bear some meaning in his mind; he would have to know that there are men who set a value on the opinion of the rest of the world; who can be made happy and satisfied with themselves rather on the testimony of other people than on their own. In reality, the source of all these differences is, that the savage lives within himself, while social man lives constantly outside himself, and only knows how to live in the opinion of others, so that he seems to receive the consciousness of his own existence merely from the judgment of others concerning him. ...

A famous author, reckoning up the good and evil of human life, and comparing the aggregates, finds that our pains greatly exceed our pleasures: so that, all things considered, human life is not at all a valuable gift. This conclusion does not surprise me; for the writer drew all his arguments from man in civilization. Had he gone back to the state of nature, his inquiries would clearly have had a different result, and man would have been seen to be subject to very few evils not of his own creation. It has indeed cost us not a little trouble to make ourselves as wretched as we are. When we consider, on the one hand, the immense labours of mankind, the many sciences brought to perfection, the arts invented, the powers employed, the deeps filled up, the mountains levelled, the rocks shattered, the rivers made navigable, the tracts of land cleared, the lakes emptied, the marshes drained, the enormous structures erected on land, and the teeming vessels that cover the sea; and, on the other hand, estimate with ever so little thought, the real advantages that have accrued from all these works to mankind, we cannot help being amazed at the vast disproportion there is between these things, and deploring the infatuation of man, which, to gratify his silly pride and vain self-admiration, induces him eagerly to pursue all the miseries he is capable of feeling, though beneficent nature had kindly placed them out of his way. ...

What, then, is to be done? Must societies be totally abolished? Must *meum* and *tuum* be annihilated, and must we return again to the forests to live among bears? This is a deduction in the manner of my adversaries, which I would as soon anticipate as let them have the shame of drawing. O you, who have never heard the voice of heaven, who think man destined only to live this little life and die in peace, you, who can resign in the midst of populous cities your fatal acquisitions, your restless spirits, your corrupt hearts and endless desires; resume, since it depends entirely on yourselves, your ancient and primitive innocence: retire to the woods, there to lose the sight and remembrance of the crimes of your contemporaries; and be not apprehensive of degrading your species, by renouncing its advances in order to renounce its vices. As for men like me, whose passions have destroyed their original simplicity, who can no longer subsist on plants or acorns, or live without laws and magistrates; those who were honoured in their first father with supernatural instructions; those who discover, in the design of giving human actions at the start a morality which they must otherwise have been so long in acquiring, the reason for a precept in itself indifferent and inexplicable on every other system; those, in short, who are persuaded that the Divine Being has called all mankind to be partakers in the happiness and perfection of celestial intelligences, all these will endeavour to merit the eternal prize they are to expect from the practice of those virtues, which they make themselves follow in learning to know them. They will respect the sacred bonds of their respective communities; they will love their fellow-citizens, and serve them with all their might: they will scrupulously obey the laws, and all those who make or administer them; they will particularly honour those wise and good princes, who find means of preventing, curing, or even palliating all these evils and abuses, by which we are constantly threatened; they will animate the zeal of their deserving rulers, by showing them, without flattery or fear, the importance of their office and the severity of their duty. But they will not therefore have less contempt for a constitution that cannot support itself without the aid of so many splendid characters, much oftener wished for than found; and from which, notwithstanding all their pains and solicitude, there always arise more real calamities than even apparent advantages.

NOTES

1 [Justin, *Hist.* ii, 2. So much more does the ignorance of vice profit the one sort than the knowledge of virtue the other.]

2 *Amour-propre* must not be confused with love of self: for they differ both in themselves and in their effects. Love of self is a natural feeling which leads every animal to look to its own preservation, and which, guided in man by reason and modified by compassion, creates humanity and virtue. *Amour-propre* is a purely relative and factitious feeling, which arises in the state of society, leads each individual to make more of himself than of any other, causes all the mutual damage men inflict one on another, and is the real source of the 'sense of honour'. This being understood, I maintain that, in our primitive condition, in the true state of nature, *amour-propre* did not exist; for as each man regarded himself as the only observer of his actions, the only being in the universe who took any interest in him, and the sole judge of his deserts, no feeling arising from comparisons he could not be led to make could take root in his soul; and for the same reason he could know neither hatred nor the desire for revenge, since these passions can spring only from a sense of injury: and as it is the contempt or the intention to hurt, and not the harm done, which constitutes the injury, men who neither valued nor compared themselves could do one another much violence, when it suited them, without feeling any sense of injury. In a word, each man, regarding his fellows almost as he regarded animals of different species, might seize the prey of a weaker or yield up his own to a stronger, and yet consider these acts of violence as mere natural occurrences, without the slightest emotion of insolence or despite, or any other feeling than the joy or grief of success or failure.

19

Of the Natural Condition of Mankind as Concerning their Felicity, and Misery

Thomas Hobbes

Hobbes's account of original man, and of life in the state of nature, differs sharply from that of Rousseau. According to Hobbes (1588–1679), the establishment of society and the constraints of law are to be commended because they rescue men from a state of constant enmity against each other, with 'continual fear, and danger of violent death'. (He ascribes this kind of life to savages in the existing world, contrary to Rousseau's favourable view of them.) However, the contrast between the two thinkers is not so straightforward. For Hobbes ascribes to pre-social man motives which, according to Rousseau, come into being only after the fatal loss of innocence; for example, 'pleasure in contemplating their own power', which, according to Hobbes, leads men to pursue their conquests 'farther than their security requires'. This is typical of the motives classified by Rousseau under amour-propre; and Rousseau himself accused Hobbes of 'having improperly admitted' such passions to his account of original man. (I have printed the reading from Rousseau first, because it gives a fuller statement of the whole subject.) In making the comparison between social and 'original' man, it is necessary to consider where the dividing line should be drawn; but this may involve difficult questions about the coherence (in the logical sense) of intermediate stages, and about the origin of language.

Nature hath made men so equal, in the faculties of the body, and mind; as that though there be found one man sometimes manifestly stronger in body, or of quicker mind than another; yet when all is reckoned together, the difference between man, and man, is not so considerable, as that one man can thereupon claim to himself any benefit, to which another may not pretend, as well as he. For as to the strength of body, the weakest has strength enough to kill the strongest, either by secret machination, or by confederacy with others, that are in the same danger with himself.

And as to the faculties of the mind, setting aside the arts grounded upon words, and especially that skill of proceeding upon general, and infallible rules, called science; which very few have, and but in few things; as being not a native faculty, born with us; nor attained, as prudence, while we look after somewhat else, I find yet a greater equality amongst men, than that of strength. For prudence, is but experience; which equal time, equally bestows on all men, in those things they equally apply themselves unto. That which may perhaps make such equality incredible, is but a vain conceit of one's own wisdom, which almost all men think they have in a greater degree, than the vulgar; that is, than all men but themselves, and a few others, whom by fame, or for concurring with themselves, they approve. For such is the nature of men, that howsoever they may acknowledge many others to be more witty, or more eloquent, or more learned; yet they will hardly believe there be many so wise as themselves; for they see their own wit at hand, and other men's at a distance. But this proveth rather that men are in that point equal, than unequal. For there is not ordinarily a greater sign of the equal distribution of any thing, than that every man is contented with his share.

From this equality of ability, ariseth equality of hope in the attaining of our ends. And therefore if any two men desire the same thing, which nevertheless they cannot both enjoy, they become enemies; and in the way to their end, which is principally their own conservation, and sometimes their delectation only, endeavour to destroy, or subdue one another. And from hence it comes to pass, that where an invader hath no more to fear, than another man's single power; if one plant, sow, build, or possess a convenient seat, others may probably be expected to come prepared with forces united, to dispossess, and deprive him, not only of the fruit of his labour, but also of his life, or liberty. And the invader again is in the like danger of another.

And from this diffidence of one another, there is no way for any man to secure himself, so reasonable, as anticipation; that is, by force, or wiles, to master the persons of all men he can, so long, till he see no other power great enough to endanger him: and this is no more than his own conservation requireth, and is generally allowed. Also because there be some, that taking pleasure in contemplating their own power in the acts of conquest, which they pursue farther than their security requires; if others, that otherwise would be glad to be at ease within modest bounds, should not by invasion increase their power, they would not be able, long time, by standing only on their defence, to subsist. And by consequence, such augmentation of dominion over men being necessary to a man's conservation, it ought to be allowed him.

Again, men have no pleasure, but on the contrary a great deal of grief, in keeping company, where there is no power able to over-awe them all. For every man looketh that his companion should value him, at the same rate he sets upon himself: and upon all signs of contempt, or undervaluing, naturally endeavours, as far as he dares (which amongst them that have no common power to keep them in quiet, is far enough to make them destroy each other) to extort a greater value from his contemners, by damage; and from others, by the example.

So that in the nature of man, we find three principal causes of quarrel. First, competition; secondly, diffidence; thirdly, glory.

The first, maketh men invade for gain; the second, for safety; and the third, for reputation. The first use violence, to make themselves masters of other men's persons, wives, children, and cattle; the second, to defend them; the third, for trifles, as a word, a smile, a different opinion, and any other sign of undervalue, either direct in their persons, or by reflection in their kindred, their friends, their nation, their profession, or their name.

Hereby it is manifest, that during the time men live without a common power to keep them all in awe, they are in that condition which is called war; and such a war, as is of every man, against every man. For WAR, consisteth not in battle only, or the act of fighting; but in a tract of time, wherein the will to contend by battle is sufficiently known: and therefore the notion of *time*, is to be considered in the nature of war; as it is in the nature of weather. For as the nature of foul weather, lieth not in a shower or two of rain; but in an inclination thereto of many days together: so the nature of war, consisteth not in actual fighting; but in the known disposition thereto, during all the time there is no assurance to the contrary. All other time is PEACE.

Whatsoever therefore is consequent to a time of war, where every man is enemy to every man; the same is consequent to the time, wherein men live without other security, than what their own strength, and their own invention shall furnish them withal. In such condition, there is no place for industry; because the fruit thereof is uncertain: and consequently no culture of the earth; no navigation, nor use of the commodities that may be imported by sea; no commodious building; no instruments of moving, and removing, such things as require much force; no knowledge of the face of the earth; no account of time; no arts; no letters; no society; and which is worst of all, continual fear, and danger of violent death; and the life of man, solitary, poor, nasty, brutish, and short.

It may seem strange to some man, that has not well weighed these things; that nature should thus dissociate, and render men apt to invade, and destroy one another: and he may therefore, not trusting to this inference, made from the passions, desire perhaps to have the same confirmed by experience. Let him therefore consider with himself, when taking a journey, he arms himself, and seeks to go well accompanied; when going to sleep, he locks his doors; when even in his house he locks his chests; and this when he knows there be laws, and public officers, armed, to revenge all injuries shall be done him; what opinion he has of his fellow-subjects, when he rides armed; of his fellow citizens, when he locks his doors; and of his children, and servants, when he locks his chests. Does he not there as much accuse mankind by his actions, as I do by my words? But neither of us accuse man's nature in it. The desires, and other passions of man, are in themselves no sin. No more are the actions, that proceed from those passions, till they know a law that forbids them: which till laws be made they cannot know: nor can any law be made, till they have agreed upon the person that shall make it.

It may peradventure be thought, there was never such a time, nor condition of war as this; and I believe it was never generally so, over all the world: but there are many places, where they live so now. For the savage people in many places of America, except the government of small families, the concord whereof dependeth on natural lust, have no government at all; and live at this day in that brutish manner, as I said before. Howsoever, it may be perceived what manner of life there would be, where there were no common power to fear, by the manner of life, which men that have formerly lived under a peaceful government, use to degenerate into, in a civil war.

But though there had never been any time, wherein particular men were in a condition of war one against another; yet in all times, kings, and persons of sovereign authority, because of their independency, are in continual jealousies, and in the state and posture of gladiators; having their weapons pointing, and their eyes fixed on one another; that is, their forts, garrisons, and guns upon the frontiers of their kingdoms; and continual spies upon their neighbours; which is a posture of war. But because they uphold thereby, the industry of their subjects; there does not follow from it, that misery, which accompanies the liberty of particular men.

To this war of every man, against every man, this also is consequent; that nothing can be unjust. The notions of right and wrong, justice and injustice have there no place. Where there is no common power, there is no law: where no law, no injustice. Force, and fraud, are in war the two cardinal virtues. Justice, and injustice are none of the faculties neither of the body, nor mind. If they were, they might be in a man that were alone in the world, as well as his senses, and passions. They are qualities, that relate to men in society, not in solitude. It is consequent also to the same condition, that there be no propriety, no dominion, no *mine* and *thine* distinct; but only that to be every man's, that he can get; and for so long, as he can keep it. And thus much for the ill condition, which man by mere nature is actually placed in; though with a possibility to come out of it, consisting partly in the passions, partly in his reason.

The passions that incline men to peace, are fear of death; desire of such things as are necessary to commodious living; and a hope by their industry to obtain them. And reason suggesteth convenient articles of peace, upon which men may be drawn to agreement.

20

Man and the State

Aristotle

On the title page of Rousseau's Discourse, *the following quotation from Aristotle (384–322 BC) appeared as a motto: 'We should consider what is natural not in things which are depraved but in those which are rightly ordered according to nature.' According to Rousseau, as we have seen, man was rightly ordered according to nature in his original state, before the emergence of societies. But Aristotle's view of nature was very different. He held that the essential nature of a thing was to be found in its potential development rather than its actual or original condition; and this was true especially of man. Man, he declares, 'is by nature a political animal', because that is where his natural* development *lies. Here we broach the idea of 'self-realization', which is taken further in section four. (The word 'political', as used by Aristotle, refers to the* polis *or city-state, such as Athens. Thus a 'political' man would be one who belongs to such an organization.)*

1252b27 The final association, formed of several villages, is the state. For all practical purposes the process is now complete; self-sufficiency[1] has been reached, and while the state came about as a means of securing life itself, it continues in being to secure the *good* life. Therefore every state exists by nature, as the earlier associations too were natural. This association is the end of those others, and nature is itself an end; for whatever is the end-product of the coming into existence of any object, that is what we call its nature – of a man, for instance, or a horse or a household. Moreover the aim and the end is perfection; and self-sufficiency is both end and perfection.[2]

1253a1 It follows that the state belongs to the class of objects which exist by nature, and that man is by nature a political animal.[3] Any one who by his nature and not simply by ill-luck has no state is either too bad or too good, either subhuman or superhuman – he is like the war-mad man condemned in Homer's words[4] as 'having no family, no law,[5] no home'; for he who is such[6] by nature is made on war: he is a non-cooperator like an isolated piece in a game of draughts.

1253a7 But obviously man is a political animal[7] in a sense in which a bee is not, or any other gregarious animal.[8] Nature, as we say, does nothing without some purpose; and she has endowed man alone among the animals with the power of speech. Speech is something different from voice, which is possessed by other animals also and used by them to express pain or pleasure; for their nature does indeed enable them not only to feel[9] pleasure and pain but to communicate these feelings to each other. Speech, on the other hand serves to indicate what is useful and what is harmful, and so also what is just and what is unjust. For the real difference between man and other animals is that humans alone have perception[10] of good and evil, just and unjust, etc. It is the sharing of a common view in *these* matters that makes a household and a state.

1253a18 Furthermore, the state has priority over the household and over any individual among us. For the whole must be prior to the part. Separate hand or foot from the whole body, and they will no longer be hand or foot except in name, as one might speak of a 'hand' or 'foot' sculptured in stone. That will be the condition of the spoilt[11] hand, which no longer has the capacity and the function which define it. So, though we may say they have the same names, we cannot say that they are, in that condition,[12] the same things. It is clear then that the state is both natural and prior to the individual. For if an individual is not fully self-sufficient after separation, he will stand in the same relationship to the whole as the parts in the other case do.[13] Whatever is incapable of participating in the association which we call the state, a dumb animal for example, and equally whatever is perfectly self-sufficient and has no need to (e.g. a god), is not a part of the state at all.

1253a29 Among all men, then, there is a natural impulse towards this kind of association; and the first man to construct a state deserves credit for conferring very great benefits. For as man is the best of all animals when he has reached his full development, so he is worst of all when divorced from law and justice. Injustice armed is hardest to deal with; and though man is born with weapons which he can use in the service of practical wisdom and virtue, it is all too easy for him to use them for the opposite purposes. Hence man without virtue is the most savage, the most unrighteous, and the worst in regard to sexual licence and gluttony. The virtue of justice is a feature of a state; for justice is the arrangement of the political association,[14] and a sense of justice decides what is just.[15]

NOTES

1 *Autarkeia*, 'political and/or economic independence'. Aristotle's use of the word here is however somewhat wider than this, and embraces opportunities to live the 'good' life according to the human virtues.

2 Aristotle makes succinct use of his teleological technicalities: the 'aim' ('that-for-the-sake-of-which', *to hou heneka*) is the 'final cause', the 'end' or purpose

towards which a process of development is directed and in which it culminates.

3   *Politikon zōon*, 'who lives/whose nature is to live, in a *polis* (state)'; cf.
    Nicomachean Ethics, I vii *ad fin.*

4   *Iliad* IX, 63.

5   *Athemistos.*

6   I.e. without a state. It is such a person's *pugnacity* that Aristotle seems to regard
    as marking him out as in some sense non-human; cf. *Nicomachean Ethics*
    1177b9.

7   See note 3.

8   A slightly comic sentence; but obviously it is the notion of the state as an
    association that Aristotle has in mind. On this sentence see R. G. Mulgan ,
    'Aristotle's doctrine that man is a political animal', *Hermes*, 102 (1974),
    pp. 438–45, and cf. Aristotle, *History of Animals* 487b33–488a13.

9   *Aisthēsis.*

10 See note 9.

11 Literally 'destroyed', 'ruined' (by the dismemberment apparently envisaged in
    the preceding sentence).

12 Of not having a function and a capacity.

13 E.g. limbs (individuals : state :: limbs : body).

14 *Politikēs koinōnias taxis*, 'the framework or organization of the association that
    takes the form of a *polis* (state)'.

15 In this paragraph *dikaiosunē*, the 'virtue' or 'sense' of justice, seems to be
    distinguished from *dikē*, 'justice', the concrete expression or embodiment of
    that virtue or sense in a legal and administrative system. 'What is just' (*dikaion*)
    evidently means particular and individual just relationships arrived at or (in
    courts) re-established by the application of *dikaiosunē* through the medium of
    the system of justice, or just system, *dikē*.

21

Nature

John Stuart Mill

The reading from Mill (1806–73) is not about the emergence of man from an original state of nature, but about the moral approbation with which nature is, in various ways, regarded. Contrary to the precept that we should 'act according to nature', he points out that to a large extent human activities represent a struggle against nature, and that we frequently admire the 'triumphs of Art over Nature'. This admiration is perhaps less common today than in Mill's time, for we have seen rather too much of the defeat of nature. But the fact remains that without the constant support of science and technology in overcoming nature (for example in the medical field) we would be deprived of many of the good things of life (and, in some cases, life itself). Turning to the case of human *nature, Mill is able to claim that crime is no less natural than virtue. 'The acquisition of virtue', he writes, 'has in all ages been accounted a work of labour and difficulty'; so in this sense too we need to overcome rather than to follow nature.*

Mill's feelings about nature are clearly very different from those of Rousseau. But what exactly is the issue on which they disagree? Rousseau might have replied that Mill's remarks apply to man as he is now, and not as he was in his original, natural state. The latter, he might say, would not need the triumphs of art over nature; and the concepts of crime or virtue would not be applicable to him, any more than to non-human animals. (A similar point is made by Hobbes: the desires and actions of men, he writes, 'are in themselves no sin ... till they know a law that forbids them'.) What about the comparison between man in the natural state and man as he is now? Rousseau's balance-sheet ('reckoning up the good and evil of human life') is clearly on the side of natural man, but Mill would give the opposite verdict. 'It is better', he writes in the extract in section four, 'to be a human being dissatisfied than a pig satisfied; better to be Socrates dissatisfied than a fool satisfied'.

Mill also draws attention to aspects of non-human nature which might be thought morally repugnant – the pain and suffering inflicted by animals on other animals (nature 'red in tooth and claw', to use Tennyson's phrase). This aspect of nature needs to be considered by those (like Singer in section two) who regard the preservation of natural habitats as a moral duty.

Nature, natural, and the group of words derived from them, or allied to them in etymology, have at all times filled a great place in the thoughts and taken a strong hold on the feelings of mankind. That they should have done so is not surprising, when we consider what the words, in their primitive and most obvious signification, represent; but it is unfortunate that a set of terms which play so great a part in moral and metaphysical speculation, should have acquired many meanings different from the primary one, yet sufficiently allied to it to admit of confusion. The words have thus become entangled in so many foreign associations, mostly of a very powerful and tenacious character, that they have come to excite, and to be the symbols of, feelings which their original meaning will by no means justify; and which have made them one of the most copious sources of false taste, false philosophy, false morality, and even bad law. ...

When it is asserted, or implied, that Nature, or the laws of Nature, should be conformed to, is the Nature which is meant, Nature in the first sense of the term, meaning all which is – the powers and properties of all things? But in this signification, there is no need of a recommendation to act according to nature, since it is what nobody can possibly help doing, and equally whether he acts well or ill. There is no mode of acting which is not conformable to Nature in this sense of the term, and all modes of acting are so in exactly the same degree. Every action is the exertion of some natural power, and its effects of all sorts are so many phenomena of nature, produced by the powers and properties of some of the objects of nature, in exact obedience to some law or laws of nature. When I voluntarily use my organs to take in food, the act, and its consequences, take place according to laws of nature: if instead of food I swallow poison, the case is exactly the same. To bid people conform to the laws of nature when they have no power but what the laws of nature give them – when it is a physical impossibility for them to do the smallest thing otherwise than through some law of nature, is an absurdity. ...

Let us then consider whether we can attach any meaning to the supposed practical maxim of following Nature, in [the] second sense of the word, in which Nature stands for that which takes place without human intervention. In Nature as thus understood, is the spontaneous course of things when left to themselves, the rule to be followed in endeavouring to adapt things to our use? But it is evident at once that the maxim, taken in this sense, is not merely, as it is in the other sense, superfluous and unmeaning, but palpably absurd and self-contradictory. For while human action cannot help conforming to nature in the one meaning of the term, the very aim and object of action is to alter and improve Nature in the other meaning. If the natural course of things were perfectly right and satisfactory, to act at all would be a gratuitous meddling, which as it could not make things better, must make them worse. Or if action at all could be justified, it would only be when in direct obedience to instincts, since these might perhaps be accounted part of the spontaneous order of Nature; but to do anything with forethought and purpose, would be a violation of that perfect order. If the artificial is not better than the natural, to what end are all the arts of life? To dig, to plough, to build, to wear clothes, are direct infringements of the injunction to follow nature.

Accordingly it would be said by every one, even of those most under the influence of the feelings which prompt the injunction, that to apply it to such cases as those just spoken of, would be to push it too far. Everybody professes to approve and admire many great triumphs of Art over Nature: the junction by bridges of shores which nature had made separate, the draining of Nature's marshes, the excavation of her wells, the dragging to light of what she has buried at immense depths in the earth; the turning away of her thunderbolts by lightning rods, of her inundations by embankments, of her ocean by breakwaters. But to commend these and similar feats, is to acknowledge that the ways of nature are to be conquered, not obeyed: that her powers are often towards man in the position of enemies, from whom he must wrest, by force and ingenuity, what little he can for his own use, and deserves to be applauded when that little is rather more than might be expected from his physical weakness in comparison to those gigantic powers. All praise of Civilization, or Art, or Contrivance, is so much dispraise of Nature; an admission of imperfection, which it is man's business, and merit, to be always endeavouring to correct or mitigate.

. . .

In considering this subject it is necessary to divest ourselves of certain preconceptions which may justly be called natural prejudices, being grounded on feelings which, in themselves natural and inevitable, intrude into matters with which they ought to have no concern. One of these feelings is the astonishment, rising into awe, which is inspired (even independently of all religious sentiment) by any of the greater natural phenomena. A hurricane; a mountain precipice; the desert; the ocean, either agitated or at rest; the solar system, and the great cosmic forces which hold it together; the boundless firmament, and to an educated mind any single star; excite feelings which make all human enterprises and powers appear so insignificant, that to a mind thus occupied it seems insufferable presumption in so puny a creature as man to look critically on things so far above him, or dare to measure himself against the grandeur of the universe. But a little interrogation of our own consciousness will suffice to convince us, that what makes these phenomena so impressive is simply their vastness. The enormous extension in space and time, or the enormous power they exemplify, constitutes their sublimity; a feeling in all cases, more allied to terror than to any moral emotion. And though the vast scale of these phenomena may well excite wonder, and sets at defiance all idea of rivalry, the feeling it inspires is of a totally different character from admiration of excellence. Those in whom awe produces admiration may be aesthetically developed, but they are morally uncultivated. It is one of the endowments of the imaginative part of our mental nature that conceptions of greatness and power, vividly realized, produce a feeling which though in its higher degrees closely bordering on pain, we prefer to most of what are accounted pleasures. But we are quite equally capable of experiencing this feeling towards maleficent power; and we never experience it so strongly towards most of the powers of the universe, as when we have most present to our consciousness a vivid sense of their capacity of inflicting evil. Because these natural powers have what we cannot imitate, enormous might, and overawe us by that one attribute, it would be a great error to infer that their other attributes are such as we ought to emulate, or that we should be justified in using our small powers after the example which Nature sets us with her vast forces.

For, how stands the fact? That next to the greatness of these cosmic forces, the quality which most forcibly strikes every one who does not avert his eyes from it, is their perfect and absolute recklessness. They go straight to their end, without regarding what or whom they crush on the road. Optimists, in their attempts to prove that 'whatever is, is right', are obliged to maintain, not that Nature ever turns one step from her path to avoid trampling us into destruction, but that it would be very unreasonable in us to expect that she should. Pope's 'Shall gravitation cease when you go by?' may be a just rebuke to any one who should be so silly as to expect common human morality from nature. But if the question were between two men, instead of between a man and a natural phenomenon, that triumphant apostrophe would be thought a rare piece of impudence. A man who should persist in hurling stones or firing cannon when another man 'goes by', and having killed him should urge a similar plea in exculpation, would very deservedly be found guilty of murder.

In sober truth, nearly all the things which men are hanged or imprisoned for doing to one another, are nature's every day performances. Killing, the most criminal act recognized by human laws, Nature does once to every being that lives; and in a large proportion of cases, after protracted tortures such as only the greatest monsters whom we read of ever purposely inflicted on their living fellow-creatures. If, by an arbitrary reservation, we refuse to account anything murder but what abridges a certain term supposed to be allotted to human life, nature also does this to all but a small percentage of lives, and does it in all the modes, violent or insidious, in which the worst human beings take the lives of one another. Nature impales men, breaks them as if on the wheel, casts them to be devoured by wild beasts, burns them to death, crushes them with stones like the first christian martyr, starves them with hunger, freezes them with cold, poisons them by the quick or slow venom of her exhalations, and has hundreds of other hideous deaths in reserve, such as the ingenious cruelty of a Nabis or a Domitian never surpassed. All this, Nature does with the most supercilious disregard both of mercy and of justice, emptying her shafts upon the best and noblest indifferently with the meanest and worst; upon those who are engaged in the highest and worthiest enterprises, and often as the direct consequence of the noblest acts; and it might almost be imagined as a punishment for them. She mows down those on whose existence hangs the well-being of a whole people, perhaps the prospects of the human race for generations to come, with as little compunction as those whose death is a relief to themselves, or a blessing to those under their noxious influence. Such are Nature's dealings with life. Even when she does not intend to kill, she inflicts the same tortures in apparent wantonness. In the clumsy provision which she has made for that perpetual renewal of animal life, rendered necessary by the prompt termination she puts to it in every individual instance, no human being ever comes into the world but another human being is literally stretched on the rack for hours or days, not unfrequently issuing in death. Next to taking life (equal to it according to a high authority) is taking the means by which we live; and Nature does this too on the largest scale and with the most callous indifference. A single hurricane destroys the hopes of a season; a flight of locusts, or an inundation, desolates a district; a trifling chemical change in an edible root, starves a million of people. The waves of the sea, like banditti seize and appropriate the wealth of the rich and the little all of the poor with the same accompaniments of stripping, wounding, and killing as their human antitypes. Everything in short, which the worst men commit either against life or property is perpetrated on a larger scale by natural agents. Nature has Noyades more fatal than those of Carrier; her explosions of fire damp are as destructive as human artillery; her plague and cholera far surpass the poison cups of the Borgias. Even the love of 'order' which is thought to be a following of the ways of Nature, is in fact a contradiction of them. All which people are accustomed to deprecate as 'disorder' and its consequences, is precisely a counterpart of Nature's ways. Anarchy and the Reign of Terror are overmatched in injustice, ruin, and death, by a hurricane and a pestilence.

But, it is said, all these things are for wise and good ends. On this I must first remark that whether they are so or not, is altogether beside the point. Supposing it true that contrary to appearances these horrors when perpetrated by Nature, promote good ends, still as no one believes that good ends would be promoted by our following the example, the course of Nature cannot be a proper model for us to imitate. Either it is right that we should kill because nature kills; torture because nature tortures; ruin and devastate because nature does the like; or we ought not to consider at all what nature does, but what it is good to do. ...

I shall not here enter into the difficult psychological question, what are, or are not instincts: the subject would require a volume to itself. Without touching upon any disputed theoretical points, it is possible to judge how little worthy is the instinctive part of human nature to be held up as its chief excellence – as the part in which the hand of infinite goodness and wisdom is peculiarly visible. Allowing everything to be an instinct which anybody has ever asserted to be one, it remains true that nearly every respectable attribute of humanity is the result not of instinct, but of a victory over instinct; and that there is hardly anything valuable in the natural man except capacities – a whole world of possibilities, all of them dependent upon eminently artificial discipline for being realized.

It is only in a highly artificialized condition of human nature that the notion grew up, or, I believe, ever could have grown up, that goodness was natural: because only after a long course of artificial education did good sentiments become so habitual, and so predominant over bad, as to arise unprompted when occasion called for them. In the times when mankind were nearer to their natural state, cultivated observers regarded the natural man as a sort of wild animal, distinguished chiefly by being craftier than the other beasts of the field; and all worth of character was deemed the result of a sort of taming; a phrase often applied by the ancient philosophers to the appropriate discipline of human beings. The truth is that there is hardly a single point of excellence belonging to human character, which is not decidedly repugnant to the untutored feelings of human nature. If there be a virtue which more than any other we expect to find, and really do find, in an uncivilized state, it is the virtue of courage. Yet this is from first to last a victory achieved over one of the most powerful emotions of human nature. If there is any one feeling or attribute more natural than all others to human beings, it is fear; and no greater proof can be given of the power of artificial discipline than the conquest which it has at all times and places shown itself capable of achieving over so mighty and so universal a sentiment. The widest difference no doubt exists between one human being and another in the facility or difficulty with which they acquire this virtue. There is hardly any department of human excellence in which difference of original temperament goes so far. But it may fairly be questioned if any human being is naturally courageous. Many are naturally pugnacious, or irascible, or enthusiastic, and these passions when strongly excited may render them insensible to fear. But take away the conflicting emotion, and fear reasserts its dominion: consistent courage is always the effect of cultivation. The courage which is occasionally though by no means generally found among tribes of savages, is as much the result of education as that of the Spartans or Romans. In all such tribes there is a most emphatic direction of the public sentiment into every channel of expression through which honour can be paid to courage and cowardice held up to contempt and derision. It will perhaps be said, that as the expression of a sentiment implies the sentiment itself, the training of the young to courage presupposes an originally courageous people. It presupposes only what all good customs presuppose – that there must have been individuals better than the rest, who set the customs going. Some individuals, who like other people had fears to conquer, must have had strength of mind and will to conquer them for themselves. These would obtain the influence belonging to heroes, for that which is at once astonishing and obviously useful never fails to be admired: and partly through this admiration, partly through the fear they themselves excite, they would obtain the power of legislators, and could establish whatever customs they pleased.

Let us next consider a quality which forms the most visible, and one of the most radical of the moral distinctions between human beings and most of the lower animals; that of which the absence, more than of anything else, renders men bestial; the quality of cleanliness. Can anything be more entirely artificial? Children, and the lower classes of most countries, seem to be actually fond of dirt: the vast majority of the human race are indifferent to it: whole nations of otherwise civilized and cultivated human beings tolerate it in some of its worst forms, and only a very small minority are consistently offended by it. Indeed the universal law of the subject appears to be, that uncleanliness offends only those to whom it is unfamiliar, so that those who have lived in so artificial a state as to be unused to it in any form, are the sole persons whom it disgusts in all forms. Of all virtues this is the most evidently not instinctive, but a triumph over instinct. Assuredly neither cleanliness nor the love of cleanliness is natural to man, but only the capacity of acquiring a love of cleanliness.

Our examples have thus far been taken from the personal, or as they are called by Bentham, the self-regarding virtues, because these, if any, might be supposed to be congenial even to the uncultivated mind. Of the social virtues it is almost superfluous to speak; so completely is it the verdict of all experience that selfishness is natural. By this I do not in any wise mean to deny that sympathy is natural also; I believe on the contrary that on that important fact rests the possibility of any cultivation of goodness and nobleness, and the hope of their ultimate entire ascendancy. But sympathetic characters, left uncultivated, and given up to their sympathetic instincts, are as selfish as others. The difference is in the *kind* of selfishness: theirs is not solitary but sympathetic selfishness; *l'egoïsme à deux, à trois*, or *à quatre*; and they may be very amiable and delightful to those with whom they sympathize, and grossly unjust and unfeeling to the rest of the world. Indeed the finer nervous organizations which are most capable of and most require sympathy, have, from their fineness, so much stronger impulses of all sorts, that they often furnish the most striking examples of selfishness, though of a less repulsive kind than that of colder natures. Whether there ever was a person in whom, apart from all teaching of instructors, friends or books, and from all intentional self-modelling according to an ideal, natural benevolence was a more powerful attribute than selfishness in any of its forms, may remain undecided. That such cases are extremely rare, every one must admit, and this is enough for the argument. ...

Veracity might seem, of all virtues, to have the most plausible claim to being natural, since in the absence of motives to the contrary, speech usually conforms to, or at least does not intentionally deviate from, fact. Accordingly this is the virtue with which writers like Rousseau delight in decorating savage life, and setting it in advantageous contrast with the treachery and trickery of civilization. Unfortunately this is a mere fancy picture, contradicted by all the realities of savage life. Savages are always liars. They have not the faintest notion of truth as a virtue. They have a notion of not betraying to their hurt, as of not hurting in any other way, persons to whom they are bound by some special tie of obligation; their chief, their guest, perhaps, or their friend: these feelings of obligation being the taught morality of the savage state, growing out of its characteristic circumstances. But of any point of honour respecting truth for truth's sake, they have not the remotest idea; no more than the whole East, and the greater part of Europe: and in the few countries which are sufficiently improved to have such a point of honour, it is confined to a small minority, who alone, under any circumstances of real temptation practise it. ...

With regard to this particular hypothesis, that all natural impulses, all propensities sufficiently universal and sufficiently spontaneous to be capable of passing for instincts, must exist for good ends, and ought to be only regulated, not repressed; this is of course true of the majority of them, for the species could not have continued to exist unless most of its inclinations had been directed to things needful or useful for its preservation. But unless the instincts can be reduced to a very small number indeed, it must be allowed that we have also bad instincts which it should be the aim of education not simply to regulate but to extirpate, or rather (what can be done even to an instinct) to starve them by disuse. Those who are inclined to multiply the number of instincts, usually include among them one which they call destructiveness: an instinct to destroy for destruction's sake. I can conceive no good reason for preserving this, no more than another propensity which if not an instinct is very like one, what has been called the instinct of domination; a delight in exercising despotism, in holding other beings in subjection to our will. The man who takes pleasure in the mere exertion of authority, apart from the purpose for which it is to be employed, is the last person in whose hands one would willingly entrust it. Again, there are persons who are cruel by character, or, as the phrase is, naturally cruel; who have a real pleasure in inflicting, or seeing the infliction of pain. This kind of cruelty is not mere hardheartedness, absence of pity or remorse; it is a positive thing; a particular kind of voluptuous excitement. The East, and Southern Europe, have afforded, and probably still afford, abundant examples of this hateful propensity. I suppose it will be granted that this is not one of the natural inclinations which it would be wrong to suppress. The only question would be whether it is not a duty to suppress the man himself along with it.

But even if it were true that every one of the elementary impulses of human nature has its good side, and may by a sufficient amount of artificial training be made more useful than hurtful; how little would this amount to, when it must in any case be admitted that without such training all of them, even those which are necessary to our preservation, would fill the world with misery, making human life an exaggerated likeness of the odious scene of violence and tyranny which is exhibited by the rest of the animal kingdom, except in so far as tamed and disciplined by man. There, indeed, those who flatter themselves with the notion of reading the purposes of the Creator in his works, ought in consistency to have seen grounds for inferences from which they have shrunk. If there are any marks at all of special design in creation, one of the things most evidently designed is that a large proportion of all animals should pass their existence in tormenting and devouring other animals. They have been lavishly fitted out with the instruments necessary for that purpose; their strongest instincts impel them to it, and many of them seem to have been constructed incapable of supporting themselves by any other food. If a tenth part of the pains which have been expended in finding benevolent adaptations in all nature, had been employed in collecting evidence to blacken the character of the Creator, what scope for comment would not have been found in the entire existence of the lower animals, divided, with scarcely an exception, into devourers and devoured, and a prey to a thousand ills from which they are denied the faculties necessary for protecting themselves! If we are not obliged to believe the animal creation to be the work of a demon, it is because we need not suppose it to have been made by a Being of infinite power. But if imitation of the Creator's will as revealed in nature, were applied as a rule of action in this case, the most atrocious enormities of the worst men would be more than justified by the apparent intention of Providence that throughout all animated nature the strong should prey upon the weak.

Pleasure, Happiness and Self-Realization

22

Pleasure and Desire

Plato

How should human beings live? Which is the way to happiness, or self-realization? Is there a general prescription for 'the good life'? These questions occupied the ancient Greek philosophers. One answer, considered in the following extract from Plato (427–347 BC), is that of satisfying one's desires and appetites. But this answer leaves us with two questions, one about quality and the other about quantity. First, are all desires equally desirable? (Is it only satisfaction that counts, regardless of the object of desire?) Secondly, is it better to have many and strong desires (assuming they can be satisfied), or few and moderate desires (assuming they can be satisfied)?

CALLICLES: What do you mean by self-mastery?

SOCRATES: Nothing in the least recondite. I use the word simply in the popular sense, of being moderate and in control of oneself and master of one's own passions and appetites.

CALLICLES: What a funny fellow you are, Socrates. The people that you call moderate are the half-witted.

SOCRATES: How so? Anybody can see that I don't mean them.

CALLICLES: Oh! but you do, Socrates. For how can a man be happy that is in subjection to anyone whatever? I tell you frankly that natural good and right consist in this, that the man who is going to live as a man ought should encourage his appetites to be as strong as possible instead of repressing them, and be able by means of this courage and intelligence to satisfy them in all their intensity by providing them with whatever they happen to desire.

For the majority, I know, this is an impossible ideal; that is why, in an endeavour to conceal their own weakness, they blame the minority whom they are ashamed of not being able to imitate, and maintain that excess is a disgraceful thing. As I said before, they try to make slaves of men of better natural gifts, and because through their own lack of manliness they are unable to satisfy their passions they praise moderation and righteousness. To those who are either of princely birth to begin with or able by their own qualities to win office or absolute rule or power what could in truth be more disgraceful or injurious than moderation, which involves their voluntary subjection to the conventions and standards and criticism of the majority, when they might enjoy every advantage without interference from anybody? How can they fail to be wretched when they are prevented by your fine righteousness and moderation from favouring their friends at the expense of their enemies, even when they are rulers in their own city?

The truth, Socrates, which you profess to be in search of is in fact this; luxury and excess and licence, provided that they can obtain sufficient backing, are virtue and happiness; all the rest is mere flummery, unnatural conventions of society, worthless cant.

SOCRATES: Your frank statement of your position, Callicles, certainly does not lack spirit. You set out plainly in the light of day opinions which other people entertain but are loth to express. Don't weaken at all, I beseech you, so that we may come to a clear conclusion how life should be lived. And tell me this. You maintain, do you not, that if a man is to be what he ought he should not repress his appetites but let them grow as strong as possible and satisfy them by any means in his power, and that such behaviour is virtue?

CALLICLES: Yes, I do.

SOCRATES: Then the view that those who have no wants are happy is wrong?

CALLICLES: Of course, at that rate stones and corpses would be supremely happy.

SOCRATES: Nevertheless even the life which you describe has its alarming side. I should not wonder if Euripides may not be right when he says:

Who knows if life be death or death be life?[1]

and if perhaps it may not be we who are in fact dead. This is a view that I have heard maintained before now by one of the pundits, who declares that we in our present condition are dead. Our body is the tomb in which we are buried,[2] and the part of the soul in which our appetites reside is liable by reason of its gullibility to be carried in the most contrary directions. This same part, because of its instability and readiness to be influenced, a witty man, Sicilian perhaps or Italian, has by a play upon words allegorically called a pitcher. In the same vein he labels fools 'uninitiated' (or 'leaky'), and that part of their soul which contains the appetites, which is intemperate and as it were the reverse of watertight, he represents as a pitcher with holes in it, because it cannot be filled up. Thus in direct opposition to you, Callicles, he maintains that of all the inhabitants of Hades – meaning by Hades the invisible world – the uninitiated are the most wretched, being engaged in pouring water into a leaky pitcher out of an equally leaky sieve. The sieve, according to my informant, he uses as an image of the soul, and his motive for comparing the souls of fools to sieves is that they are leaky and unable to retain their contents on account of their fickle and forgetful nature.[3]

This comparison is, no doubt, more or less grotesque, but it demonstrates the point which I want to prove to you, in order to persuade you, if I can, to change your mind, and, instead of a life of intemperate craving which can never be satisfied, to choose a temperate life which is content with whatever comes to hand and asks no more.

Does what I say influence you at all towards a conviction that the temperate are happier than the intemperate, or will any number of such allegories fail to convert you?

CALLICLES: The latter is nearer the truth, Socrates.

SOCRATES: Well, let me produce another simile from the same school as the first. Suppose that the two lives, the temperate and the intemperate, are typified by two men, each of whom has a number of casks. The casks of the first are sound and full, one of wine, one of honey, one of milk, and so on, but the supply of each of these commodities is scanty and he can procure them only with very great difficulty. This man, when once he has filled his casks, will not need to increase his store and give himself any further concern about it; as far as this matter goes his mind will be at rest. Now take the second man. He, like the first, can obtain a supply, though only with difficulty; but his vessels are leaky and rotten, so that if he is to avoid the extremity of privation he must be perpetually filling them, day and night. If such is the condition of the two lives respectively, can you say that the life of the intemperate man is happier than the life of the temperate? Am I making any progress towards making you admit that the temperate life is better than the intemperate, or not?

CALLICLES: No, Socrates, you are not. The man who has filled his casks no longer has any pleasure left. It is just as I said a moment ago; once his casks are filled his existence is the existence of a stone, exempt alike from enjoyment and pain. But the pleasure of life consists precisely in this, that there should be as much running in as possible.

SOCRATES: But if much is to run in much must necessarily run out, and there must be large holes for it to escape by.

CALLICLES: Certainly.

SOCRATES: Then the existence which you are describing, so far from being that of a stone or a corpse, is the existence of a greedy and dirty bird.[4] Tell me now; are you speaking of such things as being hungry and eating when one is hungry?

CALLICLES: Yes.

SOCRATES: And of being thirsty and drinking when one is thirsty?

CALLICLES: Certainly, and of having all the other appetites and being able to satisfy them with enjoyment. That is the happy life.

SOCRATES: Excellent, my good sir. Only you must stick to your point and not give way out of shame. No more must I, for that matter, it seems. Tell me first of all; can a man who itches and wants to scratch and whose opportunities of scratching are unbounded be said to lead a happy life continually scratching?

CALLICLES: How fantastic you are, Socrates, and how thoroughly vulgar.

SOCRATES: That, Callicles, is why I shocked Polus and Gorgias and made them feel shame. But you are a brave man, and will never give way to such emotions. Just answer me.

CALLICLES: Then I say that even the man who scratches lives a pleasant life.

SOCRATES: And if pleasant then happy?

CALLICLES: Of course.

SOCRATES: But suppose that the itch were not confined to his head. Must I go on with my questions? Consider what answer you will make, Callicles, if you are asked all the questions which are corollaries of this. To bring the matter to a head, take the life of a catamite,[5] is not that dreadful and shameful and wretched? Or will you dare to say that such people are happy provided that they have an abundant supply of what they want?

CALLICLES: Aren't you ashamed to introduce such subjects into the discussion, Socrates?

SOCRATES: Who is responsible for their introduction, my fine sir? I or the person who maintains without qualification that those who feel enjoyment of whatever kind are happy, and who does not distinguish between good and bad pleasures? Tell me once more; do you declare that pleasure is identical with good, or are there some pleasures which are not good? ...

NOTES

1 A fragment of the *Polyidus*, parodied by Aristophanes in the *Frogs*.

2 The idea that the body (*soma*) is a tomb (*sema*) in which the immortal soul is buried is characteristic both of the Pythagorean philosophy and of the Orphic mystery religion with which Pythagoreanism had much in common. Both had considerable influence on Plato.

3 'Sicilian' probably refers to Empedocles, who shared the view that the soul falls at birth into a state from which it must free itself. 'Italian' almost certainly means 'Pythagorean'. The sense of the passage partly depends upon plays upon words which cannot be rendered in translation. The appetitive part of the soul is called a pitcher (*pithos*) because it is readily influenced (*pithanos*); the word for 'uninitiated' (*amyetos*) is made by a fanciful derivation to bear the secondary sense of 'leaky'; Hades is equated with *aeides*, invisible. The object of initiation

is to secure the welfare of the soul in the next world, and the symbol of the leaky pitcher recalls the fate of the daughters of Danaus, whose punishment in Hades is to pour water for ever into leaky vessels. The idea that life may be death is perhaps to be interpreted in the light of this allusion; in our world an analogue to the Danaids is to be found in the behaviour of the intemperate, who may therefore be thought of as being already in Hades.

4   The bird in question (*charadrios*) is perhaps some species of plover. It is said by an ancient commentator to excrete while it eats; hence the allusion here.

5   [A catamite is a boy kept for unnatural purposes – OH.]

23

The Difference of Quality in Pleasures
and
Of What Sort of Proof the Principle of Utility is Susceptible

John Stuart Mill

Desire is also of fundamental importance in Mill's account of the 'Greatest Happiness Principle', regarded by him as 'the foundation of morals'. Why should the promotion of happiness be regarded as the supreme principle of morality? The only proof that can be given of this, replies Mill, is that happiness is what everyone desires; and he appeals to the reader's 'self-observation' and 'observation of others' to confirm that this is so. But the connection between happiness and desire is one of logic and not observation. Anyone who understands the words 'happiness' and 'desire' will be aware of the connection between them without any need for empirical evidence. A more difficult question will be: what does happiness consist in? Mill's definition of it, in terms of pleasure and pain, is likely to strike the reader as implausible. Mill is at pains, however, to explain that he would not give equal value to all pleasures; he insists that his theory can give due importance to the higher pleasures of the mind. These are distinguished, he holds, by their 'superior quality', which is such as to outweigh any considerations of quantity. In this matter he contradicts his mentor Jeremy Bentham, who had maintained that, 'quantity of pleasure being equal, push-pin is as good as poetry.'[1] According to Mill's criterion, a given pleasure is superior to another, in the relevant sense, if those acquainted with both will prefer the first, 'even though knowing it to be attended with a greater amount of discontent, and would not resign it for any quantity of the other'. It may be doubted, however, whether any pleasures would satisfy such an extreme requirement. It is also necessary to ask what is to count as 'a pleasure' – whether, for example, poetry should count as one or many (one per poet perhaps; or one per each reading, etc.); and similarly with push-pin or any other example.

In this passage, Mill also declares his preference for the human life over that of a pig, and the Socratic life over that of a fool (as previously quoted). These lives are better, he maintains, even if the balance of satisfaction and dissatisfaction is against them; and he tries to show that, contrary to appearances, this preference is compatible with the Greatest Happiness Principle. Be that as it may, most readers will probably agree with Mill that the first kind of life, in each pair, is the better one. This may be, to some extent, because of the derogatory connotations of 'pig' and 'fool'. But what if the comparisons were made without such connotations? Is it better to be a human being dissatisfied than, say, a zebra satisfied? (And, similarly, the word 'fool' might be replaced by 'person of moderate intellect', in making the comparison with Socrates.) Even so, many readers would share Mill's preference. But to find a justification for the preference is no easy matter. The opposite view was well expressed by Thomas Gray: 'Where ignorance is bliss, 'tis folly to be wise.'

NOTE

1   See 'Mill on Bentham' in *Utilitarianism*, ed. Mary Warnock (Collins, 1962), 123. These are Bentham's words as remembered by Mill, and not exactly what he said.

The Difference of Quality in Pleasures

The creed which accepts as the foundation of morals, Utility, or the Greatest Happiness Principle, holds that actions are right in proportion as they tend to promote happiness, wrong as they tend to produce the reverse of happiness. By happiness is intended pleasure, and the absence of pain; by unhappiness, pain, and the privation of pleasure. To give a clear view of the moral standard set up by the theory, much more requires to be said; in particular, what things it includes in the ideas of pain and pleasure; and to what extent this is left an open question. But these supplementary explanations do not affect the theory of life on which this theory of morality is grounded – namely, that pleasure, and freedom from pain, are the only things desirable as ends; and that all desirable things (which are as numerous in the utilitarian as in any other scheme) are desirable either for the pleasure inherent in themselves, or as means to the promotion of pleasure and the prevention of pain.

Now, such a theory of life excites in many minds, and among them in some of the most estimable in feeling and purpose, inveterate dislike. To suppose that life has (as they express it) no higher end than pleasure – no better and nobler object of desire and pursuit – they designate as utterly mean and grovelling; as a doctrine worthy only of swine, to whom the followers of Epicurus were, at a very early period, contemptuously likened; and modern holders of the doctrine are occasionally made the subject of equally polite comparisons by its German, French and English assailants.

When thus attacked, the Epicureans have always answered, that it is not they, but their accusers, who represent human nature in a degrading light; since the accusation supposes human beings to be capable of no pleasures except those of which swine are capable. If this supposition were true, the charge could not be gainsaid, but would then be no longer an imputation; for if the sources of pleasure were precisely the same to human beings and to swine, the rule of life which is good enough for the one would be good enough for the other. The comparison of the Epicurean life to that of beasts is felt as degrading, precisely because a beast's pleasures do not satisfy a human being's conception of happiness. Human beings have faculties more elevated than the animal appetites, and when once made conscious of them, do not regard anything as happiness which does not include their gratification. I do not, indeed, consider the Epicureans to have been by any means faultless in drawing out their scheme of consequences from the utilitarian principle. To do this in any sufficient manner, many Stoic, as well as Christian elements require to be included. But there is no known Epicurean theory of life which does not assign to the pleasures of the intellect, of the feelings and imagination, and of the moral sentiments, a much higher value as pleasures than to those of mere sensation. It must be admitted, however, that utilitarian writers in general have placed the superiority of mental over bodily pleasures chiefly in the greater permanency, safety, uncostliness, etc., of the former – that is, in their circumstantial advantages rather than in their intrinsic nature. And on all these points utilitarians have fully proved their case; but they might have taken the other, and, as it may be called, higher ground, with entire consistency. It is quite compatible with the principle of utility to recognize the fact, that some *kinds* of pleasure are more desirable and more valuable than others. It would be absurd that while, in estimating all other things, quality is considered as well as quantity, the estimation of pleasures should be supposed to depend on quantity alone.

If I am asked, what I mean by difference of quality in pleasures, or what makes one pleasure more valuable than another, merely as a pleasure, except its being greater in amount, there is but one possible answer. Of two pleasures, if there be one to which all or almost all who have experience of both give a decided preference, irrespective of any feeling of moral obligation to prefer it, that is the more desirable pleasure. If one of the two is, by those who are competently acquainted with both, placed so far above the other that they prefer it, even though knowing it to be attended with a greater amount of discontent, and would not resign it for any quantity of the other pleasure which their nature is capable of, we are justified in ascribing to the preferred enjoyment a superiority in quality, so far outweighing quantity as to render it, in comparison, of small account.

Now it is an unquestionable fact that those who are equally acquainted with, and equally capable of appreciating and enjoying, both, do give a most marked preference to the manner of existence which employs their higher faculties. Few human creatures would consent to be changed into any of the lower animals, for a promise of the fullest allowance of a beast's pleasures; no intelligent human being would consent to be a fool, no instructed person would be an ignoramus, no person of feeling and conscience would be selfish and base, even though they should be persuaded that the fool, the dunce, or the rascal is better satisfied with his lot than they are with theirs. They would not resign what they possess more than he for the most complete satisfaction of all the desires which they have in common with him. If they ever fancy they would, it is only in cases of unhappiness so extreme, that to escape from it they would exchange their lot for almost any other, however undesirable in their own eyes. A being of higher faculties requires more to make him happy, is capable probably of more acute suffering, and certainly accessible to it at more points, than one of an inferior type; but in spite of these liabilities, he can never really wish to sink into what he feels to be a lower grade of existence. We may give what explanation we please of this unwillingness; we may attribute it to pride, a name which is given indiscriminately to some of the most and to some of the least estimable feelings of which mankind are capable: we may refer it to the love of liberty and personal independence, an appeal to which was with the Stoics one of the most effective means for the inculcation of it; to the love of power, or to the love of excitement, both of which do really enter into and contribute to it: but its most appropriate appellation is a sense of dignity, which all human beings possess in one form or another, and in some, though by no means in exact, proportion to their higher faculties, and which is so essential a part of the happiness of those in whom it is strong, that nothing which conflicts with it could be, otherwise than momentarily, an object of desire to them. Whoever supposes that this preference takes place at a sacrifice of happiness – that the superior being, in anything like equal circumstances, is not happier than the inferior – confounds the two very different ideas, of happiness, and content. It is indisputable that the being whose capacities of enjoyment are low, has the greatest chance of having them fully satisfied; and a highly endowed being will always feel that any happiness which he can look for, as the world is constituted, is imperfect. But he can learn to bear its imperfections, if they are at all bearable; and they will not make him envy the being who is indeed unconscious of the imperfections, but only because he feels not at all the good which those imperfections qualify. It is better to be a human being dissatisfied than a pig satisfied; better to be Socrates dissatisfied than a fool satisfied. And if the fool, or the pig, are of a different opinion, it is because they only know their own side of the question. The other party to the comparison knows both sides.

Of What Sort of Proof the Principle of Utility is Susceptible

It has already been remarked, that questions of ultimate ends do not admit of proof, in the ordinary acceptation of the term. To be incapable of proof by reasoning is common to all first principles; to the first premises of our knowledge, as well as to those of our conduct. But the former, being matters of fact, may be the subject of a direct appeal to the faculties which judge of fact – namely, our sense, and our internal consciousness. Can an appeal be made to the same faculties on questions of practical ends? Or by what other faculty is cognizance taken of them?

Questions about ends are, in other words, questions what things are desirable. The utilitarian doctrine is, that happiness is desirable, and the only thing desirable, as an end; all other things being only desirable as means to that end. What ought to be required of this doctrine – what conditions is it requisite that the doctrine should fulfil – to make good its claim to be believed?

The only proof capable of being given that an object is visible, is that people actually see it. The only proof that a sound is audible, is that people hear it: and so of the other sources of our experience. In like manner, I apprehend, the sole evidence it is possible to produce that anything is desirable, is that people do actually desire it. If the end which the utilitarian doctrine proposes to itself were not, in theory and in practice, acknowledged to be an end, nothing could ever convince any person that it was so. No reason can be given why the general happiness is desirable, except that each person, so far as he believes it to be attainable, desires his own happiness. This, however, being a fact, we have not only all the proof which the case admits of, but all which it is possible to require, that happiness is a good: that each person's happiness is a good to that person, and the general happiness, therefore, a good to the aggregate of all persons. Happiness has made out its title as *one* of the ends of conduct, and consequently one of the criteria of morality.

But it has not, by this alone, proved itself to be the sole criterion. To do that, it would seem, by the same rule, necessary to show, not only that people desire happiness, but that they never desire anything else. Now it is palpable that they do desire things which, in common language, are decidedly distinguished from happiness. They desire, for example, virtue, and the absence of vice, no less really than pleasure and the absence of pain. The desire of virtue is not as universal, but it is as authentic a fact, as the desire of happiness. And hence the opponents of the utilitarian standard deem that they have a right to infer that there are other ends of human action besides happiness, and that happiness is not the standard of approbation and disapprobation.

But does the utilitarian doctrine deny that people desire virtue, or maintain that virtue is not a thing to be desired? The very reverse. It maintains not only that virtue is to be desired, but that it is to be desired disinterestedly, for itself. Whatever may be the opinion of utilitarian moralists as to the original conditions by which virtue is made virtue; however they may believe (as they do) that actions and dispositions are only virtuous because they promote another end than virtue; yet this being granted, and it having been decided, from considerations of this description, what *is* virtuous, they not only place virtue at the very head of the things which are good as means to the ultimate end, but they also recognize as a psychological fact the possibility of its being, to the individual, a good in itself, without looking to any end beyond it; and hold, that the mind is not in a right state, not in a state conformable to Utility, not in the state most conducive to the general happiness, unless it does love virtue in this manner – as a thing desirable in itself, even although, in the individual instance, it should not produce those other desirable consequences which it tends to produce, and on account of which it is held to be virtue. This opinion is not, in the smallest degree, a departure from the Happiness principle. The ingredients of happiness are very various, and each of them is desirable in itself, and not merely when considered as swelling an aggregate. The principle of utility does not mean that any given pleasure, as music, for instance, or any given exemption from pain, as for example health, is to be looked upon as means to a collective something termed happiness, and to be desired on that account. They are desired and desirable in and for themselves; besides being means, they are a part of the end. Virtue, according to the utilitarian doctrine, is not naturally and originally part of the end, but it is capable of becoming so; and in those who love it disinterestedly it has become so, and is desired and cherished, not as a means to happiness, but as a part of their happiness.

To illustrate this farther, we may remember that virtue is not the only thing, originally a means, and which if it were not a means to anything else, would be and remain indifferent, but which by association with what it is a means to, comes to be desired for itself, and that too with the utmost intensity. What, for example, shall we say of the love of money? There is nothing originally more desirable about money than about any heap of glittering pebbles. Its worth is solely that of the things which it will buy; the desires for other things than itself, which it is a means of gratifying. Yet the love of money is not only one of the strongest moving forces of human life, but money is, in many cases, desired in and for itself; the desire to possess it is often stronger than the desire to use it, and goes on increasing when all the desires which point to ends beyond it, to be compassed by it, are falling off. It may, then, be said truly, that money is desired not for the sake of an end, but as part of the end. From being a means to happiness, it has come to be itself a principal ingredient of the individual's conception of happiness. The same may be said of the majority of the great objects of human life – power, for example, or fame; except that to each of these there is a certain amount of immediate pleasure annexed, which has at least the semblance of being naturally inherent of fame, is the immense aid they give to the attainment of in them; a thing which cannot be said of money. Still, however, the strongest natural attraction, both of power and our other wishes; and it is the strong association thus generated between them and all our objects of desire, which gives to the direct desire of them the intensity it often assumes, so as in some characters to surpass in strength all other desires. In these cases the means have become a part of the end, and a more important part of it than any of the things which they are means to. What was once desired as an instrument for the attainment of happiness, has come to be desired for its own sake. In being desired for its own sake it is, however, desired as *part* of happiness. The person is made, or thinks he would be made, happy by its mere possession; and is made unhappy by failure to obtain it. The desire of it is not a different thing from the desire of happiness, any more than the love of music, or the desire of health. They are included in happiness. They are some of the elements of which the desire of happiness is made up. Happiness is not an abstract idea, but a concrete whole; and these are some of its parts. And the utilitarian standard sanctions and approves their being so. Life would be a poor thing, very ill provided with sources of happiness, if there were not this provision of nature, by which things originally indifferent, but conducive to, or otherwise associated with, the satisfaction of our primitive desires, become in themselves sources of pleasure more valuable than the primitive pleasures, both in permanency, in the space of human existence that they are capable of covering, and even in intensity.

Virtue, according to the utilitarian conception, is a good of this description. There was no original desire of it, or motive to it, save its conduciveness to pleasure, and especially to protection from pain. But through the association thus formed, it may be felt a good in itself, and desired as such with as great intensity as any other good; and with this difference between it and the love of money, of power, or of fame, that all of these may, and often do, render the individual noxious to the other members of the society to which he belongs, whereas there is nothing which makes him so much a blessing to them as the cultivation of the disinterested love of virtue. And consequently, the utilitarian standard, while it tolerates and approves those other acquired desires, up to the point beyond which they would be more injurious to the general happiness than promotive of it, enjoins and requires the cultivation of the love of virtue up to the greatest strength possible, as being above all things important to the general happiness.

It results from the preceding considerations, that there is in reality nothing desired except happiness. Whatever is desired otherwise than as a means to some end beyond itself, and ultimately to happiness, is desired as itself a part of happiness, and is not desired for itself until it has become so. Those who desire virtue for its own sake, desire it either because the consciousness of it is a pleasure, or because the consciousness of being without it is a pain, or for both reasons united; as in truth the pleasure and pain seldom exist separately, but almost always together, the same person feeling pleasure in the degree of virtue attained, and pain in not having attained more. If one of these gave him no pleasure, and the other no pain, he would not love or desire virtue, or would desire it only for the other benefits which it might produce to himself or to persons whom he cared for.

We have now, then, an answer to the question, of what sort of proof the principle of utility is susceptible. If the opinion which I have now stated is psychologically true – if human nature is so constituted as to desire nothing which is not either a part of happiness or a means of happiness, we can have no other proof, and we require no other, that these are the only things desirable. If so, happiness is the sole end of human action, and the promotion of it the test by which to judge of all human conduct; from whence it necessarily follows that it must be the criterion of morality, since a part is included in the whole.

And now to decide whether this is really so; whether mankind do desire nothing for itself but that which is a pleasure to them, or of which the absence is a pain; we have evidently arrived at a question of fact and experience, dependent, like all similar questions, upon evidence. It can only be determined by practised self-consciousness and self-observation, assisted by observation of others. I believe that these sources of evidence, impartially consulted, will declare that desiring a thing and finding it pleasant, aversion to it and thinking of it as painful, are phenomena entirely inseparable, or rather two parts of the same phenomenon; in strictness of language, two different modes of naming the same psychological fact: that to think of an object as desirable (unless for the sake of its consequences), and to think of it as pleasant, are one and the same thing; and that to desire anything, except in proportion as the idea of it is pleasant, is a physical and metaphysical impossibility.

So obvious does this appear to me, that I expect it will hardly be disputed: and the objection made will be, not that desire can possibly be directed to anything ultimately except pleasure and exemption from pain, but that the will is a different thing from desire; that a person of confirmed virtue, or any other person whose purposes are fixed, carries out his purposes without any thought of the pleasure he has in contemplating them, or expects to derive from their fulfilment; and persists in acting on them, even though these pleasures are much diminished, by changes in his character or decay of his passive sensibilities, or are out-weighed by the pains which the pursuit of the purposes may bring upon him. All this I fully admit, and have stated it elsewhere, as positively and emphatically as any one. Will, the active phenomenon, is a different thing from desire, the state of passive sensibility, and though originally an offshoot from it, may in time take root and detach itself from the parent stock; so much so, that in the case of an habitual purpose, instead of willing the thing because we desire it, we often desire it only because we will it. This, however, is but an instance of that familiar fact, the power of habit, and is nowise confined to the case of virtuous actions. Many indifferent things, which men originally did from a motive of some sort, they continue to do from habit. Sometimes this is done unconsciously, the consciousness coming only after the action: at other times with conscious volition, but volition which has become habitual, and is put in operation by the force of habit, in opposition perhaps to the deliberate preference, as often happens with those who have contracted habits of vicious or hurtful indulgence. Third and last comes the case in which the habitual act of will in the individual instance is not in contradiction to the general intention prevailing at other times, but in fulfilment of it; as in the case of the person of confirmed virtue, and of all who pursue deliberately and consistently any determinate end. The distinction between will and desire thus understood is an authentic and highly important psychological fact; but the fact consists solely in this – that will, like all other parts of our constitution, is amenable to habit, and that we may will from habit what we no longer desire for itself, or desire only because we will it. It is not the less true that will, in the begining, is entirely produced by desire; including in that term the repelling influence of pain as well as the attractive one of pleasure. Let us take into consideration, no longer the person who has a confirmed will to do right, but him in whom that virtuous will is still feeble, conquerable by temptation, and not to be fully relied on; by what means can it be strengthened? How can the will to be virtuous, where it does not exist in sufficient force, be implanted or awakened? Only by making the person *desire* virtue – by making him think of it in a pleasurable light, or of its absence in a painful one. It is by associating the doing right with pleasure, or the doing wrong with pain, or by eliciting and impressing and bringing home to the person's experience the pleasure naturally involved in the one or the pain in the other, that it is possible to call forth that will to be virtuous, which, when confirmed, acts without any thought of either pleasure or pain. Will is the child of desire, and passes out of the dominion of its parent only to come under that of habit. That which is the result of habit affords no presumption of being intrinsically good; and there would be no reason for wishing that the purpose of virtue should become independent of pleasure and pain, were it not that the influence of the pleasurable and painful associations which prompt to virtue is not sufficiently to be depended on for unerring constancy of action until it has acquired the support of habit. Both in feeling and in conduct, habit is the only thing which imparts certainty; and it is because of the importance to others of being able to rely absolutely on one's feelings and conduct, and to oneself of being able to rely on one's own, that the will to do right ought to be cultivated into this habitual independence. In other words, this state of the will is a means to good, not intrinsically a good; and does not contradict the doctrine that nothing is a good to human beings but in so far as it is either itself pleasurable, or a means of attaining pleasure or averting pain.

But if this doctrine be true, the principle of utility is proved. Whether it is or not must now be left to the consideration of the thoughtful reader.

24

The Experience Machine

Robert Nozick

Everyone desires to be happy. But is it only happiness we desire? Is it better to be a happy fool than an unhappy Socrates? One might prefer the latter. Again, a person with brain damage might be described as happy (if he has all he needs, is not in pain, etc.), but few people would desire such happiness. It might be thought that what is needed in addition is some qualification about the quality of experiences, of the kind attempted by Mill. But Nozick's thought-experiment, in the reading that follows, is designed to show that what we value about life goes beyond any set of experiences, however 'superior' they might be.

Suppose there were an experience machine that would give you any experience you desired. Superduper neuropsychologists could stimulate your brain so that you would think and feel you were writing a great novel, or making a friend, or reading an interesting book. All the time you would be floating in a tank, with electrodes attached to your brain. Should you plug into this machine for life, preprogramming your life's experiences? If you are worried about missing out on desirable experiences, we can suppose that business enterprises have researched thoroughly the lives of many others. You can pick and choose from their large library or smorgasbord of such experiences, selecting your life's experiences for, say, the next two years. After two years have passed, you will have ten minutes or ten hours out of the tank, to select the experiences of your *next* two years. Of course, while in the tank you won't know that you're there; you'll think it's all actually happening. Others can also plug in to have the experiences they want, so there's no need to stay unplugged to serve them. (Ignore problems such as who will service the machines if everyone plugs in.) Would you plug in? *What else can matter to us, other than how our lives feel from the inside?* Nor should you refrain because of the few moments of distress between the moment you've decided and the moment you're plugged. What's a few minutes of distress compared to a lifetime of bliss (if that's what you choose), and why feel any distress at all if your decision *is* the best one?

What does matter to us in addition to our experiences? First, we want to *do* certain things, and not just have the experience of doing them. In the case of certain experiences, it is only because first we want to do the actions that we want the experiences of doing them or thinking we've done them. (But *why* do we want to do the activities rather than merely to experience them?) A second reason for not plugging in is that we want to *be* a certain way, to be a certain sort of person. Someone floating in a tank is an indeterminate blob. There is no answer to the question of what a person is like who has long been in the tank. Is he courageous, kind, intelligent, witty, loving? It's not merely that it's difficult to tell; there's no way he is. Plugging into the machine is a kind of suicide. It will seem to some, trapped by a picture, that nothing about what we are like can matter except as it gets reflected in our experiences. But should it be surprising that what *we are* is important to us? Why should we be concerned only with how our time is filled, but not with what we are?

Thirdly, plugging into an experience machine limits us to a man-made reality, to a world no deeper or more important than that which people can construct. There is no *actual* contact with any deeper reality, though the experience of it can be simulated. Many persons desire to leave themselves open to such contact and to a plumbing of deeper significance.[1] This clarifies the intensity of the conflict over psychoactive drugs, which some view as mere local experience machines, and others view as avenues to a deeper reality; what some view as equivalent to surrender to the experience machine, others view as following one of the reasons *not* to surrender!

We learn that something matters to us in addition to experience by imagining an experience machine and then realizing that we would not use it. We can continue to imagine a sequence of machines each designed to fill lacks suggested for the earlier machines. For example, since the experience machine doesn't meet our desire to *be* a certain way, imagine a transformation machine which transforms us into whatever sort of person we'd like to be (compatible with our staying us). Surely one would not use the transformation machine to become as one would wish, and thereupon plug into the experience machine![2] So something matters in addition to one's experiences *and* what one is like. Nor is the reason merely that one's experiences are unconnected with what one is like. For the experience machine might be limited to provide only experiences possible to the sort of person plugged in. Is it that we want to make a difference in the world? Consider then the result machine, which produces in the world any result you would produce and injects your vector input into any joint activity. We shall not pursue here the fascinating details of these or other machines. What is most disturbing about them is their living of our lives for us. Is it misguided to search for *particular* additional functions beyond the competence of machines to do for us? Perhaps what we desire is to live (an active verb) ourselves, in contact with reality. (And this, machines cannot do *for* us.)

NOTES

1 Traditional religious views differ on the *point* of contact with a transcendent reality. Some say that contact yields eternal bliss or Nirvana, but they have not distinguished this sufficiently from merely a *very* long run on the experience machine. Others think it is intrinsically desirable to do the will of a higher being which created us all, though presumably no one would think this if we discovered we had been created as an object of amusement by some superpowerful child from another galaxy or dimension. Still others imagine an eventual merging with a higher reality, leaving unclear its desirability, or where that merging leaves *us*.

2 Some wouldn't use the transformation machine at all; it seems like *cheating*. But the one-time use of the transformation machine would not remove all challenges; there would still be obstacles for the new us to overcome, a new plateau from which to strive even higher. And is this plateau any the less earned or deserved than that provided by genetic endowment and early childhood environment? But if the transformation machine could be used indefinitely often, so that we could accomplish anything by pushing a button to transform ourselves into someone who could do it easily, there would remain no limits we *need* to strain against or try to transcend. Would there be anything left *to do*? Do some theological views place God outside of time because an omniscient omnipotent being couldn't fill up his days?

25

How Should a Man Live?

Aristotle

In his preference for the intellectual life, Mill was following a long tradition going back to Aristotle and beyond. The best life, according to Aristotle, 'is the life of the intellect, since the intellect is in the fullest sense the man'. As can be seen from this quotation, Aristotle (unlike Mill) put forward an argument in support of his preference, and this is expounded at length in the following reading. His prescription for the good life for man was deduced from the essential nature *of man. And as mentioned in the introduction to the previous reading from Aristotle (section three), he understood 'nature' in a developmental sense. His conclusion there was in favour of the 'political' life; but he regarded this as connected with 'the life of the intellect', as recommended below. In this reading he speaks of a 'function' of man. Just as an artist or craftsman has a certain function, which determines the right conduct of his life, so it is, according to Aristotle, with man in general. And in each case the function is correlated with a 'distinctive excellence', so that the best life consists in developing this function as fully as possible. What is the characteristic function of man? It must be that in which he differs from other animals; and according to Aristotle, this is the activity of reason or intellect. The rational life is peculiar to man, and therefore fulfilment and happiness are to be found in perfecting it as far as possible.*

The analogy between the artist and craftsman, and man in general, is not as perfect as Aristotle seems to have thought. The function of the former, it may be said, is to serve the needs of others, in certain specialized ways; but we cannot say this of man in general and his intellectual 'function'. A good carpenter or flautist will be one who performs that specialized function as well as possible; but we cannot similarly say that a good man is one who performs the special function of man as well as possible. It may still be held, however, that the way to happiness is to do well whatever we are specially qualified to do. The functional view of man is also connected with what is nowadays called 'self-realization'. In educating our children, we regard it as a duty to realize what is potentially in them, and to a large extent (though not entirely) we think of this in terms of the intellectual function (though not necessarily in the form or forms described by Aristotle).

Nowadays we might think of 'the good life' as being about moral rather than intellectual virtue. Aristotle, however, regarded the former as being of secondary

*importance. In the intellectual life (which he identified with a life of contemplation)
man approaches as nearly as possible to a godlike existence. But this could not be
so in the case of moral virtues, for there would be no place for these among the
gods; among them, he argued, there would be no place for notions like justice or
the returning of deposits. This may seem, to the modern reader, a rather fanciful
argument; but a somewhat similar one might be put forward without recourse to
the gods. Moral virtues, it might be said, are correlative with vice and (rather
differently) with suffering; in a perfect world these would not exist, and neither
would there be a need for moral virtue. (More would need to be said, however,
in order to reach Aristotle's conclusion.)*

*In the final extract (which has been transposed from the order in the original),
Aristotle gives an account of personal integration, and this is largely in terms of
moral goodness. The integrated person, he points out, can view himself and his
life with pleasure; but this satisfaction is not available to wicked people: 'possessing
no lovable qualities, they feel no affection for themselves.' Here is one kind of
happiness that is not available to the wicked, however successful they may be in
other respects.*

*The reading from Aristotle is probably the most difficult in this volume. His
arguments are often hard to follow, and some of his remarks will seem implausible
or even quaint to a modern reader. There are also questions about the translations
of some of his key terms, for example 'happiness'. For a better appreciation, it is
advisable to read a longer introduction, such as that of Jonathan Barnes to the
volume from which our extracts are taken, or J. L. Ackrill's* Aristotle the
Philosopher.

EUDEMIAN ETHICS

[1215b] About many things it is not easy to judge correctly, but it is especially
difficult to do so in regard to that which everyone thinks is most easy and
within anyone's capacity to know; namely, which of the things in life is
worth choosing, and such that one who obtains it will have his desire
fulfilled. After all, many things that happen are such as to induce people
to abandon life – disease, extremes of pain, storms, for example; so that it
is evident that, on account of those things at any rate, it would, given the
choice, have been worth choosing not to be born in the first place. Again,
⟨there is⟩ the life which men lead while they are still children. For no one
in his right mind would tolerate a return to that sort of existence. Moreover,
many of the things that involve neither pleasure nor pain, or involve
pleasure, but of a reprehensible sort, are enough to make not existing at
all preferable to being alive. In general, if we put together all the things
that everyone does or undergoes, but not voluntarily (because they are not
done or undergone for their own sake), and an infinite stretch of time were

provided in addition, no one would choose in order to have *them* to be alive, rather than not. Nor again would anyone who was not a complete slave prefer to live solely for the pleasure associated with nutrition and sex, if all the pleasures were removed that knowing or seeing or any of the other senses bestow upon human beings; for it is evident that, for a man who made such a choice as *this* for himself, it would make no difference whether he were born a beast or a man. Certainly the ox in Egypt, which they honour as the god Apis, has a greater abundance of several of such things than many sovereigns. Similarly, no one would prefer life for the pleasure of sleep; for what difference is there between sleeping without ever waking from one's first day to one's last, over a period of ten thousand years – or however many one likes – and living the life of a plant? Certainly plants seem to have a share in some such sort of life, as do infants. Babies indeed when they first come to be inside the mother exist in their natural state, but asleep all the time. So all this makes it clear that what the well and the good is in life eludes those who investigate the subject.

They say that Anaxagoras, when someone raised just these puzzles and asked him what it was for which a person would choose to be born rather than not, answered that it would be 'in order to apprehend the heavens and the order in the whole universe'. So *he* thought that it was knowledge that made the choice of life worth making; on the other hand, those who admire Sardanapallus, or Smindurides of Sybara or one or other of those who live the pleasure-loving life, all appear to place happiness in enjoyment, but others again would choose neither wisdom nor bodily pleasures of any kind in preference to virtuous actions. ...

NICOMACHEAN ETHICS

But what is happiness? If we consider what the function of man is, we find that happiness is a virtuous activity of the soul

... Presumably to say that happiness is the supreme good seems a platitude, and some more distinctive account of it is still required. This might perhaps be achieved by grasping what is the function of man. If we take a flautist or a sculptor or any artist – or in general any class of men who have a specific function or activity – his goodness and proficiency is considered to lie in the performance of that function; and the same will be true of man, assuming that man has a function. But is it likely that whereas joiners and shoemakers have certain functions or activities, man as such has none, but has been left by nature a functionless being? Just as we can see that eye and hand and foot and every one of our members has some function, should we not assume that in like manner a human being has a function over and above these particular functions? What, then, can this possibly be? Clearly life is a thing shared also by plants, and we are looking for man's *proper* function; so we must exclude [1098a] from our definition the life that consists in nutrition and growth. Next in order would be a sort of sentient life; but this too we see is shared by horses and cattle and animals of all kinds. There remains, then, a practical life of the rational part. (This has two aspects: one amenable to reason, the other possessng it and initiating thought.) As this life also has two meanings, we must lay down that we intend here life determined by activity, because this is accepted as the stricter sense.[1] Now if the function of man is an activity of the soul in accordance with, or implying, a rational principle; and if we hold that the function of an individual and of a good individual of the same kind – e.g. of a harpist and of a good harpist, and so on generally – is generically the same, the latter's distinctive excellence being attached to the name of the function (because the function of the harpist is to play the harp, but that of the good harpist is to play it well); and if we assume that the function of man is a kind of life, viz., an activity or series of actions of the soul, implying a rational principle; and if the function of a good man is to perform these well and rightly; and if every function is performed well when performed in accordance with its proper excellence; if all this is so, the conclusion is that the good for man is an activity of soul in accordance with virtue, or if there are more kinds of virtue than one, in accordance with the best and most perfect kind.

There is a further qualification: in a complete lifetime. One swallow does not make a summer; neither does one day. Similarly neither can one day, or a brief space of time, make a man blessed and happy. ...

Recapitulation: the nature of happiness

Now that we have finished our discussion of the virtues, of friendship, and of pleasures, it remains for us to give an outline account of happiness, since we hold it to be the end of human conduct. It may make our treatment of the subject more concise if we recapitulate what has been said already.

We said, then, that happiness is not a *state*, since if it were it might belong even to a man who slept all through his life, passing a vegetable existence; or to a victim of the greatest misfortunes. So if this [1176b] is unacceptable, and we ought rather to refer happiness to some activity, as we said earlier; and if activities are either necessary and to be chosen for the sake of something else, or to be chosen for themselves: clearly we must class happiness as one of those to be chosen for themselves, and not as one of the other kind, because it does not need anything else: it is self-sufficient. The activities that are to be chosen for themselves are those from which nothing is required beyond the exercise of the activity; and such a description is thought to fit actions that accord with goodness; because the doing of fine and good actions is one of the things that are to be chosen for themselves.

Happiness must be distinguished from amusement

Pleasant amusements are also thought to belong to this class, because they are not chosen as means to something else: in fact their effects are more harmful than beneficial, since they make people neglect their bodies and their property. However, most of those who are regarded as happy have recourse to such occupations, and that is why those who show some dexterity in them are highly esteemed at the courts of tyrants; they make themselves agreeable by providing the sort of entertainment that their patrons want, and such persons are in demand. So these amusements are thought to be conducive to happiness, because men in positions of power devote their leisure to them. But what people of this kind do is probably no evidence, because virtue and intelligence, which are the sources of serious activities, do not depend upon positions of power; and if these persons, never having tasted pure and refined pleasure, have recourse to physical pleasures, that is no reason why the latter should be regarded as worthier of choice. Children, too, believe that the things they prize are the most important; so it is natural that just as different things seem valuable to children and adults, so they should seem different also to good and bad men. Thus, as we have often said, it is the things that seem valuable and pleasant to the good man that are really such. But to each individual it is the activity in accordance with his own disposition that is most desirable, and therefore to the good man virtuous activity is most desirable. It follows that happiness does not consist in amusement. Indeed it would be paradoxical if the end were amusement; if we toiled and suffered all our lives long to amuse ourselves. For we choose practically everything for the sake of something else, except happiness, because it is the end. To spend effort and toil for the sake of amusement seems silly and unduly childish; but on the other hand the maxim of Anacharsis, 'Play to work harder', seems to be on the right lines, because amusement is a form of relaxation, and people need relaxation because they cannot exert themselves continuously. Therefore relaxation [1177a] is not an end, because it is taken for the sake of the activity. But the happy life seems to be lived in accordance with goodness, and such a life implies seriousness and does not consist in amusing oneself. Also we maintain that serious things are better than those that are merely comical and amusing, and that the activity of a man, or part of a man, is always more serious in proportion as it is better. Therefore the activity of the better part is superior, and *eo ipso* more conducive to happiness.

Anybody can enjoy bodily pleasures – a slave no less than the best of men – but nobody attributes a part in happiness to a slave, unless he also attributes to him a life of his own.[2] Therefore happiness does not consist in occupations of this kind, but in activities in accordance with virtue, as we have said before.

Happiness and contemplation

If happiness is an activity in accordance with virtue, it is reasonable to assume that it is in accordance with the highest virtue, and this will be the virtue of the best part of us. Whether this is the intellect or something else that we regard as naturally ruling and guiding us, and possessing insight into things noble and divine – either as being actually divine itself or as being more divine than any other part of us – it is the activity of this part, in accordance with the virtue proper to it, that will be perfect happiness.

We have already said that it is a contemplative activity. This may be regarded as consonant both with our earlier arguments and with the truth. For contemplation is both the highest form of activity (since the intellect is the highest thing in us, and the objects that it apprehends are the highest things that can be known), and also it is the most continuous, because we are more capable of continuous contemplation than we are of any practical activity. Also we assume that happiness must contain an admixture of pleasure; now activity in accordance with ⟨philosophic⟩ wisdom is admittedly the most pleasant of the virtuous activities; at any rate philosophy is held to entail pleasures that are marvellous in purity and permanence; and it stands to reason that those who possess knowledge pass their time more pleasantly than those who are still in pursuit of it. Again, the quality that we call self-sufficiency will belong in the highest degree to the contemplative activity. The wise man, no less than the just one and all the rest, requires the necessaries of life; but, given an adequate supply of these, the just man also needs people with and towards whom he can perform just actions, and similarly with the temperate man, the brave man, and each of the others; but the wise man can practise contemplation by himself, and the wiser he is, the more he can do it. No doubt he does it better with the help of fellow-workers; but for all that he is the [1177b] most self-sufficient of men. Again, contemplation would seem to be the only activity that is appreciated for its own sake; because nothing is gained from it except the act of contemplation, whereas from practical activities we expect to gain something more or less over and above the action.

Since happiness is thought to imply leisure, it must be an intellectual, not
a practical activity

Also it is commonly believed that happiness depends on leisure; because
we occupy ourselves so that we may have leisure, just as we make war in
order that we may live at peace. Now the exercise of the practical virtues
takes place in politics or in warfare, and these professions seem to have no
place for leisure. This is certainly true of the military profession, for nobody
chooses to make war or provokes it for the sake of making war; a man
would be regarded as a bloodthirsty monster if he made his friends[3] into
enemies in order to bring about battles and slaughter. The politician's
profession also makes leisure impossible, since besides the business of
politics it aims at securing positions of power and honour, or the happiness
of the politician himself and of his fellow-citizens – a happiness separate
from politics, and one which we clearly pursue as separate.

If, then, politics and warfare, although pre-eminent in nobility and
grandeur among practical activities in accordance with goodness, are
incompatible with leisure and, not being desirable in themselves, are
directed towards some other end, whereas the activity of the intellect is
considered to excel[4] in seriousness, taking as it does the form of
contemplation, and to aim at no other end beyond itself, and to possess a
pleasure peculiar to itself, which intensifies its activity; and if it is evident
that self-sufficiency and leisuredness and such freedom from fatigue as is
humanly possible, together with all the other attributes assigned to the
supremely happy man, are those that accord with this activity; then this
activity will be the perfect happiness for man – provided that it is allowed
a full span of life; for nothing that pertains to happiness is incomplete.

Life on this plane is not too high for the divine element in human
nature

But such a life will be too high for human attainment; for any man who
lives it will do so not as a human being but in virtue of something divine
within him, and in proportion as this divine element is superior to the
composite being,[5] so will its activity be superior to that of the other kind
of virtue.[6] So if the intellect is divine compared with man, the life of the
intellect must be divine compared with the life of a human being. And we
ought not to listen to those who warn us that 'man should think the thoughts
of man', or 'mortal thoughts fit mortal minds';[7] but we ought, so far as in
us lies, to put on immortality, and do all that we can to live in conformity
with the highest that is in us; for even if it [1178a] is small in bulk, in power
and preciousness it far excels all the rest. Indeed, it would seem that this

is the true self of the individual, since it is the authoritative and better part of him; so it would be an odd thing if a man chose to live someone else's life instead of his own. Moreover, what we said above will apply here too: that what is best and most pleasant for any given creature is that which is proper to it. Therefore for man, too, the best and most pleasant life is the life of the intellect, since the intellect is in the fullest sense the man. So this life will also be the happiest.

Moral activity is secondary happiness

Life in conformity with the other kind of virtue will be happy in a secondary degree, because activities in accordance with it are human.[8] It is in our dealings with one another that we act justly and bravely and display the other virtues, observing what is due to each person in all contracts and mutual services and actions of every kind, and in our feelings too; and all these are obviously *human* experiences. Some of them are even thought to have a physical origin, and moral goodness is considered to be intimately connected in various ways with the feelings. Prudence, too, is closely linked with moral goodness, and moral goodness with prudence, since the first principles of prudence are given by the moral virtues, and the right standard for the virtues is set by prudence. These moral virtues, being bound up with the feelings too, will also belong to the composite person.[9] But the virtues of the composite person are human. Therefore the life that conforms with these virtues, and the happiness that belongs to it, are also human. But the happiness of the intellect is separate. ...

The view that happiness is contemplation is confirmed by other arguments

That perfect happiness is a kind of contemplative activity may be shown [1178b] also from the following argument. The gods in our conception of them are supremely happy and blessed, but what kind of actions should we attribute to them? If we say 'Just actions', surely we shall be confronted by the absurdity of their making contracts and returning deposits and all that sort of thing. Well, shall we say 'Brave actions' – facing terrors and risking their persons in the cause of honour? What of liberal actions? They will have nobody to give to; and it is absurd that they should actually have coined money or its equivalent. What form could their temperate actions take? Surely it would be cheap praise,[10] since they have no evil desires! If we went through the whole list we should find that the practical details of these actions are petty and unworthy of gods. On the other hand men have always conceived of them as at least living beings, and therefore active; for we cannot suppose that they spend their time in sleeping, like Endymion.[11] But if a living being is deprived of action, and still further of production, what is left but contemplation? It follows, then, that the activity of God, which is supremely happy, must be a form of contemplation; and therefore among human activities that which is most akin to God's will be the happiest.

This view is further supported by the fact that the lower animals have no share in happiness, being completely incapable of such an activity. The life of the gods is altogether happy, and that of man is happy in so far as it contains something that resembles the divine activity; but none of the lower animals is happy, because they have no way of participating in contemplation. Happiness, then, is co-extensive with contemplation, and the more people contemplate, the happier they are; not incidentally, but in virtue of their contemplation, because it is in itself precious. Thus happiness is a form of contemplation. ...

[1166a] People define a friend as (*a*) one who wishes and effects the good, or apparent good, of another for the sake of that other; or (*b*) one who wishes for the existence and preservation of his friend for the friend's sake – the same attitude as mothers have towards their children, or as old friends have towards those with whom they have fallen out. Others define him as (*c*) one who spends all his time with another, and (*d*) chooses the same things as he does, or as (*e*) one who shares his friend's joys and sorrows (this also is a very special trait of mothers). Friendship, too, is defined by one or another of these characteristics. But each one of them applies to the good man in relation to himself (and applies to others in so far as they suppose themselves to be good; in every case, as we have said, the standard seems to be ⟨moral⟩ goodness or the good man). For he is completely integrated[12] and desires the same things with every part of his soul. Also he wishes and effects the things that are or seem to be good for him[13] (for it is the mark of a good man to direct his energies to what is good) and he does it for his own sake (for he does it on account of the intellectual part of him, which is held to be the self of the individual). Also he desires his own life and safety,[14] especially that of his rational part; because for the good man existence is good, and everyone wishes his own good – nobody would choose to have all the good things in the world at the price of becoming somebody else (for as it is God possesses the good[15]), but only while remaining himself, whatever he is. And it would seem that the thinking part is, or most nearly is, the individual self. Such a person likes his own company,[16] because he enjoys being by himself, since he has entertaining memories of the past and good hopes for the future, and these afford him pleasure; also his mind is well furnished with subjects for contemplation. And he has the fullest consciousness of his joys and sorrows,[17] for it is always the same things that vex or please him, and not

different things at different times; because he virtually never changes his mind. . . .

[1166b] It seems, however, that the qualities that we have been describing belong also to the majority of people, bad as they are. Probably they share in them only in so far as they are self-satisfied and suppose themselves to be respectable; because nobody who is utterly bad and evil has them, or even the semblance of them. It is hardly too much to say that not even ⟨moderately⟩ bad people have them, because they are in conflict with themselves;[18] they desire one thing and will another, like the incontinent, who choose harmful pleasures instead of what they themselves believe to be good. There are others again who through cowardice and indolence shirk doing what they believe is in their own best interests. Others who have committed many fearful crimes and are hated for their villainy actually run away from life[19] and commit suicide. Also bad people seek constant companionship and avoid their own society,[20] because when they are by themselves they recall many disagreeable experiences and expect to have more of the same kind, whereas when they are with others they can forget. Possessing no lovable quality, they feel no affection for themselves;[21] consequently such people have no sympathetic consciousness of their own joys and sorrows,[22] because their soul is in a state of conflict: one part of it through depravity feels pain in abstaining from certain things, and another feels pleasure; one pulls this way and the other that, as if they would tear it apart. If it is impossible to feel pleasure and pain at the same time, at any rate such a person is very soon sorry that he was glad, and wishes that he had never taken pleasure in such things; for bad men are full of regrets.

It seems, then, that a bad man is not even amicably disposed towards himself, because he has no lovable quality. So if this state is the height of misery, one ought to strain every nerve to avoid wickedness and try to be a man of good character; for in that way one can both be on good terms with oneself and become the friend of somebody else.

NOTES

1 The other being life as a *state*, implying no more than the possession of reason.
2 Which he does not; cf. *Politics* 1280a32.
3 i.e. friendly states.
4 To excel other leisured occupations.
5 Probably composite soul, although the word (*suntheton*) is generally used of the composite whole consisting of soul and body.
6 Moral virtue.
7 Cf. *Rhetoric* 1394b24, Pindar, *Isthmians* v.20; similar maxims are common in the dramatists.
8 Whereas intellectual activity is divine.
9 The concrete man, embodied soul.

10   To impute self-control to them.

11   He was loved by the moon-goddess (in some versions of the story by Artemis or Diana) and granted immortality, but at the price of unconsciousness.

12   He has no inner conflict; see (*d*) above.

13   See (*a*) above.

14   See (*b*) above.

15   And *only* God possesses the supreme good; so to wish for all good, with a change of personality, would mean wishing to be God – which is no more sensible than wishing one's friend to be a god.

16   See (*c*) above.

17   See (*e*) above.

18   See (*d*) above.

19   See (*b*) above.

20   See (*c*) above.

21   See (*a*) above.

22   See (*c*) above.

26

My Station and its Duties

F. H. Bradley

F. H. Bradley (1846–1924) was another thinker who derived a prescription for the good life from man's nature and function as he saw them. He points out that a human being 'is born not into a desert, but into a living world'; he is necessarily part of a larger whole, member of a particular society; and his proper function is to be found in the station in which he is placed. Bradley's argument is about self-realization in a very specific way. He points out that what a person is depends on his place in society; there are no 'mere individuals' in the abstract. Hence there is no conflict between a person's interests and the demands of his station; for it is in acting out his station that he realizes himself. There are obvious affinities between Bradley's position and that of Aristotle. Both insist on the nature of man as a social being (or 'political animal'), and both argue from the nature and function of man to a conclusion about the good life. However, whereas Aristotle's argument yields a single prescription for man as such, Bradley's will vary according to the station in which one is placed. What is universally true is that we are all placed in some station or other.

And to confine the subject, and to keep to what is familiar, we will not call to our aid the life of animals, nor early societies, nor the course of history, but we will take men as they are now; we will take ourselves, and endeavour to keep wholly to the teaching of experience.

Let us take a man, an Englishman as he is now, and try to point out that, apart from what he has in common with others, apart from his sameness with others, he is not an Englishman – nor a man at all; that if you take him as something by himself, he is not what he is. Of course we do not mean to say that he can not go out of England without disappearing, nor, even if all the rest of the nation perished, that he would not survive. What we mean to say is, that he is what he is because he is a born and educated social being, and a member of an individual social organism; that if you make abstraction of all this, which is the same in him and in others, what you have left is not an Englishman, nor a man, but some I know not what residuum, which never has existed by itself, and does not so exist. If we suppose the world of relations, in which he was born and bred, never to have been, then we suppose the very essence of him not to be; if we take that away, we have taken him away; and hence he now is not an individual, in the sense of owing nothing to the sphere of relations in which he finds himself, but does contain those relations within himself as belonging to his very being; he is what he is, in brief, so far as he is what others also are. ...

Thus the child is at birth; and he is born not into a desert, but into a living world, a whole which has a true individuality of its own, and into a system and order which it is difficult to look at as anything else than an organism, and which, even in England, we are now beginning to call by that name. And I fear that the 'individuality' (the particularness) which the child brought into the light with him, now stands but a poor chance, and that there is no help for him until he is old enough to become a 'philosopher'. We have seen that already he has in him inherited habits, or what will of themselves appear as such; but, in addition to this, he is not for one moment left alone, but continually tampered with; and the habituation which is applied from the outside is the more insidious that it answers to this inborn disposition. Who can resist it? Nay, who but a 'thinker' could wish to have resisted it? And yet the tender care that receives and guides him is impressing on him habits, habits, alas, not particular to himself, and the 'icy chains' of universal custom are hardening themselves round his cradled life. As the poet tells us, he has not yet thought of himself; his earliest notions come mixed to him of things and persons, not distinct from one another, nor divided from the feeling of his own existence. The need that he can not understand moves him to foolish, but not futile, cries for what only another can give him; and the breast of his mother, and the soft warmth and touches and tones of his nurse, are made one with the feeling of his own pleasure and pain; nor is he yet a moralist to beware of such illusion, and to see in them mere means to an end without them in his separate self. For he does not even think of his separate self; he grows with his world, his mind fills and orders itself; and when he can separate himself from that world, and know himself apart from it, then by that time his self, the object of his self-consciousness, is penetrated, infected, characterized by the existence of others. Its content implies in every fibre relations of community. He learns, or already perhaps has learnt, to speak, and here he appropriates the common heritage of his race, the tongue that he makes his own is his country's language, it is (or it should be) the same that others speak, and it carries into his mind the ideas and sentiments of the face (over this I need not stay), and stamps them in indelibly. He grows up in an atmosphere of example and general custom, his life widens out from one little world to other and higher worlds, and he apprehends through successive stations the whole in which he lives, and in which he has lived. Is he now to try and develop his 'individuality', his self which is not the same as other selves? Where is it? What is it? Where can he find it? The soul within him is saturated, is filled, is qualified by, it has assimilated, has got its substance, has built itself up from, it *is* one and the same life with the universal life, and if he turns against this he turns against himself; if he thrusts it from him, he tears his own vitals; if he attacks it, he sets his weapon against his own heart. He has found his life in the life of the whole, he lives that in himself, 'he is a pulse-beat of the whole system, and himself the whole system.' ...

We have seen that the 'individual' apart from the community is an abstraction. It is not anything real, and hence not anything that we can realize, however much we may wish to do so. We have seen that I am myself by sharing with others, by including in my essence relations to them, the relations of the social state. If I wish to realize my true being, I must therefore realize something beyond my being as a mere this or that; for my true being has in it a life which is not the life of any mere particular, and so must be called a universal life.

What is it then that I am to realize? We have said it in 'my station and its duties'. To know what a man is (as we have seen) you must not take him in isolation. He is one of a people, he was born in a family, he lives in a certain society, in a certain state. What he has to do depends on what his place is, what his function is, and that all comes from his station in the organism. Are there then such organisms in which he lives, and if so, what is their nature? Here we come to questions which must be answered in full by any complete system of Ethics, but which we can not enter on. We must content ourselves by pointing out that there are such facts as the family, then in a middle position a man's own profession and society, and, over all, the larger community of the state. Leaving out of sight the question of a society wider than the state, we must say that a man's life with its moral duties is in the main filled up by his station in that system of wholes which the state is, and that this, partly by its laws and institutions, and still more by its spirit, gives him the life which he does live and ought to live. That objective institutions exist is of course an obvious fact; and it is a fact which every day is becoming plainer that these institutions are organic, and further, that they are moral. The assertion that communities have been manufactured by the addition of exclusive units is, as we have seen, a mere fable; and if, within the state, we take that which seems wholly to depend on individual caprice, e.g. marriage,[1] yet even here we find that a man does give up his self so far as it excludes others; he does bring himself under a unity which is superior to the particular person and the impulses that belong to his single existence, and which makes him fully as much as he makes it. In short, man is a social being; he is real only because he is social, and can realize himself only because it is as social that he realizes himself. The mere individual is a delusion of theory; and the attempt to realize it in practice is the starvation and mutilation of human nature, with total sterility or the production of monstrosities. ...

'My station and its duties' teaches us to identify others and ourselves with the station we fill; to consider that as good, and by virtue of that to consider others and ourselves good too. It teaches us that a man who does his work in the world is good, notwithstanding his faults, if his faults do not prevent him from fulfilling his station. It tells us that the heart is an idle abstraction; we are not to think of it, nor must we look at our insides, but at our work and our life, and say to ourselves, Am I fulfilling my appointed function or not? Fulfil it we can, if we will: what we have to do is not so much better than the world that we can not do it; the world is there waiting for it; my duties are my rights. On the one hand, I am not likely to be much better than the world asks me to be; on the other hand, if I can take my place in the world I ought not to be discontented. Here we must not be misunderstood; we do not say that the false self, the habits and desires opposed to the good will, are extinguished. Though negated, they never are all of them entirely suppressed, and can not be. Hence we must not say that any man really does fill his station to the full height of his capacity; nor must we say of any man that he can not perform his function better than he does, for we all can do so, and should try to do so. We do not wish to deny what are plain moral facts, nor in any way to slur them over.

How then does the contradiction disappear? It disappears by my identifying myself with the good will that I realize in the world, by my refusing to identify myself with the bad will of my private self. So far as I am one with the good will, living as a member in the moral organism, I am to consider myself real, and I am not to consider the false self real. That can not be attributed to me in my character of member in the organism. Even in me the false existence of it has been partly suppressed by that organism; and, so far as the organism is concerned, it is wholly suppressed, because contradicted in its results, and allowed no reality. Hence, not existing for the organism, it does not exist for me as a member thereof; and only as a member thereof do I hold myself to be real. And yet this is not justification by faith, for we not only trust, but see, that despite our faults the moral world stands fast, and we in and by it. It is like faith, however, in this, that not merely by thinking ourselves, but by willing ourselves as such, can we look on ourselves as organs in a good whole, and so ourselves good. And further, the knowledge that as members of the system we are real, and not otherwise, encourages us more and more to identify ourselves with that system; to make ourselves better, and so more real, since we see that the good is real, and that nothing else is.

Or, to repeat it, in education my self by habituation has been growing into one with the good self around me, and by my free acceptance of my lot hereafter I consciously make myself one with the good, so that, though bad habits cling to and even arise in me, yet I can not but be aware of myself as the reality of the good will. That is my essential side; my imperfections are not, and practically they do not matter. The good will in the world realizes itself by and in imperfect instruments, and in spite of them. The work is done, and so long as I will my part of the work and do it (as I do), I feel that, if I perform the function, I *am* the organ, and that my faults, if they do not matter to my station, do not matter to me. My heart I am not to think of, except to tell by my work whether it is in my work, and one with the moral whole; and if that is so, I have the consciousness of absolute reality in the good because of and by myself, and in myself because of and through the good; and with that I am satisfied, and have no right to be dissatisfied.

The individual's consciousness of himself is inseparable from the knowing himself as an organ of the whole; and the residuum falls more and more into the background, so that he thinks of it, if at all, not as himself, but as an idle appendage. For his nature now is not distinct from his 'artificial self'. He is related to the living moral system not as to a foreign body; his relation to it is 'too inward even for faith,' since faith implies a certain separation. It is no other-world that he can not see but must trust to: he feels himself in it, and it in him; in a word, the self-consciousness of himself *is* the self-consciousness of the whole in him, and his will is the will which sees in him its accomplishment by him; it is the free will which knows itself as the free will, and, as this, beholds its realization and is more than content.

NOTE

1 Marriage is a contract, a contract to pass out of the sphere of contract; and this is possible only because the contracting parties are already beyond and above the sphere of mere contract.

27

Freedom and Bad Faith

Jean-Paul Sartre

The arguments of Rousseau, Aristotle and Bradley may all be described as 'essentialist', since they proceed from claims about the essential nature of man. This approach is rejected in the 'existentialism' of Jean-Paul Sartre (1905–80). To suppose that a recipe for living, a 'function of man', can be deduced from man's essential nature is to treat him as if he were an artefact made for a purpose. Such an approach might be appropriate if one believes in God ('the supreme artisan'), but not otherwise. There is, according to Sartre, no answer to the question how we should live, once that belief is given up. Nor is there any moral code to which one can appeal for guidance, for it is always up to the individual to judge whether a given moral code or imperative is acceptable. Thus we are left with a total freedom of choice, and it is self-deception (or 'bad faith') to pretend that it is otherwise. 'No limits to my freedom can be found except freedom itself or, if you prefer ..., we are not free to cease being free'.[1] One of Sartre's examples of bad faith, reprinted below, is that of the café waiter who gives himself up to that role as if he were bound by it. Bradley would have commended the man for living according to his station and in that way achieving self-realization. But according to Sartre such fulfilment is not possible for human beings, who are conscious, and cannot avoid being conscious, of their freedom with regard to any given role or station. Using the word 'I' in two senses, Sartre expresses the human capacity for self-reflection thus: 'It is precisely this person who I have to be *(if I am the waiter in question) and who I am not.'*

The alternative to bad faith is 'sincerity' – facing up fully to one's predicament as a self-reflective human being, not tied by any essence, social role or moral code. This, according to Sartre, is the only virtue that is left once we have faced up to the full implications of our freedom. But this is not sincerity in the sense of being true to one's nature; for what is required is to transcend one's nature, as a being of this or that type. We 'surpass this being – and that not toward another being but toward emptiness, toward nothing.' *Sartre's writings (especially his novels and plays) contain vivid portrayals of people who, conscious of their all-embracing freedom, cannot make their minds up to any course of action. One example, reprinted below, is that of the student who came to him for advice in a case of moral conflict – advice that Sartre was not prepared to give.*

Sartre's philosophy is especially a philosophy of the modern world in which we live, and in which, indeed, we often experience an excess of freedom. Religion is largely abandoned, social roles have become more fluid than ever before, moral principles seem to have lost their certainty. What is left for us to live by? It may be questioned, however, whether our freedom, even after these changes, is really as absolute as Sartre sees it. Of course decisions are often difficult, especially where reasons are in conflict or insufficient. But this is not always so. For example, if I have borrowed some money, then I ought (other things being equal) to repay it; and, in reasoning thus, I would not need to appeal to any moral code or essentialist philosophy. Perhaps Sartre would reply that the very idea of acting for a reason is incompatible with our freedom.

The waiter in Sartre's example 'plays with his condition in order to realize *it.' He plays his role as intensively as he can, attempting to really be a waiter and nothing else; and herein lies his bad faith. Yet in another part of his book Sartre speaks approvingly of play, regarding it as an expression of freedom. Here he contrasts play with 'the spirit of seriousness'. The 'serious man', he says, 'is in* bad faith' *because, taking the world seriously, he hides his independence of it from himself. This account of play versus seriousness may be compared with Schlick's account of play versus 'the curse of purposes' in section one; and also with Huizinga's conception of man as* homo ludens, *in the reading after Sartre.*

NOTE

1 *Being and Nothingness*, 439 (London, Methuen 1958); not reprinted here.

If one considers an article of manufacture – as, for example, a book or a paper-knife – one sees that it has been made by an artisan who had a conception of it; and he has paid attention, equally, to the conception of a paper-knife and to the pre-existent technique of production which is a part of that conception and is, at bottom, a formula. Thus the paper-knife is at the same time an article producible in a certain manner and one which, on the other hand, serves a definite purpose, for one cannot suppose that a man would produce a paper-knife without knowing what it was for. Let us say, then, of the paper-knife that its essence – that is to say the sum of the formulae and the qualities which made its production and its definition possible – precedes its existence. The presence of such-and-such a paper-knife or book is thus determined before my eyes. Here, then, we are viewing the world from a technical standpoint, and we can say that production precedes existence.

When we think of God as the creator, we are thinking of him, most of the time, as a supernal artisan. Whatever doctrine we may be considering, whether it be a doctrine like that of Descartes, or of Leibnitz himself, we always imply that the will follows, more or less, from the understanding or at least accompanies it, so that when God creates he knows precisely what he is creating. Thus, the conception of man in the mind of God is comparable to that of the paper-knife in the mind of the artisan; God makes man according to a procedure and a conception, exactly as the artisan manufactures a paper-knife, following a definition and a formula. Thus each individual man is the realization of a certain conception which dwells in the divine understanding. In the philosophic atheism of the eighteenth century, the notion of God is suppressed, but not, for all that, the idea that essence is prior to existence; something of that idea we will still find everywhere, in Diderot, in Voltaire and even in Kant. Man possesses a human nature; that 'human nature', which is the conception of human being, is found in every man; which means that each man is a particular example of an universal conception, the conception of Man. In Kant, this universality goes so far that the wild man of the woods, man in the state of nature and the bourgeois are all contained in the same definition and have the same fundamental qualities. Here again, the essence of man precedes that historic existence which we confront in experience.

Atheistic existentialism, of which I am a representative, declares with greater consistency that if God does not exist there is at least one being whose existence comes before its essence, a being which exists before it can be defined by any conception of it. That being is man or, as Heidegger has it, the human reality. What do we mean by saying that existence precedes essence? We mean that man first of all exists, encounters himself, surges up in the world – and defines himself afterwards. If man as the existentialist sees him is not definable, it is because to begin with he is nothing. He will not be anything until later, and then he will be what he makes of himself. Thus, there is no human nature, because there is no God to have a conception of it. Man simply is. Not that he is simply what he conceives himself to be, but he is what he wills, and as he conceives himself after already existing – as he wills to be after that leap towards existence. Man is nothing else but that which he makes of himself. That is the first principle of existentialism. And this is what people call its 'subjectivity', using the word as a reproach against us. But what do we mean to say by this, but that man is of a greater dignity than a stone or a table? For we mean to say that man primarily exists – that man is, before all else, something which propels itself towards a future and is aware that it is doing so. Man is, indeed, a project which possesses a subjective life, instead of being a kind of moss, or a fungus or a cauliflower. Before that projection of the self nothing exists; not even in the heaven of intelligence: man will only attain existence when he is what he purposes to be. Not, however, what he may wish to be. For what we usually understand by

wishing or willing is a conscious decision taken – much more often than
not – after we have made ourselves what we are. I may wish to join a party,
to write a book or to marry – but in such a case what is usually called my
will is probably a manifestation of a prior and more spontaneous decision.
If, however, it is true that existence is prior to essence, man is responsible
for what he is. Thus, the first effect of existentialism is that it puts every
man in possession of himself as he is, and places the entire responsibility
for his existence squarely upon his own shoulders. ...

You know the story: An angel commanded Abraham to sacrifice his son:
and obedience was obligatory, if it really was an angel who had appeared
and said, 'Thou, Abraham, shalt sacrifice thy son.' But anyone in such a
case would wonder, first, whether it was indeed an angel and secondly,
whether I am really Abraham. Where are the proofs? A certain mad woman
who suffered from hallucinations said that people were telephoning to her,
and giving her orders. The doctor asked, 'But who is it that speaks to you?'
She replied: 'He says it is God.' And what, indeed, could prove to her that
it was God? If an angel appears to me, what is the proof that it is an angel;
or, if I hear voices, who can prove that they proceed from heaven and not
from hell, or from my own subconsciousneses or some pathological
condition? Who can prove that they are really addressed to me? ...
    Dostoyevsky once wrote 'If God did not exist, everything would be
permitted'; and that, for existentialism, is the starting point. Everything is
indeed permitted if God does not exist, and man is in consequence forlorn,
for he cannot find anything to depend upon either within or outside himself.
He discovers forthwith, that he is without excuse. For if indeed existence
precedes essence, one will never be able to explain one's action by reference
to a given and specific human nature; in other words, there is no determinism
– man is free, man *is* freedom. Nor, on the other hand, if God does not
exist, are we provided with any values or commands that could legitimize
our behaviour. Thus we have neither behind us, nor before us in a luminous
realm of values, any means of justification or excuse. We are left alone,
without excuse. That is what I mean when I say that man is condemned
to be free. Condemned, because he did not create himself, yet is nevertheless
at liberty, and from the moment that he is thrown into this world he is
responsible for everything he does. The existentialist does not believe in
the power of passion. He will never regard a grand passion as a destructive
torrent upon which a man is swept into certain actions as by fate, and
which, therefore, is an excuse for them. He thinks that man is responsible
for his passion. Neither will an existentialist think that a man can find help
through some sign being vouchsafed upon earth for his orientation: for he
thinks that the man himself interprets the sign as he chooses. He thinks
that every man, without any support or help whatever, is condemned at

every instant to invent man. As Ponge has written in a very fine article, 'Man is the future of man.' That is exactly true. Only, if one took this to mean that the future is laid up in heaven, that God knows what it is, it would be false, for then it would no longer even be a future. If, however, it means that, whatever man may now appear to be, there is a future to be fashioned, a virgin future that awaits him – then it is a true saying. But in the present one is forsaken.

As an example by which you may the better understand this state of abandonment, I will refer to the case of a pupil of mine, who sought me out in the following circumstances. His father was quarrelling with his mother and was also inclined to be a 'collaborator'; his elder brother had been killed in the German offensive of 1940 and this young man, with a sentiment somewhat primitive but generous, burned to avenge him. His mother was living alone with him, deeply afflicted by the semi-treason of his father and by the death of her eldest son, and her one consolation was in this young man. But he, at this moment, had the choice between going to England to join the Free French Forces or of staying near his mother and helping her to live. He fully realized that this woman lived only for him and that his disappearance – or perhaps his death – would plunge her into despair. He also realized that, concretely and in fact, every action he performed on his mother's behalf would be sure of effect in the sense of aiding her to live, where as anything he did in order to go and fight would be an ambiguous action which might vanish like water into sand and serve no purpose. For instance, to set out for England he would have to wait indefinitely in a Spanish camp on the way through Spain; or, on arriving in England or in Algiers he might be put into an office to fill up forms. Consequently, he found himself confronted by two very different modes of action; the one concrete, immediate, but directed towards only one individual; and the other an action addressed to an end infinitely greater, a national collectivity, but for that very reason ambiguous– and it might be frustrated on the way. At the same time, he was hesitating between two kinds of morality; on the one side the morality of sympathy, of personal devotion and, on the other side, a morality of wider scope but of more debatable validity. He had to choose between those two. What could help him to choose? Could the Christian doctrine? No. Christian doctrine says: Act with charity, love your neighbour, deny yourself for others, choose the way which is hardest, and so forth. But which is the harder road? To whom does one owe the more brotherly love, the patriot or the mother? Which is the more useful aim, the general one of fighting in and for the whole community, or the precise aim of helping one particular person to live? Who can give an answer to that *a priori*? No one. Nor is it given in any ethical scripture. The Kantian ethic says, Never regard another as a means, but always as an end. Very well; if I remain with my mother, I shall be regarding her as an end and not as a means: but by the same token I am in danger of treating as means those who are fighting on my behalf; and the converse is also true, that if I go to the aid of the combatants I shall be treating them as the end at the risk of treating my mother as a means.

If values are uncertain, if they are still too abstract to determine the particular, concrete case under consideration, nothing remains but to trust in our instincts. That is what this young man tried to do; and when I saw him he said, 'In the end, it is feeling that counts; the direction in which it is really pushing me is the one I ought to choose. If I feel that I love my mother enough to sacrifice everything else for her – my will to be avenged, all my longings for action and adventure – then I stay with her. If, on the contrary, I feel that my love for her is not enough, I go.' But how does one estimate the strength of a feeling? The value of his feeling for his mother was determined precisely by the fact that he was standing by her. I may say that I love a certain friend enough to sacrifice such or such a sum of money for him, but I cannot prove that unless I have done it. I may say, 'I love my mother enough to remain with her', if actually I have remained with her. I can only estimate the strength of this affection if I have performed an action by which it is defined and ratified. But if I then appeal to this affection to justify my action, I find myself drawn into a vicious circle. . . .

Man makes himself; he is not found ready-made; he makes himself by the choice of his morality, and he cannot but choose a morality, such is the pressure of circumstances upon him. We define man only in relation to his commitments; it is therefore absurd to reproach us for irresponsibility in our choice.

In the second place, people say to us, 'You are unable to judge others.' This is true in one sense and false in another. It is true in this sense, that whenever a man chooses his purpose and his commitment in all clearness and in all sincerity, whatever that purpose may be, it is impossible to prefer another for him. It is true in the sense that we do not believe in progress. Progress implies amelioration; but man is always the same, facing a situation which is always changing, and choice remains always a choice in the situation. The moral problem has not changed since the time when it was a choice between slavery and anti-slavery – from the time of the war of Secession, for example, until the present moment when one chooses between the MRP[1] and the Communists.

We can judge, nevertheless, for, as I have said, one chooses in view of others, and in view of others one chooses himself. One can judge, first – and perhaps this is not a judgment of value, but it is a logical judgment – that in certain cases choice is founded upon an error, and in others upon the truth. One can judge a man by saying that he deceives himself. Since we have defined the situation of man as one of free choice, without excuse and without help, any man who takes refuge behind the excuse of his passions, or by inventing some deterministic doctrine, is a self-deceiver. One may object: 'But why should he not choose to deceive himself?' I reply that it is not for me to judge him morally, but I define his self-deception as an error. Here one cannot avoid pronouncing a judgment of truth. The self-deception is evidently a falsehood, because it is a dissimulation of man's complete liberty of commitment. Upon this same level, I say that it is also a self-deception if I choose to declare that certain values are incumbent upon me; I am in contradiction with myself if I will these values and at the same time say that they impose themselves upon me. If anyone says to me, 'And what if I wish to deceive myself?' I answer, There is no reason why you should not, but I declare that you are doing so, and that the attitude of strict consistency alone is that of good faith. Furthermore, I can pronounce a moral judgment. For I declare that freedom, in respect of concrete circumstances, can have no other end and aim but itself; and when once a man has seen that values depend upon himself, in that state of forsakenness he can will only one thing, and that is freedom as the foundation of all values. That does not mean that he wills it in the abstract: it simply means that the actions of men of good faith have, as their ultimate significance, the quest of freedom itself as such. ...

PATTERNS OF BAD FAITH

Let us consider this waiter in the café. His movement is quick and forward, a little too precise, a little too rapid. He comes toward the patrons with a step a little too quick. He bends forward a little too eagerly; his voice, his eyes express an interest a little too solicitous for the order of the customer. Finally there he returns, trying to imitate in his walk the inflexible stiffness of some kind of automaton while carrying his tray with the recklessness of a tight-rope-walker by putting it in a perpetually unstable, perpetually broken equilibrium which he perpetually reestablishes by a light movement of the arm and hand. All his behavior seems to us a game. He applies himself to chaining his movements as if they were mechanisms, the one regulaing the other; his gestures and even his voice seem to be mechanisms; he gives himself the quickness and pitiless rapidity of things. He is playing, he is amusing himself. But what is he playing? We need not watch long before we can explain it: he is playing at *being* a waiter in a café. There is nothing there to surprise us. The game is a kind of marking out and investigation. The child plays with his body in order to explore it, to take inventory of it; the waiter in the café plays with his condition in order to *realize* it. This obligation is not different from that which is imposed on all tradesmen. Their condition is wholly one of ceremony. The public demands of them that they realize it as a ceremony; there is the dance of the grocer, of the tailor, of the auctioneer, by which they endeavour to persuade their clientele that they are nothing but a grocer, an auctioneer, a tailor. A grocer who dreams is offensive to the buyer, because such a grocer is not wholly a grocer. Society demands that he limit himself to his function as a grocer, just as the soldier at attention makes himself into a soldier-thing with a direct regard which does not see at all, which is no longer meant to see, since it is the rule and not the interest of the moment which determines the point he must fix his eyes on (the sight 'fixed at ten paces'). There are indeed many precautions to imprison a man in what he is, as if we lived in perpetual fear that he might escape from it, that he might break away and suddenly elude his condition.

In a parallel situation, from within, the waiter in the café can not be immediately a café waiter in the sense that this inkwell *is* an inkwell, or the glass is a glass. It is by no means that he can not form reflective judgments or concepts concerning his condition. He knows well what it 'means:' the obligation of getting up at five o'clock, of sweeping the floor of the shop before the restaurant opens, of starting the coffee pot going, etc. He knows the rights which it allows: the right to the tips, the right to belong to a union, etc. But all these concepts, all these judgments refer to the transcendent. It is a matter of abstract possibilities, of rights and duties conferred on a 'person possessing rights.' And it is precisely this person *who I have to be* (if I am the waiter in question) and who I am not. It is not that I do not wish to be this person or that I want this person to be different. But rather there is no common measure between his being and mine. It is a 'representation' for others and for myself, which means that I can be he only in *representation*. But if I represent myself as him, I am not he; I am separated from him as the object from the subject, separated *by nothing* but this nothing isolates me from him. I can not be he, I can only play at *being* him; that is, imagine to myself that I am he. And thereby I affect him with nothingness. In vain do I fulfil the functions of a café waiter. I can be he only in the neutralized mode, as the actor is Hamlet, by mechanically making the *typical gestures of* my state and by aiming at myself as an imaginary café waiter through those gestures taken as an 'analogue.' What I attempt to realize is a being-in-itself of the café waiter, as if it were not just in my power to confer their value and their urgency upon my duties and the rights of my position, as if it were not my free choice to get up each morning at five o'clock or to remain in bed, even though it meant getting fired. As if from the very fact that I sustain this role in existence I did not transcend it on every side, as if I did not constitute myself as one *beyond* my condition. Yet there is no doubt that I *am* in a sense a café waiter – otherwise could I not just as well call myself a diplomat or a reporter? But if I am one, this can not be in the mode of being in itself. I am a waiter in the mode of *being what I am not*. ...

There remains one type of activity which we willingly admit is entirely gratuitous; the activity of *play* and the 'drives' which relate back to it. Can we discover an appropriate drive in sport? To be sure, it must be noted first that play as contrasted with the spirit of seriousness appears to be the least possessive attitude; it strips the real of its reality. The serious attitude involves starting from the world and attributing more reality to the world than to oneself; at the very least the serious man confers reality on himself to the degree to which he belongs to the world. It is not by chance that materialism is serious; it is not by chance that it is found at all times and places as the favourite doctrine of the revolutionary. This is because revolutionaries are serious. They come to know themselves first in terms of the world which oppresses them, and they wish to change this world. In this one respect they are in agreeement with their ancient adversaries, the possessors, who also come to know themselves and appreciate themselves in terms of their position in the world. Thus all serious thought is thickened by the world; it coagulates; it is a dismissal of human reality in favour of the world. The serious man is 'of the world' and has no resource in himself. He does not even imagine any longer the possibility of *getting out* of the world, for he has given to himself the type of existence of the rock, the consistency, the inertia, the opacity of being-in-the-midst-of-the-world. It is obvious that the serious man at bottom is hiding from himself the consciousness of his freedom; he is in *bad faith* and his bad faith aims at presenting himself to his own eyes as a consequence; everything is a consequence for him, and there is never any beginning. That is why he is so concerned with the consequences of his acts. Marx proposed the original dogma of the serious when he asserted the priority of object over subject. Man is serious when he takes himself for an object.

Play, like Kierkegaard's irony, releases subjectivity. What is play indeed if not an activity of which man is the first origin, for which man himself sets the rules, and which has no consequences except according to the rules posited? As soon as a man apprehends himself as free and wishes to use his freedom, a freedom, by the way, which could just as well be his anguish, then his activity is play. The first principle of play is man himself; through it he escapes his natural desire; he himself sets the value and rules for his acts and consents to play only according to the rules which he himself has established and defined. As a result, there is in a sense 'little reality' in the world. It might appear then that when a man is playing, bent on discovering himself as free in his very action, he certainly could not be concerned with *possessing* a being in the world. His goal, which he aims at through sports or pantomime or games, is to attain himself as a certain being, precisely the being which is in question in his being.

NOTES

1   Mouvement Républicain Populaire.
2   Cf. *L'Imaginaire*, Conclusion.

28

Homo Ludens

J. Huizinga

The book Homo Ludens, *from which the next reading is taken, is a wide-ranging study of human activities in different ages, with the aim of showing that 'the great archetypal activities of human society are all permeated with play'. Like Sartre (in the final extract), Huizinga sees play as an expression of freedom. But play can itself be taken seriously; 'the contrast between play and seriousness is always fluid.' In comparing the various discussions of play, it must be borne in mind that play can mean different things. A distinction must be made, for example, between childish play (as advocated by Schlick in section one) and the playing of games in which procedures and aims are laid down by strict rules. The latter would not conform to Schlick's renunciation of the schema of means and ends ('the curse of purposes'); but they are satisfying in another way, introducing a kind of order that is not found elsewhere. And the same is true of the type of play discussed by Huizinga. 'Into an imperfect world and into the confusions of life it brings a temporary, a limited perfection.'*

The great archetypal activities of human society are all permeated with play from the start. Take language, for instance – that first and supreme instrument which man shapes in order to communicate, to teach, to command. Language allows him to distinguish, to establish, to state things; in short, to name them and by naming them to raise them into the domain of the spirit. In the making of speech and language the spirit is continually 'sparking' between matter and mind, as it were, playing with this wondrous nominative faculty. Behind every abstract expression there lie the boldest of metaphors, and every metaphor is a play upon words. Thus in giving expression to life man creates a second, poetic world alongside the world of nature.

Or take myth. This, too, is a transformation or an 'imagination' of the outer world, only here the process is more elaborate and ornate than is the case with individual words. In myth, primitive man seeks to account for the world of phenomena by grounding it in the Divine. In all the wild imaginings of mythology a fanciful spirit is playing on the border-line between jest and earnest. Or finally, let us take ritual. Primitive society performs its sacred rites, its sacrifices, consecrations and mysteries, all of which serve to guarantee the well-being of the world, in a spirit of pure play truly understood.

Now in myth and ritual the great instinctive forces of civilized life have their origin: law and order, commerce and profit, craft and art, poetry, wisdom and science. All are rooted in the primaeval soil of play. ...

First and foremost, then, all play is a voluntary activity. Play to order is no longer play: it could at best be but a forcible imitation of it. By this quality of freedom alone, play marks itself off from the course of the natural process. It is something added thereto and spread out over it like a flowering, an ornament, a garment. Obviously, freedom must be understood here in the wider sense that leaves untouched the philosophical problem of determinism. It may be objected that this freedom does not exist for the animal and the child; they *must* play because their instinct drives them to it and because it serves to develop their bodily faculties and their powers of selection. The term 'instinct', however, introduces an unknown quantity, and to presuppose the utility of play from the start is to be guilty of a *petitio principii*. Child and animal play because they enjoy playing, and therein precisely lies their freedom.

Be that as it may, for the adult and responsible human being play is a function which he could equally well leave alone. Play is superfluous. The need for it is only urgent to the extent that the enjoyment of it makes it a need. Play can be deferred or suspended at any time. It is never imposed by physical necessity or moral duty. It is never a task. It is done at leisure, during 'free time'. Only when play is a recognized cultural function – a rite, a ceremony– is it bound up with notions of obligation and duty.

Here, then, we have the first main characteristic of play: that it is free, is in fact freedom. A second characteristic is closely connected with this, namely, that play is not 'ordinary' or 'real' life. It is rather a stepping out of 'real' life into a temporary sphere of activity with a disposition all of its own. Every child knows perfectly well that he is 'only pretending', or that it was 'only for fun'. How deep-seated this awareness is in the child's soul is strikingly illustrated by the following story, told to me by the father of the boy in question. He found his four-year-old son sitting at the front of a row of chairs, playing 'trains'. As he hugged him the boy said: 'Don't kiss the engine, Daddy, or the carriages won't think it's real'. This 'only pretending' quality of play betrays a consciousness of the inferiority of play compared with 'seriousness', a feeling that seems to be something as primary as play itself. Nevertheless, as we have already pointed out, the consciousness of play being 'only a pretend' does not by any means prevent it from proceeding with the utmost seriousness, with an absorption, a devotion that passes into rapture and, temporarily at least, completely abolishes that troublesome 'only' feeling. Any game can at any time wholly run away with the players. The contrast between play and seriousness is always fluid. The inferiority of play is continually being offset by the corresponding superiority of its seriousness. Play turns to seriousness and seriousness to play. Play may rise to heights of beauty and sublimity that leave seriousness far beneath. ...

Play begins, and then at a certain moment it is 'over'. It plays itself to an end. While it is in progress all is movement, change, alternation, succession, association, separation. But immediately connected with its limitation as to time there is a further curious feature of play: it at once assumes fixed form as a cultural phenomenon. Once played, it endures as a new-found creation of the mind, a treasure to be retained by the memory. It is transmitted, it becomes tradition. It can be repeated at any time, whether it be 'child's play' or a game of chess, or at fixed intervals like a mystery. In this faculty of repetition lies one of the most essential qualities of play. It holds good not only of play as a whole but also of its inner structure. In nearly all the higher forms of play the elements of repetition and alternation (as in the *refrain*), are like the warp and woof of a fabric.

More striking even than the limitation as to time is the limitation as to space. All play moves and has its being within a playground marked off beforehand either materially or ideally, deliberately or as a matter of course. Just as there is no formal difference between play and ritual, so the 'consecrated spot' cannot be formally distinguished from the play-ground. The arena, the card-table, the magic circle, the temple, the stage, the screen, the tennis court, the court of justice, etc., are all in form and function play-grounds, i.e. forbidden spots, isolated, hedged round, hallowed, within which special rules obtain. All are temporary worlds within the ordinary world, dedicated to the performance of an act apart.

Inside the play-ground an absolute and peculiar order reigns. Here we come across another, very positive feature of play: it creates order, *is* order. Into an imperfect world and into the confusion of life it brings a temporary, a limited perfection. Play demands order absolute and supreme. The least deviation from it 'spoils the game', robs it of its character and makes it worthless. The profound affinity between play and order is perhaps the reason why play, as we noted in passing, seems to lie to such a large extent in the field of aesthetics. Play has a tendency to be beautiful. It may be that this aesthetic factor is identical with the impulse to create orderly form, which animates play in all its aspects. The words we use to denote the elements of play belong for the most part to aesthetics, terms with which we try to describe the effects of beauty: tension, poise, balance, contrast, variation, solution, resolution, etc. Play casts a spell over us; it is 'enchanting', 'captivating'. It is invested with the noblest qualities we are capable of perceiving in things: rhythm and harmony. ...

Ritual is seriousness at its highest and holiest. Can it nevertheless be play? We began by saying that all play, both of children and of grown-ups, can be performed in the most perfect seriousness. Does this go so far as to imply that play is still bound up with the sacred emotion of the sacramental act? Our conclusions are to some extent impeded by the rigidity of our accepted ideas. We are accustomed to think of play and seriousness as an absolute antithesis. It would seem, however, that this does not go to the heart of the matter.

Let us consider for a moment the following argument. The child plays in complete – we can well say, in sacred – earnest. But it plays and knows that it plays. The sportsman, too, plays with all the fervour of a man enraptured, but he still knows that he is playing. The actor on the stage is wholly absorbed in his playing, but is all the time conscious of 'the play'. The same holds good of the violinist, though he may soar to realms beyond this world. The play-character, therefore, may attach to the sublimest forms of action. Can we now extend the line to ritual and say that the priest performing the rites of sacrifice is only playing? At first sight it seems preposterous, for if you grant it for one religion you must grant it for all. Hence our ideas of ritual, magic, liturgy, sacrament and mystery would all fall within the play-concept. In dealing with abstractions we must always guard against over-straining their significance. We would merely be playing with words were we to stretch the play-concept unduly. But, all things considered, I do not think we are falling into that error when we characterize ritual as play. The ritual act has all the formal and essential characteristics of play which we enumerated above, particularly in so far as it transports the participants to another world. This identity of ritual and play was unreservedly recognized by Plato as a given fact. He had no hesitation in comprising the *sacra* in the category of play. 'I say that a man must be serious with the serious,' he says (*Laws*, vii, 803). 'God alone is worthy of supreme seriousness, but man is made God's plaything, and that is the best part of him. Therefore every man and woman should live life accordingly, and play the noblest games and be of another mind from what they are at present. ... For they deem war a serious thing, though in war there is neither play nor culture worthy the name [ουτ' ουϑ παιδιὰ ... ουτ' αυ παιδεία], which are the things *we* deem most serious. Hence all must live in peace as well as they possibly can. What, then, is the right way of living? Life must be lived as play, playing certain games, making sacrifices, singing and dancing, and then a man will be able to propitiate the gods, and defend himself against his enemies, and win in the contest.'[1]

NOTE

1 Cf. *Laws*, vii, 796, where Plato speaks of the sacred dances of the Kouretes of Crete, calling them ἐνοπλια παλγβια.

29

Moral Tradition

John Kekes

Huizinga speaks of the power of play to assume a 'fixed form' and become part of a tradition. Tradition is the topic of our final reading. According to John Kekes, what is needed for a 'healthy society' is the existence of traditional ways of doing things, which are accepted in a 'largely unreflective and spontaneous' way. To be contrasted with these is the type of radical questioning (as advocated by Sartre) which would 'make our children free without teaching them how to use their freedom'. There is a resemblance between Kekes's position and that of Bradley; in both cases adherence to existing arrangements is seen as the remedy against moral confusion. However, Kekes is not a relativist, claiming that all traditions are equally good. His traditionalism is compatible, he argues, with adherence to certain absolute standards, and a given tradition may be criticized if it falls short of these.

I

In a healthy society, moral conduct is largely unreflective and spontaneous. People pay their debts, tell the truth, keep promises, help each other if they can without too much trouble, do their jobs, and do not think much about it. True, complications inevitably arise, conflicts and temptations occasionally disturb the even surface of moral life. But these ripples are exceptional, smoothness is the rule. Extreme situations and men devoid of conscience are remote and rarely demand attention. The prevalent moral failings are not monstrous, and guilt, shame, fear, self-respect, and lucky circumstances conspire to keep them that way.

What guides moral conduct in this desirable way? The network of customs that constitutes a moral tradition. 'Custom', I say with Hume, 'is the great guide of human life.'[1] This is not a widely shared view in contemporary moral thinking. The received opinion is that moral conduct is guided primarily by principles or ideals.

The guiding principle is said by some to be the categorical imperative; others think it is the greatest happiness; one recent proposal combines two of them; the equal liberty and the difference principles; and there are many other candidates as well. The content of these principles does not affect the objection to regarding them as fundamental moral guides, nor does it matter whether they are said to be one or many. What does matter is the explanation of how they guide moral conduct. This they are said to do both consciously and unconsciously.

The principles are taught unconsciously in moral education. Underlying the many dos and don'ts of a moral tradition, there is the pervasive influence of the basic principles. Secondary moral rules reflect the primary ones. And a morally well-trained person, having acquired the secondary rules, naturally, without thinking or deliberation, follows the primary ones. This is all that most people most of the time need to do to behave in a morally praiseworthy way. But the basic principles can also be, and occasionally need to be, conscious guides. For the secondary principles may conflict; they may be challenged internally by people wishing to know why they should follow a principle that obliges them to go against their desires; and they may also be challenged externally by coming into contact with another moral tradition. When this happens, primary principles are appealed to as justifications of secondary ones, and this, of course, requires the conscious recognition of their guiding force.

It is true that principles guide conduct. But they cannot be the basic guides they are supposed to be for three reasons. First, how do principles come to be formulated and accepted? The reasonable answer is that they are extracted from the conventional conduct of members of some more or less stable society. Thus formulated, the principles find general acceptance, because they exemplify what people have been doing anyway. The principles grow out of the practice they aim to guide. If the moral tradition of a people does not already embody, say, the Golden Rule, then it is useless to try to graft on to it the alien principle. The graft will take only if the host is receptive. Thus practice is primary and principles are secondary. And the practice from which moral principles are extracted is the customary conduct of people in a moral tradition.

Secondly, potential principles for a moral tradition may be rejected, accepted, or revised. How could this be if the principles were basic? The answer, of course, is that they are not basic, customary conduct is, and the fate of a newly proposed principle depends on how well it reflects prevailing practice. Lastly, the application of the principle presupposes approval of the practice the principle is supposed to legitimate. For cases must be recognized as coming under the jurisdiction of a principle before they can be evaluated in its terms. I can follow the principle of paying debts only if I recognize that what I received from you constitutes indebtedness. If I do not recognize it, the principle will not help; and if I do recognize it, I do not need the principle.

Principles, therefore, cannot be basic guides of conduct. They are useful only as formulae that can be taught in the early stages of moral education and as efficient ways in which participants in a moral tradition can communicate to each other the grounds of their approval or disapproval.

Nor do ideals fare better. It is supposed that ideals guide moral conduct by inspiring one to improve himself so as to approximate more closely some end he values. These ends may be happiness, one of the many forms of perfection, or service to some cause or another. It is necessary, of course, to make the ideal concrete. For unless this is done, anything anyone does can be taken as an exemplification. We need to be told in some detail what happiness, perfection, or the cause amount to before we can understand the thesis. However, as soon as this is done, the supposed primacy of the ideal over customary practice disappears.

To begin with, an ideal does not exist in the abstract; it can inspire conduct only if it is embodied. This usually takes the form of a real or fictional person whose life or conduct is an exemplary representation of the ideal. But the explanation of what makes a life or an action exemplary cannot merely be that it was inspired by the ideal; the explanation must show what a person did in the various circumstances of his life that constitute the substance of being inspired by that ideal. And this means that ideals, like principles, owe their origin to conduct that must first occur, before it can instantiate anything.

Furthermore, when a person is inspired to live in accordance with an ideal exemplified in someone else's life, he must find that the ideal is appropriate to his life and circumstances. But he cannot judge its appropriateness without first having some practical knowledge of what it is like to live in accordance with the ideal. His imaginative appreciation must grow out of some of the actual practices prevailing in his context; only because he is familiar with some practices of the relevant sort can the ideal strike a receptive chord. If one is not already favourably disposed to contemplation, he will not find the life of Montaigne, Spinoza, or Hume inspiring; and if one is not compelled by his own creative urges to ignore conventional conduct, he will not find in the life of Gauguin or Rimbaud a liberating influence. The inspiration of an ideal requires at least a weak pre-existing pattern of action according to it. Only by drawing on someone else's conduct and on one's own previous conduct can a person become devoted to an ideal.

The inspiration of ideals is an important part of moral life. But ideals do not inspire by being abstract representations of untried possibilities. They inspire by people having observed others in their society live according to them and by judging their own character and conduct sufficiently similar to the observed ones to find that they are appropriate objects of emulation. Ideals, therefore, are convenient labels for complicated conventional patterns of conduct one finds attractive. To say that ideals inspire is a short way of saying that one wishes to conduct himself as a person does whose conduct he admires. Once again, customary conduct precedes what is supposed to guide it.

II

Moral ideals and principles grow out of and receive sustenance from customary conduct. If conduct ceases to be customary, the ideals based on it become hollow and the principles lose their force. The result is chaos, for people could not then know what to expect of each other. Suspicion would replace trust, friendliness would turn into hostility, politeness, sympathy, altruism would become unaffordable luxuries. The great importance of a moral tradition is that it protects a society from this kind of dissolution.

A moral tradition is the network of a certain sort of customary conduct that exists in a society. A society is an association of people; it has a history; most of its members are born into it; it occupies a more or less clearly defined geographical area; its members speak the same language; and they participate in common political, legal, and moral practices. The people of a nation typically form a society; but groups within a nation, such as Creoles, or international groups, like Freemasons, may also do so.

Following Oakeshott,[2] I shall distinguish between two kinds of tradition. The first is an association of people guided by a specific and common goal. The tradition provides the framework in which they aim to achieve whatever this goal happens to be. It may be profit, world domination, the composition, performance, and appreciation of music, historical research, athletic achievement, helping the poor, and so on. There will be many such traditions in a society. The other is an association in which the necessary conditions are maintained for the continued existence of the first kind of traditions. This sort of tradition does not aim to achieve a specific goal, it aims to create a context in which specific goals can be achieved. Legal, political, managerial, and law enforcement traditions are examples of it. And it is to this class that moral traditions also belong. Moral traditions, then, are ground-clearing rather than architectural; enabling rather than productive; protective rather than venturesome. A moral tradition has achieved its purpose if no one in a society needs to be aware of its existence. For the society, then, shows itself to be morally untroubled and people can live their lives in the framework thus established.

It is a great and rare achievement if a society reaches this state of moral harmony. Our society and the vast majority of societies in recorded history fall more or less short. The approximation of this desirable state depends, in the first instance, on moral education. It consists in handing down the moral tradition from generation to generation in a society. This is the context in which principles acquire importance. For moral education begins with imitation, but that cannot go very far. A morally well-trained person does not merely know how to do what others had done in his situation; he also knows how to recognize situations as calling for specific types of moral response. Principles and ideals help to advance a person's moral initiation from mere imitation to intelligent performance. But such performance is more than knowing how to follow principles and ideals, it also involves knowing how to conduct oneself in new situations. This kind of knowledge cannot be based on generalizations from the past, it requires creative participation in the tradition. It is based on experience, requires good judgment and a deep appreciation of the spirit of one's tradition. It calls for judging which of several conflicting ideals and principles should guide one in a particular situation, when to adhere steadfastly to a moral guide and when consistency turns into soulless ritual, when the letter of the moral tradition is at odds with its spirit, when an individual's interest should take precedence over the common good, when the good to be achieved is great enough to risk the evil failure may produce, what kindness, justice, or charity actually come to in the case confronting one. These are difficult matters to judge and moral knowledge is hard to acquire.

One reason for making the required effort is that a moral tradition is inspiring. A moral education is an initiation into a vision of the possibilities of human life; it is a training in the development of a sensibility in terms of which one perceives good and evil for himself and others. Thus allegiance to a moral tradition is not merely habitual conformity to customary conduct, but, in addition, to be motivated by a moral vision to do so, and the sharing of that vision by fellow members of the tradition.

Vision is perhaps too chiliastic a term to describe what I have in mind. People in a moral tradition are rarely visionaries; in fact, moral traditions usually exercise a restraining influence on the millennial flights of fancy of their members. Yet one receives more from a moral tradition than an outlook. An outlook need not guide action, it need not inspire, it need not provide a framework for interpretation and evaluation, and it can leave one's emotions unengaged. But a moral tradition provides all this.

The evaluative dimension of a sound tradition is deep. It goes beyond knowing how to use such terms as good and evil, or right and wrong. The depth comes from familiarity with the discriminations, nuances, judgments of importance and priority, and from an aliveness to sources of conflict and tension, all of which form the texture of the moral life guided by the tradition. What one knows is not merely that this person is good and that evil, but also what makes them so, and why one is better or worse, more or less culpable or admirable, weaker or stronger, more capable of improvement or hopelessly corrupt than another person in similar circumstances. It is to know what is outrageous, shocking, offensive rather than sophomoric attempt to provoke, an assertion of independence, or a cry for help.

A full-fledged participant in a moral tradition knows these and thousands of similar things in a particular manner. He does not know them as a judge knows the law; he does not reflect and then carefully select the appropriate rule or precedent that best fits the case at hand. Moral knowledge of the sort I have in mind has become his second nature. Making the distinctions, noticing the nuances, being alive to the conflicts, priorities, and temptations no longer requires reflection. Just as an accomplished violinist knows how to play adagio and a rock climber knows how to manage an overhang, so a moral agent knows about moral matters. Of course, he may have to stop and think. But that happens only in difficult cases, the daily flow of moral life can be handled spontaneously by members of a sound moral tradition.

Nor is the knowledge like that of an anthropologist observing a society. The crucial difference is that the anthropologist stands outside of what he observes. He may approve or disapprove of the tradition, he may feel sympathy, revulsion, or be indifferent, he may compare it favourably or unfavourably to other traditions. A participant in a moral tradition is necessarily inside it. He can observe it perhaps as accurately as any anthropologist. But he cannot be indifferent. Now I do not mean that he is bound to judge his own tradition superior to others. What I mean is that whatever moral judgment he makes is made in terms the tradition provides. His belonging to it means that he sees the moral aspect of the world in that way.

This should not be confused with relativism. Moral relativists believe that moral judgments can be justified only within the tradition in which they are made and, therefore, an independent moral judgment of a tradition is impossible. It is true, I think, that moral judgments are made in the context of a tradition, but it does not follow that some traditions cannot reasonably be judged morally superior to others. The reason for this is twofold.

First, as we have seen, a moral tradition is intended to establish the conditions in which members of a society can pursue whatever they regard as good lives. But there are some conditions which any moral tradition must guarantee, such as, for instance, safeguarding the lives, security, property, and some freedom of its members, having some institution for the adjudication of conflicts, having a recognized authority in charge of performing such services as are judged to be in the common good, and so on. Now a moral tradition guaranteeing these conditions can reasonably be said to be superior to one that does not. And one that guarantees more is superior to one that guarantees fewer.

Secondly, moral traditions grow out of a physical context. Societies occupy land and are subject to climatic, geographical, demographic, and other influences, and have certain natural resources, and they emerge at a certain time. These physical conditions are different for many societies, but they are also comparable for others. We can consider two societies in roughly similar physical contexts, such as Sparta and Athens, Brazil and the United States, the Ottoman and the Hapsburg Empires, Quebec and Ontario, and ask which moral tradition enabled these societies to make better use of their similar physical endowments. And by better I do not, of course, mean morally better, but better in finding, developing, and distributing the natural resources among their citizens. The welfare of a people partly depends on the organization of their resources, and since this is strongly influenced by their moral tradition, we are afforded another basis upon which reasonable evaluation of the comparative merits of different traditions is possible.

My account of moral traditions, therefore, is not committed to moral relativism. At the same time, I want to stress that a person cannot be indifferent to the moral tradition that has his allegiance, for the tradition engages the feelings of those who belong to it. Nor could this be otherwise. For one is given by his tradition the conception of what makes life worth living, what it is to be a good man, what personal characteristics are virtuous and admirable, how people should treat others, what the acceptable forms of personal relationships are, how to cope with misfortune, adversity, and the prospect of failure, and what the duties and privileges are of the various stations in life his society affords. These constitute the substance of his moral life and inform the sensibility in terms of which he interprets and evaluates whatever happens. Indifference would mean the loss of one's evaluative dimension.

Allegiance to a moral tradition will, then, shape how a person thinks and feels about his own life and how he judges the disclosures of his experiences. But by being so shaped, one becomes part of a moral community whose members share the vision and sensibility of their common tradition. A tradition, then, not only defines the moral identity of its members, it also unites them in virtue of their common way of judging and responding to the world. At other times, when societies were smaller and more homogeneous, members of a moral community were likely to know each other personally or by reputation, and if they did not, their clothing, demeanour, and language identified their belongingness. This has been changing, because societies have grown larger, more impersonal, and because only the most blatant outward manifestation is a reliable indicator of inner processes. Yet moral communities need visible marks of belongingness and these, in our times, are behavioural clues, rituals, and ceremonies.

The behavioural clues are the gestures, frowns, smiles, nods, scowls, laughter and tears, sniffings and cluckings, winkings, head scratchings, yawns, clearings of throat, stares, gazes, looks and taking care not to look, gaze or stare, the speed and emphasis with which something is said, the occasion and direction in which it is said, flushes, blushes, blanches, and the multitude of other ways in which people emphasize, embellish, soften, indicate the seriousness or levity of what they say and do. But the clues are appropriate only if they communicate what was intended or meant by them, and this, of course, requires that the actor and the spectator, the agent and the recipient should share an interpretation of the significance of what has passed between them. This, once again, is rarely a conscious reflective process. The clues are frequently given and understood without either party being aware of their passage. To a very considerable extent, people in a moral tradition are united, feel comfortable and familiar with each other, because they can depend on this being understood.

This sense of belongingness is enhanced by the rituals that permeate everyday life: the how-are-yous, handshakes, openings of doors, taking off of hats, coats, jackets, the sharing of a meal, having coffee or a drink together, the kisses and the embraces, the telling of secrets, sharing confidences, exchanging gossip, the use of formulae for expressing respect, condolence, enmity, or sympathy, the occasions and manner of congratulations for success and commiseration for failure or misfortune. And the ceremonies marking significant occasions like birth, marriage, death, graduation, birthdays, anniversaries, arrivals and departures, promotion and retirement, holidays and festivities, are similarly unifying forces. Fellow members of a moral tradition recognize their connectedness, because they share knowledge of what is appropriate to the events of their lives and they share also knowledge of the manner in which these events are to be marked. And this remains true even of those rebels, eccentrics, non-conformists, and iconoclasts who refuse to do what is appropriate. For the moral tradition against which they protest determines the occasions on which they can express their disdain. Only genuine indifference, uninvolvement, and ignorance of what is appropriate place one outside of a moral tradition.[3]

Thus the basis of a moral community, the source that sustains a tradition, is not that its members know, love, or even like each other; there is no fundamental principle to which they have sworn allegiance; there is no overarching ideal whose inspirational force establishes their solidarity. There is largely spontaneous, unreflective, customary conduct, the unarticulated feeling of ease in each other's company, because there is much that need not be said, and there is knowledge that when something needs to be done, they know how to do it. The signs of connectedness are the behavioural clues, rituals, and ceremonies, and their consequences are that people recognized as fellow members are given the benefit of the doubt, and they are treated in a friendly polite way. The categorical imperative, liberty, equality, and fraternity, the happiness of mankind, the imitation of Christ are intellectual abstractions that derive what force they may have from the concrete good will that participants in a moral tradition spontaneously have toward each other. Without this good will, the abstractions ring hollow. And this is why Hume is right in regarding custom as the great guide of life.[4]

III

I have been stressing the conventional and emotive aspects of moral traditions, but they are also evaluative and practical. They are evaluative, because they concern moral good and evil, and they are practical, because they influence conduct.

By good and evil I understand benefit and harm to human beings, and by moral good and evil, benefit and harm to human beings produced by human agency. My present concern is exclusively with moral good and evil. What makes a tradition moral is that it encourages customary conduct that leads to as favourable a balance of good over evil for its members as possible given the context. I shall make use of the Aristotelian distinction between external and internal goods to discuss this feature of traditions.[5]

External and internal goods are benefits obtainable through participation in a moral tradition. External goods are related to traditions as ends are to means. The many types of customary conduct that make up a moral tradition are instrumental to obtaining such benefits as protection of life, security, property, safeguard against the unfair use of power, assurance of some freedom for exercising choices in directing one's life, at least a modicum of good will shown by others to oneself, and so on. Any sound moral tradition will aim to provide these benefits. They are the requirements for the flourishing of any human life. Periclean Athens, Confucian China, early medieval Christendom, Puritan New England, Victorian England all had moral traditions which provided external goods for their members. Of course, these moral traditions were vastly different, but their differences were not on account of the identity of external goods. A moral tradition is needed to supply external goods, but any tradition doing so is acceptable. The pursuit of external goods, therefore, is utilitarian. What matters is the achievement of ends, and not the nature of the means.

Internal goods are related to tradition as parts are to a whole: they constitute it. Thus the identity of a moral tradition is logically connected with the identity of the internal goods obtainable through it. But obtaining internal goods is not like winning a prize, enjoying a musical performance, or solving a difficult problem to one's satisfaction. Internal goods are enjoyed by being forms a good life may take. These forms are manners of living, acting, and being connected with others. They are the forms of customary conduct that jointly compose a tradition. A person more or less consciously inherits a conception of a good life from his tradition – a conception that is his special individual amalgam of such opportunities, defined and made possible by his tradition, as he finds attractive and applicable to his own case.

We can tell, in general terms, that a satisfactory conception of a good life must include, first, self-direction. That is, some view of what a person wants to make of himself and what character-traits he needs to have and cultivate to achieve it. One must ask and answer such questions as whether he wants to live a retiring private or a gregarious public life, whether he has the talents and personality required by his chosen form of life, whether that form will be scholarly, artistic, commercial, or athletic, whether he prizes achievement, contemplation, service, risk-taking, casting his net wide, or specializing in a distinct endeavour, whether he aims at exercising power, enjoying luxuries wealth can provide, receiving the recognition status and prestige bestow, basking in the reciprocated love of a few intimates, or devoting himself to a cause.

Secondly, a conception of good life must leave room for intimate personal relationships based on love and friendship; without them, a life cannot be satisfactory. But whether the satisfaction will be derived from marriage, parenthood, solidarity with comrades in a joint cause, shared admiration of some ideal, love affairs, discipleship to a great man, or from the affection and loyalty of one's students will vary from life to life.

Thirdly, one cannot have a good life unless he has settled on an acceptable way of relating to the vast majority of people in his society whom he does not know and yet continually encounters in the routine conduct of his affairs. The desired attitude here is decency, that is, appropriate conduct as judged by the customs of one's society. Its marks are casual friendliness, spontaneous good will, politeness, giving others the benefit of the doubt, or negatively, the absence of hostility, distrust, suspicion, and of the litigious disposition bent on exacting one's pound of flesh.

The internal goods of a moral tradition, then, are the forms of self-direction, intimacy, and decency that a society provides for its members. Conceptions of good life in a moral tradition will be combinations of the forms a person consciously or otherwise aims to follow in his life. In a sound moral tradition, the available forms are much more numerous than what a person can reasonably aspire to follow. In a society enjoying such a rich tradition, customary conduct does not appear as rigid codes, rules that bind, or ideals demanding obeisance; customary conduct will seem to provide different ways, and the option to follow them, in which a person can make a good life for himself. Such a society will be pluralistic, in virtue of the multiplicity of available forms of conduct, and it will be free, because its members can choose among the forms their lives could take. A moral tradition, therefore, is not an enemy of individuality, but a necessary condition of its development.

I have already stressed the importance of moral education as an initiation into the moral tradition of a society. I can expand my previous remarks now by saying that this initiation involves acquainting the young with the available forms of self-direction, intimacy, and decency. Moral education imparts knowledge of the possible forms of moral life. This knowledge will increase the freedom of its recipients, because what they come to know is that their lives may take more forms than they can possibly realize. So in becoming aware of the riches of their own tradition, they are maximizing their own chances of living a satisfactory life.

Moral education can be better or worse. It is better, if it acquaints its recipients with as many forms of traditional life as possible, and if the forms are presented in a way that appeals to their imagination and sensibility. No one individual is likely to be able to provide a full moral education for others, since personal experience of forms of life and the ability to convey what it is like to live them is bound to be limited. A society, therefore, is well-advised to institutionalize its moral education.

Before we began to lose sight of it, this was the role liberal education was supposed to play in our society. The intention was to teach the classic works of our cultural tradition; works that are classics, partly because they depict enduring human options in a sufficiently evocative manner to inspire succeeding generations to enjoy and emulate them as part of their inheritance. To a considerable extent, our present moral confusions, and their destructive consequences, are due to having forgotten that liberal education is moral education. We make our children free without teaching them how to use their freedom. The bogey of indoctrination so frightens us that we become afraid to hand down to the next generation the accumulated wisdom of our moral tradition.

IV

This brings us to the question of the rationality of moral traditions. I have rejected moral relativism on the ground that moral traditions can be judged rationally by examining whether they guarantee the minimum conditions without which no human life can be good. So we already have an independent standard of rational appraisal. But this will not take us very far, because moral traditions provide much more than the minimum conditions; the customary forms of conduct prevailing in a tradition strongly influence the conceptions of good life members will have. Different traditions provide different conceptions, and it is proper to ask whether these conceptions can be rationally judged. I think that they can be, but only negatively. Moral traditions can be criticized. But if one's moral tradition is acquitted upon rational scrutiny, it is reasonable to live according to it. This view supports the supposition that there is a plurality of rational traditions prevailing in different societies. The relativistic conclusion that we cannot tell that some traditions are irrational, however, does not follow from it.

Moral traditions can be criticized by showing them to be self-defeating. An irrational moral tradition cannot achieve its own purposes, because features internal to it stand in the way. The form of particular criticisms will depend on what features of a moral tradition handicap it. And since many features may, possible criticisms of moral traditions are not delimitable *a priori*. Nevertheless, there are some fairly standard defects and I shall discuss some of them by way of illustrating how a moral tradition can be criticized.

The simplest form is pointing out that the benefits inherent in a moral tradition about good and evil are false. It will be recalled that moral good and evil are understood as benefit and harm to human beings produced by human agency. If it turns out that what members of a tradition think benefits or harms themselves and others does not, then their tradition cannot achieve its purpose of providing internal and external goods for its members.

Take the case of external goods first. Some conditions are required by any life, if it is to be good. Life, security, property, and some freedom, for instance, must be protected. If a moral tradition incorporates customary practices that violate these external goods, it fails in its own terms. Examples of this are not hard to find: slavery, foot binding, female circumcision, torture, human sacrifice, enticing the young to drug addiction are harmful, and thus evil. A moral tradition fostering them, therefore, undermines rather than guarantees the minimum conditions of its members living good lives.[6]

If these judgments grate on some relativistic ears, their owners should ask whether these barbaric practices are anywhere defended as good. The answer is that they are not. Those who perpetrate them either deny that they are doing so, or defend them as necessary evils, or proceed without regard to morality. My claim is that if a moral tradition, necessarily having regard for morality, fosters such practices, and they are recognized for what they are, then there can be no doubt about their being evil, even if necessary evils. But necessary or not, a moral tradition is defective if it permits evil to be customary practice. The road to improvement lies through pointing out as forcefully as possible that the practice is evil and explaining why it is so.

Let us now consider less clearcut cases in which a moral tradition is committed to providing external goods for its members, but it is faulty on account of its provision of internal goods. The situation I am describing is one in which the minimum conditions for a good life are guaranteed, but the tradition incorporates defective forms such lives may take.

The most obvious case in point is a tradition that has only a very limited number of forms. In such a context, a person's freedom to choose between different forms of life is severely reduced and so, therefore, are his chances of making for himself a good life. Such traditions are rigid; they have an impoverished conception of human possibilities. The rigidity may be due to adverse physical conditions forcing members of a society to adhere to activities directly related to maintaining subsistence. Or the rigidity may be imposed by some orthodoxy that has achieved unquestioned authority. Turnbull's description of the Ik in *The Mountain People* and the horrendous vision of Orwell in *1984* are examples of these aberrations. But however it comes about, its fault is a reduction of human options, a curtailment of the directions in which members can develop themselves. Since the purpose of the tradition is to increase the opportunities for pursuing internal and external goods, and since rigidity leads to decreasing the stock of internal goods, a rigid moral tradition is faulty in its own terms.

Another source of weakness is if a moral tradition fails to inspire its members. Recall the realization that preceded Mill's crisis; he asked himself: '"Suppose that all your objects in life were realized; that all the changes in institutions and opinions which you are looking forward to, could be completely effected at this instant: would this be a great joy and happiness to you?" And an irrepressible self-consciousness distinctly answered, "No!" At this my heart sank within me: the whole foundation on which my life was constructed fell down. ... I seemed to have nothing left to live for.' (*Autobiography*, Chapter V.)

This passage describes a personal experience. Imagine, however, that the experience is not due to psychological factors peculiar to one person, but to a realistic appraisal of one's moral tradition. The signs of this happening are widespread boredom, *ennui, anomie*, decadence, the feverish pursuit of thrills. When this happens, and its cause is internal to a tradition rather than the fault of some of its members, the tradition is played out. It is supposed to move its members to action by appealing to their imagination, exciting them to admiration, inspiring their feelings by giving a cast to their emotional life in which feeling and doing, imagining options and being moved to realize them are inseparable. A tradition that fails to inspire, fails to be action-guiding. Its more conscientious members may continue to carry on in a desultory way, but the soul of it is gone. This, I think, is what happened to the Roman tradition, due largely to the impact of Christianity, and to the *ancien régime* before the blood of the Revolution washed it away.

These are some of the ways in which traditions can come to grief. Other ways can be added, because there are as many potential criticisms of a tradition as there are contexts and aspirations. They can fail by allowing custom to turn into a ritual whose point is forgotten, by the breakdown of its institutions for adjudicating conflicts, by cataclysmic changes to which it cannot respond, by the appearance of another tradition which does better justice to the experience and aspirations of its members, and so on. The upshot is that since a tradition can be successfully criticized, it can be rational. But if the available criticisms do not convict a tradition, then it is reasonable to adhere to it. A rational tradition provides for its members rich opportunities for self-direction, forms intimate personal relationships can take, and so participants in it have good will toward each other, and thus decency prevails. A society, therefore, is justified in jealously guarding its moral tradition, if it is sound, and improving it, if it is defective.

V

If a moral tradition is in order, people are barely aware of it. For they have translated customary conduct into personal habits, and living according to their individual amalgam of the forms provided by the tradition has become second nature. Of course, not even the best moral tradition can prevent some of its members from making a mess of their lives. The tradition merely provides opportunities and the forms, their realization may be prevented by bad judgment, misfortune, stupidity, or lack of discipline. Traditions, however, are rarely free of defect, and though human frailty inevitably takes its toll, the blame for failure does not exclusively rest with individuals. It is very difficult to judge how responsibility for failure should be apportioned among tradition, personal defects, and circumstances beyond anyone's control. Nevertheless, if there is widespread failure, it is reasonable to suspect that the tradition is not as it should be. The signs are that people wonder about the meaning and purpose of their lives, that intimacy is increasingly based on joining forces better to pursue self-interest, and that incivility, rather than decency, prevails in impersonal social relationships. When these signs are much in evidence, people begin to question their moral tradition. Spontaneity disappears and self-consciousness takes its place. Self-consciousness, then, is a danger signal; it betokens, if it is widespread, doubts about the tradition. This is what occasions the demand for justification.

The tragedy is that once the demand is generally felt, it can no longer be satisfied. Defenders of the tradition can, of course, offer arguments, give reasons for adhering to customary conduct, point out that everyone's welfare is connected with the tradition, show how moral possibilities, a sense of identity, and being at home in the world depend on sharing the traditional vision. But these arguments will not assuage the doubt. For its fundamental source is that many people want and do not get the internal goods from their tradition. Thus the justification will ring hollow in their ears.

Of course, part of what I have been doing in this paper is to offer a
justification for our moral tradition. And if this were all, my conclusion
would doom the justification to futility. But I have been doing something
else as well: diagnose the source of the present malaise. The diagnosis is
that our moral education is at fault. It fails to convey to the young how
fine the tradition is. If this diagnosis is correct, the remedy is obvious.

NOTES

1 D. Hume, *Enquiries Concerning the Principles of Morals* (Oxford: Clarendon,
   1961), ed. L. A. Selby-Bigge, 44.
2 M. Oakeshott, 'On the Civil Condition', *On Human Conduct* (Oxford: Clarendon,
   1975). My thinking about moral traditions is deeply influenced by Oakeshott,
   especially by the essays in *Rationalism in Politics* (London: Methuen, 1962).
3 E. Goffman perceptively describes these rituals, clues, and ceremonies in many
   works. See, for instance, *The Presentation of Self in Everyday Life* (New York:
   Doubleday, 1959) and *Interaction Ritual* (New York: Pantheon, 1967).
4 For a general account of tradition from a sociological perspective, see E. Shils,
   Tradition (Chicago: University of Chicago Press, 1981).
5 The distinction is in Book 1 of *Nicomachean Ethics*. I say that the distinction is
   Aristotelian, not Aristotle's, because I find it obscure in Aristotle's writings and
   I have not hesitated to adapt it to my own purposes. In doing so, I have been
   influenced by A. MacIntyre's *After Virtue* (Notre Dame: University of Notre
   Dame Press, 1981).
6 In *The Moral Rules* (New York: Harper, 1973). B. Gert gives an excellent
   account of what these minimum conditions are and why their violation is evil.

Index

Index compiled by Justyn Balinski